The Writer's Reader

Who will apologise for children's lives lost in Iraq? How do you force a big company to take responsibility for damaging the health of its workers? What do you do when you suspect a famous author is a fake? How does it feel to be on the receiving end of police crowd control? Or on a hillside, spellbound and fearful, watching the light being sucked from the sky during an eclipse?

Top writers and journalists who have written about events and issues big and small talk frankly about how they approach the task in this highly readable new collection. *The Writer's Reader* combines selected non-fiction articles with interviews with authors reflecting on the process of writing. Academic writing can be dry and dull, but this refreshingly accessible anthology values straight talking about writing and argues that if you want to write, then you should be reading.

Susie Eisenhuth is a lecturer in journalism at the University of Technology, Sydney.

Willa McDonald is a lecturer in media and writing at Macquarie University.

The Writer's Reader

Understanding Journalism and Non-Fiction

Susie Eisenhuth
Willa McDonald

CAMBRIDGE UNIVERSITY PRESS
Cambridge, New York, Melbourne, Madrid, Cape Town, Singapore, São Paulo

Cambridge University Press
477 Williamstown Road, Port Melbourne, Vic 3207, Australia

Published in the United States of America by Cambridge University Press, New York

www.cambridge.org
Information on this title: www.cambridge.org/9780521700337

First published 2007

Printed in Australia by Ligare

A catalogue record for this book is available from the British Library

National Library of Australia Cataloguing in Publication data

Eisenhuth, Susie.
The writer's reader: understanding journalism and non-fiction
ISBN 13 978-0-52170-033-7 paperback
ISBN 10 0-52170-033-7 paperback
1. Academic writing 2. Journalism I. McDonald. Willa–
II. Title.
808.066

ISBN-13 978-0-52170-033-7
ISBN-10 0-52170-033-7

This book is dedicated with love to our children Tian and Toby.
And with gratitude to those writers whose storytelling enriches all our lives.

Contents

Preface ix

1 News and Follow-ups 1
Turning news into features *Susie Eisenhuth* 1
Michael Southwell 6
Robert Fisk 10
David Marr and Marian Wilkinson 25
Discussion question 37
Further reading 37

2 New Journalism and Its Legacy 38
Looking back and forward *Susie Eisenhuth* 38
Joan Didion 43
Barry Siegel 55
Discussion question 76
Further reading 76

3 Profiles 77
Talking to people/beyond celebrity flimflam *Susie Eisenhuth* 77
Greg Bearup 81
Tony Squires 92
Discussion question 97
Further reading 97

4 Investigations 98
'Muckraking' with honour *Susie Eisenhuth* 98
Jessica Mitford 102
Malcolm Knox 116

Discussion questions 124
Further reading 124

5 Essays 125
Turning personal stories into reflective writing *Willa McDonald* 125
John Birmingham 130
Arundhati Roy 140
David Sedaris 144
Discussion questions 147
Further reading 147

6 Memoir 148
Examining our own lives *Willa McDonald* 148
Kathy Evans 153
Helen Garner 160
Mark Mordue 167
Discussion questions 172
Further reading 172

7 Writing about Place 173
Placing readers in the world *Willa McDonald* 173
Ashley Hay 177
Annie Dillard 187
Discussion questions 197
Further reading 197

8 Travel Writing 198
Taking to the road to learn about ourselves *Willa McDonald* 198
Pico Iyer 202
Discussion questions 215
Further reading 215

Notes 216

Sources 220

Index 223

Preface

Our intention in putting this collection of non-fiction together was to put the focus squarely on the importance of reading other writers. We asked a lot of writers what their best advice to aspiring writers would be. 'Reading, reading, reading', said Pulitzer Prize winning US journalist and author Barry Siegel. 'You need a sense of story. Where do you get a sense of story? You get a sense of story by reading stories.' Non-fiction author and journalist Helen Garner offered almost the self-same mantra. 'Read', she said. 'Read, read, read.' She put an extra 'read' in there for emphasis, we noted, along with a very Garneresque addendum '(And don't use too many adverbs.)'

Writer and journalist John Birmingham, known for tilting at traditional boundaries and urging an edgier approach to non-fiction in general, nonetheless came on like a martinet on this question, recommending a punishing regime of 'four hours a day reading, four hours a day writing'. ('And a cup of tea in between.') Journalist and non-fiction author Mark Mordue, whose music journalism helped to fund his early writing career, cites the influence of British *New Musical Express* writer Paul Morley, 'whose wit and intelligence demonstrated that a good magazine article or review could have all the grace and structure of a fine short story or essay'. He was also an avid reader of writers Hunter S. Thompson, Jack Kerouac and Charles Bukowski. (Not to mention the poetry of Baudelaire and the piano's-been-drinking lyrics of Tom Waits.)

Siegel, looking back to the 1960s and 1970s, describes Tom Wolfe, Joan Didion and John McPhee as his 'textbooks'. Essayist and journalist Pico Iyer cites writers such as Graham Greene, V. S. Naipaul and W. G. Sebald, but also notes that his close study of the strictly fact-checked model of *Time* magazine gave him a crash course in concision, clarity and 'telling a story through details and particulars'.

The same advice can be heard across the spectrum. Susan Sontag, writing about writing for the *New York Times*, observed that 'the impulse to write is almost always fired by reading. Reading, the love of reading is what makes you dream of becoming a writer.' And bestselling author Stephen King, whose book *On Writing* offers useful tips for both fiction and non-fiction writers, says he first began to learn the lesson that 'good description begins with clear seeing and ends with clear writing' by reading Raymond Chandler, Dashiell Hammett and Ross McDonald. But 'I gained perhaps even more respect for the power of compact descriptive language from reading T. S. Eliot (those ragged claws scuttling across the ocean floor; those coffee spoons) and William Carlos Williams (white chickens, red wheelbarrow, the plums that were in the ice box, so sweet and so cold)'.

Looking across so many stories, we were by no means attempting a best of the best. As journalists who teach both writing and journalism at university we know the value of guest lectures where published writers come in and talk to the students about their craft. We hope that, in part, our book serves as a forum where the voices of some eminent 'guests' and their invaluable advice will be accessible along with their stories. As to the selection of stories, the longer we looked the more we realised how much the various non-fiction categories overlap, as beloved as they may be by those whose expertise depends on policing their margins. We wanted to explore a continuum where fine writing skills come together in the art of storytelling, whether the telling stories that result come from the urgent narrative of history-in-a-hurry in news writing, or the more ruminative meditations of essays and memoir.

It seemed obvious that the same sorts of skills translate across the categories. When reporters chase down the news, both deftly telegrammed events and artful writing can be in evidence. Good journalists, like good fiction writers, can frame a dramatic story – even re-create it scene by scene if they're blessed with the space – people it with characters, record their thoughts and feelings, layer in backgrounding context and sound resonating echoes of other, past stories. (Important stories, as the late Graham Perkin, editor of the Melbourne *Age*, memorably observed, have roots in the past and a stake in the future.)

If a non-fiction writer produces a densely researched story that focuses on ideas as much as events, the reader is unlikely to care if it is tap-dancing between feature story and essay. Likewise journalists and essayists can take on hot political topics, and both can pull back from the narrative for a lyrical meditation on the details that make place and time resonate for the reader. Nor is opinion necessarily the exclusive preserve of the essay or column writer. A piece of feature writing fuelled by meticulous research that flags its intention to take a stand – as clearly as it does its sources – doesn't shed its cred because some commentators cling doggedly to the bogus notion that objectivity is an outcome that can actually be attained, rather than a useful reminder to aim, always, for balance. The same blurring of the lines can be seen with essays, memoir and travel. Should the travel writers who spin rich yarns interwoven with history and cultural conjecture be pigeonholed with some of the advertorial writing that bulks out the travel sections? If essayists veer into their own history – or the world's – are they operating in the land of memoir (and are memoirs, as Clive James suggests, unreliable)?

Who is to say where journalism ends and writing begins? Or when writing ascends into the rarefied realms of literature? For us, fine storytelling is the key to fine writing. And people are always to the fore. And that's what we looked for. Most of the writers included here engage in both journalism and other sorts of non-fiction. Their pieces show us writers breaking conventions, telling untold stories, writing artfully, honestly, amusingly, about their own predelictions, pitching us into other people's lives, offering us insights into our own. Some set out to expose spin, some, fired up by the watchdog notion of public interest, take a fierce stand against the powerful, pushing to provide a voice for the powerless.

We see them responding to all sorts of challenges. How do you get at the truth behind the Tampa headlines? How do you force a big company to admit to endangering the health of its workers? What do you do when you suspect a famous book is a fake? How does it feel to be on the receiving end of police crowd control? Or on a hillside, like Annie Dillard, spellbound and fearful, watching the light being sucked from the sky during an eclipse? What makes ordinary people commit murder? And what, as a hungry David Sedaris wants to know, makes fancy restaurants think a huge plate with a tarted-up tidbit in the middle will pass for a good feed?

Non-fiction stories, like fiction stories, stand or fall – as they always have – on whether or not they are a good read, whether they grip us, inspire us, surprise us, inform us, fire up our imaginations (or our hackles), or home in with so much heart on human frailties or foibles that they move us to laughter or tears. Read, enjoy, reflect, have a go yourself. But above all, read.

With thanks

There are many people who have helped us with advice and assistance during this project, in particular: Philip Bell, Aileen Berry, Peter Craven, Jenny Cullen, Mitchell Dean, Carol Elliott, Mandy van den Elshout, Helen Freidman, Damian Grace, Ashley Hay, Robyn and John Paul Healy, Pico Iyer, Alexandra Jones, Christine Jones, Debra Jopson, Noel King, Caro Llewellyn, David McKnight, Kathryn Millard, Mark Mordue, Penny O'Donnell, Susan Omundsen, John Potts, Tony Stephens, Michael Visontay, Julia Wee, Amanda Wilson and Susan Wyndham.

Our families and friends provided care and encouragement that kept us going and the team at Cambridge helped to smooth our way.

We would also like to thank Macquarie University and the University of Technology, Sydney (UTS), who gave invaluable advice, time and funding, and the University of NSW, where Susie Eisenhuth was a Visiting Fellow in 2006 during the preparation of this book.

Finally, the authors compiled the featured interviews together and we are grateful to the writers for their patience with our questioning. We thank all the writers of these stories who have so generously allowed us to reproduce their work. It is their skill, their dedication and their love of storytelling that we honour in this book and share with our readers.

Chapter 1
News and Follow-ups

Turning news into features

Susie Eisenhuth

In April 1996 a news story was filed from a Lebanon racked with violence. Like many others at the time it recorded in a few terse paragraphs the latest bloody incident to which journalists had been witness: a number of civilians had been killed in a rocket attack on their vehicle near the village of Mansouri in southern Lebanon. The vehicle was an ambulance, the rocket fired by an Israeli helicopter. The dead, two women and four children, were among a small group using the ambulance to flee the area under fire.

That was the news. The conflict rolled on. And the presses. Out here in reader land, most of us would have filed the incident under 'Middle East conflict', the ubiquitous news-speak label that so helpfully dissolves not only national boundaries and complex political issues but also the need to explain them. Another day, another shelling – and who knew what exactly was going on in those 'Middle East' killing fields so far away?

Yet on this occasion, the news item would not be the end of the story. As the UN peacekeepers were picking through the blast site for evidence, British journalist Robert Fisk, arriving from an assignment nearby, met a Reuters camerawoman with harrowing footage of the events on video. Fisk looked closely at the missile fragments the UN ordnance officers were collecting, one still bearing the nameplate and code that would ultimately identify it as a Hellfire anti-armour missile, manufactured in the United States and allocated to US forces. That discovery marked the beginning of a long journey for the veteran Middle East correspondent, which would lead to the remarkable feature story published in the London *Independent* over a year later.[1]

In that feature, Fisk would convert the basic facts into a story that went way beyond the confines of a routine report from the front. It would buy into the bigger issues behind the headlines, about war and weaponry, soldiers and civilians, and the companies who profit from the weapons that can kill both indiscriminately. Tracking across the world to confront the missile makers in their US headquarters, Fisk would ultimately engage them in a debate about the morality of the war business, summoning up the shade of George Bernard Shaw, whose play *Major Barbara* gave us, years earlier, the character of Undershaft the armaments manufacturer, and his silken defence of might is right.

If this is so, then what?

The story of Fisk's Mansouri feature goes to the heart of what makes good journalism great writing. Revisiting the site of events that might otherwise pass us by, seeking out background, shading in context and exploring nuance, such writers at their best end up telling us important stories about the human condition, about the choices we make and the actions we take. About who we are. If news is history on the run – the frail first draft – feature writing follows at a more measured pace, examining the detail, chronicling the consequences, conjecturing about responsibility. If this is so, it asks, then what? If this happened, what does it mean, why does it matter, and to whom?

Such storytellers are part writer, part sleuth, part social historian. Their stock in trade is detail. With the bogus notion of total objectivity unlikely to be achieved by any mere mortal, their stories must proceed with the same honest push for accuracy, clarity, fairness and balance that good journalism brings to the simplest news story. But for the story to come convincingly to life they need the details. They need the wide shots *and* the close-ups, the small moments, the anecdotes – a depth of information that will layer meaning into the story. They need to supplement the who, what, when and where with as much contextualising how and why as they can muster.

Seeking out detail/taking us there

Good storytellers know they need to take us there – and the fuel is the power of the specific, showing rather than telling the reader what it was like, how it felt to be there. The detail is what anchors us in reality and if we're lucky – and the writer's arsenal includes a touch of artistry, or even poetry – those details will resonate with deeper meanings that make us pause, make us care.

Fisk's eye for the indelible image – the kind of detail that brings real humanity to reportage – is always in evidence. The extended features that form the chapters of his recent book about reporting the Middle East, *The Great War for Civilisation*, read like on-the-spot history laced with incident, anecdote and detail. Reflecting on the 'titanic bloodbath' of the Iran–Iraq war, he singles out in one battle zone the image of the body of a young man 'curled up like a child', a wedding ring on his finger. 'I am mesmerised by the ring,' he tells us. 'On this hot, golden morning, it glitters and sparkles with freshness and life.' He wonders if the young Iraqi is Sunni or Shia, Christian or Kurd, and he wonders about his wife. 'Somewhere to the north of us, his wife is waking the children, making breakfast, glancing at her husband's photograph on the wall, unaware that she is already a widow and that her husband's wedding ring, so bright with love for her on this glorious morning, embraces a dead finger.'[2]

Going beyond the givens

The best journalism is about going beyond the givens. That is, going beyond the information that is generated as news events occur, often speeded on its way by PR spin that pushes a particular line. That line, uncontested, can assume the status of a given. Like Fisk's story, Seymour Hersh's 2004 *New Yorker* features chronicling the occupation of Iraq went, startlingly, beyond the givens, revealing – as in the Abu Ghraib prison stories – deeper issues, darker secrets.[3] Likewise John Cassidy's extended feature, 'The David Kelly Affair',[4] went behind the givens strenuously asserted by the Blair Government when it was accused of 'sexing up' the issue of Iraqi weapons of mass destruction. Cassidy's careful assembly of the detailed backstory not only put the lie to the government's denial, but also sounded a touching lament for the death of David Kelly, the British scientist caught up in the controversy.

In Australia, in 2005, several journalists – broadcasters, reporters and feature writers – went tenaciously behind the political givens, chipping away at the stony façade of the Immigration Department's denial of the casual cruelty and ineptitude – later officially acknowledged – in its handling of the people caught up in its system. Among them was the *Sydney Morning Herald* team of Marian Wilkinson and David Marr, whose feature stories – including the shabby saga of the Australian Wheat Board and bribes for Saddam Hussein – are characterised by a forensic examination of the record and a focus on the kind of good solid storytelling that makes complex issues accessible.

The same patient accumulation of detail was in evidence when they took up the earlier story of the refugees caught up in the *Tampa* rescue and the 'children overboard' myth – when Australia's government nailed its colours to the mast on asylum seekers. Bit by resolute bit, their features provided a fascinating counterpoint to the spin gushing from the national capital. 'We love detail', Marr says. 'Complex details don't necessarily produce complex narratives. Often the reverse: from a blizzard of detail comes the simple, true story.'[5]

Courage under pressure

Going beyond the givens is not easy terrain in the post 9/11 world, where governments are often unnervingly eager to foster fear and lower a blanket of secrecy over public interest issues that are quite properly the domain of journalism. The pressure to toe the 'official' line can be fierce, as we saw when the spinmeisters closed ranks in the runup to the Iraq invasion. Journalists who begged to differ, discharging their ethical duty to question authority – to 'monitor the centres of power', as the courageous Israeli journalist Amira Hass describes it – were less likely to earn plaudits than to be labelled as biased and even unpatriotic.

Taking on the powerful in any arena is a tough gig, as the *West Australian*'s Michael Southwell found when he pursued his news story about the mining giant Alcoa and the legacy of its toxic fallout. Southwell's lone investigation had all the makings of an Erin Brockovich saga as he tracked down the people behind the fears surfacing within the local community and then pushed for hard evidence to substantiate their claims. In the end, both the big corporate citizen and the government were forced to take action. The series of stories won Southwell a swag of national awards, including the prestigious national Walkley for news, yet the personal toll was heavy. Efforts to undermine him and pressure to lay off the story came from government and corporate sources and even from inside the paper and he resigned soon after to work independently. 'In the end it just got too hard, too much of a problem . . . It really opened up my eyes about how things work in the world and that you have to work outside the system if you want to challenge authority and challenge the status quo.'[6]

Telling it longer: turning features into books

Apart from the pressures that arise when journalists pursue volatile issues, it is dispiriting that the space for in-depth stories is increasingly shrink-wrapped across the media. Virtual pages are on offer via blogs and online publications of varying sophistication, but more writers are also opting to extend their stories into non-fiction books. The Marr–Wilkinson features on asylum seekers grew into a powerful non-fiction book, *Dark Victory*,[7] which flagged the seismic changes those controversial events presaged for Australia's image at home and abroad. *Dark Victory* joined the ranks of other stories that first appeared as features yet had an undertow that cried out for a longer telling: Truman Capote's *In Cold Blood*, Sebastian Junger's *The Perfect Storm*, John Bryson's Chamberlain saga *Evil Angels*, Margaret Simons' *Fit to Print*, Helen Garner's *Joe Cinque's Consolation*. In a fitting postscript to the problematic Alcoa series, Michael Southwell decided that the murky undertow of that story – and his fight to get it told – was worth more detail. He is writing a non-fiction book about the story. It is called *White Lies*. White, he explains, is the colour of Alcoa's prized alumina. The lies, he adds, speak for themselves.

Michael Southwell

Michael Southwell joined the *West Australian* in 1988. He later worked as an investigative reporter on the *Sunday Times* and political reporter for Nine News in Perth before re-joining the *West* in 1999. In 2002 his two-year pursuit of Alcoa on pollution, despite heavy pressure to drop the story, won the Munster Prize for Independent Journalism and the national Walkley Award for News. The Walkley citation called the stories (three appear here) 'a courageous series of lone-hand reporting that relentlessly pursued allegations against a very big corporate citizen'. It noted the lasting impact Southwell's crusading series had on public policy and the community. Southwell left the *West* soon after and is writing a non-fiction book, *White Lies*, about the story behind the story.

TOXIC FALLOUT NEAR ALCOA

Michael Southwell

West Australian, September 22, 2001

Alcoa Incorporated denies emissions from its alumina refinery are causing health problems. Its claim is supported by the Western Australian (WA) Department of Environmental Protection (DEP), which has taken part in a working group along with Alcoa and community representatives.

The group's interim report states alumina dust is found two kilometres from the refinery and abnormal levels of heavy metals occur up to six kilometres away. Air samples contain sulphur dioxide above the World Health Organization's recommended limits and aldehyde gas levels are higher on adjacent farms than at the refinery. The report, however, recommends no further testing.

A University of WA community survey concluded there is a mucous membrane irritant in the atmosphere. Chemistry Centre senior chemist, Doug Ingraham, says there is definitely a link between emissions from the refinery and health problems among Wagerup residents.

CANCER SECRET

Michael Southwell

West Australian, November 29, 2001

MINING giant Alcoa has known for years that pollution from its Kwinana and Wagerup alumina refineries could cause cancer, leukaemia and other health problems, according to confidential company documents.

The documents, provided to a parliamentary inquiry yesterday, reveal the company was aware as early as 1990 that its liquor-burning units produce large concentrations of compounds known to cause cancer.

A memo written in July, 1990, by Alcoa research scientists said several cancer-causing compounds had been found in the liquor-burner smoke stack at Kwinana. 'We should do some homework on how we communicate this information since many of these compounds are known carcinogens, some of them potent carcinogens,' the memo states.

Alcoa spokesman Brian Doy yesterday acknowledged some emissions from the refineries were known to be cancer-causing, but said air samples taken around the plants had shown these were not present at harmful levels. 'The levels found are within every health and safety standard,' Mr Doy said.

The first liquor-burner was installed at the Kwinana refinery in 1989. Another bigger one began operation at Wagerup in late 1996. Since then, there has been a dramatic increase in complaints from Wagerup workers and surrounding residents experiencing headaches, nausea and burning eyes, nose and throat.

The documents were produced by Australian Manufacturing Workers Union health and safety representative Bill Vanderpal as part of his evidence to the Legislative Council's environment and public affairs committee, which is probing Wagerup refinery emissions and health impacts.

Mr Vanderpal, who has worked at the Wagerup plant for 17 years, told the committee he had been warned several times by Alcoa staff that if he made the documents public, he would face legal action.

'I've been sitting on this, waiting for an opportunity to bring it forward,' Mr Vanderpal said.

Mr Vanderpal produced an Alcoa document prepared for a presentation to Kwinana refinery employees which suggested workers should be told that the liquor-burner produced emissions including an alkaline dust, a caustic mist and benzene, which was known to cause cancer.

He said the information was never given to employees. The committee was also shown a report prepared for Alcoa in 1997 by occupational health consultant Brian Galton-Fenzi.

It detailed strategies to overcome 'outrage' about the liquor-burner emissions in the community around the Wagerup refinery.

The report said the burner reduced impurities in alumina and was imperative for improved productivity and reduced overall costs of aluminium production.

Complaints from employees and nearby communities had the potential to threaten this process.

'Any unusual diseases (lymphomas, cancers) and possibly the more common ones (asthma, bronchitis) may have to be defended in court, again likely to be costly in time, resources and public relations,' the report said.

'Cancer is a major concern to all communities. This is best managed by legitimising the dread. Take the dread seriously and discuss the likelihood of the disease, which could arise from exposure to high concentrations of the gases/chemicals, and have them put in context.'

Documents attached to the report detail various long- and short-term health effects known to be associated with liquor-burner emissions, including leukaemia.

Dr Galton-Fenzi is now the chief occupational physician at the Department of Minerals and Energy.

ALCOA TOLD OF HEALTH ISSUES

Michael Southwell

West Australian, May 24, 2002

A LEAKED internal memo shows Alcoa knew in January 1998 that emissions from its Kwinana and Wagerup alumina refineries appeared to be harming workers.

It discusses the possibility that liquor-burner emissions at the Kwinana refinery are 'hurting our people' and compares the situation to the Wagerup refinery where a liquor-burner had been temporarily shut to minimise the impact on workers and nearby residents.

Alcoa is considering ex-gratia payments of $350,000 to several former Wagerup workers who developed multiple chemical sensitivity after exposure to fumes from the liquor-burner. Alcoa says only one Kwinana worker has been diagnosed with the condition.

No compensation has been paid.

The memo from Alcoa Kwinana's then head of research and development, Peter Forster, was sent to company doctor Steve Ormonde and six other Alcoa executives including refinery manager Hamish Petrie.

Mr Forster says he has been told by a union representative that about 30 Kwinana workers claimed to have suffered adverse health effects from liquor-burner emissions.

'Given the extreme sensitivity at Wagerup with liquor-burner emissions and alleged adverse health effects, I thought it wise to alert you . . .' the memo says.

'If these are genuine (in that a link to liquor-burner emissions can be established) then I believe that this is a serious concern, in that we may be hurting our people as well as having a deficiency in the reporting and recording of these incidents.

'Obviously, we don't want to hurt people from exposure to emissions but we don't want to get into the Wagerup situation where liquor-burner availability is severely restricted (i.e. completely offline) to minimise the impact of the emissions on our people or the surrounding community.'

Other Alcoa documents show that in 1998, the liquor-burner at Kwinana was emitting more than 3 kg per hour of cancer-causing benzene and other toxic compounds. The concentration of benzene was almost five times the recommended maximum occupational exposure limit.

A former shift foreman at the plant, Dave Thompson, has taken Alcoa to court over chemical injuries he claims were a result of exposure to refinery fumes in early 1998.

Mr Thompson said he knew of about 35 other past and present Kwinana employees who had illnesses, including cancer, which could be attributed to chemical emissions.

'The company should have investigated what was making those workers ill and told the rest of us about the concerns,' he said. 'They should have come clean with us.'

Australian Workers Union organiser Henry Rozmianiec said he was not aware of any workers injured by emissions at Kwinana, apart from Mr Thompson.

Alcoa spokesman Brian Doy said an AWU site representative had raised concerns in 1998 about liquor burning. These were investigated and resolved to the union's satisfaction.

Robert Fisk

Journalist and author Robert Fisk is the Beirut-based Middle East correspondent for the *Independent* newspaper in London. He has lived in the Middle East for almost three decades and holds more British and international awards than any other foreign correspondent. His last book, *Pity the Nation: Lebanon at war*, a history of the Lebanon war, was published in 1990 and revised in 2001. He is the author of *The Point of No Return: The strike which broke the British in Ulster*, and *In Time of War: Ireland, Ulster and the price of neutrality 1939–45*. His latest book, *The Great War for Civilisation: The conquest of the Middle East*, which chronicles his three decades of reporting the Middle East, was published in 2005.

IS THIS SOME KIND OF CRUSADE?

Robert Fisk

Independent On Sunday, May 18, 1997

All morning, the Israelis had shelled Mansouri. Thirty-two-year-old Fadila al-Oglah had spent the night with her aunt Nowkal, cowering in the barn close to the village donkeys and cows. But on Saturday morning, 13 April 1996, she came out of hiding because there was no more bread in the village and the Israeli artillery rounds were landing between the grimy concrete houses. Abbas Jiha, a farmer who acted as volunteer ambulance driver for the Shia Muslim village, had spent the night with his 27-year-old wife Mona, their three small daughters – Zeinab, Hanin and baby Mariam – and their six-year-old son Mehdi in the family's one-room hut above an olive grove, listening to the threats broadcast by the Voice of Hope radio station (which is run by Israel in the 10 per cent of Lebanese territory it occupies north of its border). 'The Israelis kept saying over the radio that the people of the villages must flee their homes,' Abbas Jiha recalls. 'They named Mansouri as one of those villages. They were telling us to escape. They were saying that they wouldn't attack the cars that were leaving the villages. And when I opened the door, I saw that the shelling was coming into Mansouri.'

Across all of southern Lebanon on that spring morning last year, towering clouds of black and grey smoke drifted towards the Mediterranean as thousands of Israeli shells poured into the little hill villages. The sky was alive with the sound of supersonic F-16 fighter-bombers, while several thousand feet above the hamlets and laneways hovered the latest and most ferocious addition to Israel's armoury – the American-made Apache helicopters whose firepower had proved so deadly to the retreating Iraqi army in Kuwait five years before. Just four days earlier, a 14-year-old Lebanese boy had been torn to pieces by a booby-trap bomb hidden beside a wall in the nearby village of Bradchit; the pro-Iranian Hizballah militia, accusing Israel of responsibility, sought revenge by firing Katyusha rockets across the border into Israel, wounding several civilians. In response,

Israeli prime minister Shimon Peres – vainly seeking re-election by portraying himself as a soldier-statesman at war with Hizballah 'terrorism' – ordered the mass bombardment of southern Lebanon from the air, sea and land.

The United States meekly called for both sides to 'exercise restraint' but publicly sympathised with Israel. The Hizballah, according to the US State Department, were ultimately to blame for the death of all those civilians – there were to be almost 200 within the next three weeks – killed by Israeli fire. Although Washington was officially neutral, the Lebanese found it difficult to dissociate their latest war from the United States. The Voice of Hope radio station ordering them to flee their homes was partly funded by right-wing American evangelists. The 155 mm artillery shells hissing over their villages were made in America. So were the F-16 jets and the Apache helicopters hovering like wasps in the pale blue skies above them. Even the name chosen by Shimon Peres for Israel's latest adventure in Lebanon – 'Operation Grapes of Wrath' – appeared to be influenced by America. If it did not come from the Book of Deuteronomy, then it was inspired by Julia Howe's 19th-century Battle Hymn of the Republic – where the Lord is seen 'trampling out the vintage where the grapes of wrath are stored' – or by the best-selling novel of the American writer John Steinbeck, who once described Arabs as 'the dirtiest people in the world and among the smelliest'.

The fruits of the operation could already be seen in Mansouri. Shortly after dawn on 13 April, a shell had struck a house on the edge of the village, wounding Abdulaziz Mohsen, a 23-year-old farmer and former Lebanese army conscript. Despite the gunfire, Abbas Jiha ran from his home to ask for the keys of the Mansouri ambulance from the village mukhtar (mayor). The battered, white-painted Volvo – a gift to the people of Mansouri from villagers who had made money after emigrating to west Africa – had two empty stretchers lying on the back floor and Jiha pushed Mohsen into the vehicle, setting off through the shellfire to the city of Tyre, up the Mediterranean coast to the north-west. In Tyre, he bought sacks of flat Arabic bread for the marooned villagers of Mansouri and arrived back by nine in the morning. He was handing out the bread when another shell hit a laneway, wounding a two-month-old baby called Ali Modehi. Back Abbas Jiha drove once more in the old village ambulance, its blue light flashing on the roof, until he had safely delivered Ali to the Tyre hospital. He bought yet more bread for the families of Mansouri, then set off again for the village.

As he did so, Najla Abujahjah, a young Reuters camerawoman, was on an equally dangerous mission, driving through the foothills east of Mansouri in an attempt to film the Israeli air attacks for the British news agency. Unwilling to leave the battlezone, Abujahjah – a resourceful and brave young woman who will never forget the terrible event she was shortly to witness – headed west to a road near Mansouri where she caught sight of two more Apaches that appeared to be watching something – 'almost stationary in the sky but moving a few metres backwards and then a few metres forwards'.

Abbas Jiha was now back in the centre of Mansouri, enveloped in a scene of mass panic. 'Many people had already fled their homes but a few were left, including my own family, and the shells were falling all over the place. A jet came and dropped a bomb on the edge of the village. So I said the people could get into the ambulance and I'd take them to safety. I got Mona and our children.' Abbas Jiha says that just as he put nine-year-old Zeinab, five-year-old Hanin and two-month-old Mariam, along with their brother Mehdi into the back of the ambulance, he saw two helicopters. 'They were low and the pilots seemed to be watching us,' he says.

Fadila al-Oglah bought two bags of bread from Abbas but was herself now fearful of the planes. 'Although the Israelis said we would not be attacked if we fled our houses, the Apaches were strafing the roads with bullets, and shells were bursting around our homes,' she was to recall later. 'My brothers had left in a pick-up and other people had escaped in farm tractors. My parents told me: "Leave and follow your brothers." I went down to the village to look for another pick-up but then I saw Abbas Jiha driving the village ambulance with his wife and family inside. I asked if he would take me and he said, "No problem."'

By the time Abbas Jiha left Mansouri, he had 13 terrified passengers crammed into the vehicle. There was his wife Mona and their four children, Fadila and her aunt Nowkal, Mohamed Hisham, a window repairman, and five members of the al-Khaled family – 22-year-old Nadia, who was Nowkal's daughter, and her four nieces, Sahar (three), Aida (seven), Hudu (11) and Manar (13). Abbas and Mohamed Hishem, the only male adults, sat in the front of the ambulance along with six-year-old Mehdi; the rest sat pressed together in the back. 'Can you imagine what it was like with 14 people in the vehicle?' Fadila asks. Abbas Jiha remembers that part of the village was now on fire, the smoke curling over the fields. 'We left in a convoy of tractors and cars and headed for Amriyeh where there was a UN post with Fijian soldiers on the main coast road to Tyre. The shells were falling all round us in the fields.'

Najla Abujahjah was herself now standing in front of the Fijian position – UN Checkpoint 1–23 – taking still pictures of refugee traffic on the road, her friend holding her videocamera. 'There were two helicopters in the sky, watching the checkpoint,' she says. 'I was worried about those helicopters, about what they were doing there. I saw an ambulance coming down the road and thought it must have wounded on board but then saw it was full of women and children. There was another car moving in the opposite direction and the ambulance driver was waving with his hand, telling it to turn back.' The videotape record of those moments shows the ambulance passing the UN checkpoint, as Abbas Jiha's hand comes from the window, urging the car to stop.

It was then that Abbas Jiha heard the women in the back of his ambulance shouting at him. 'One of them was crying out to me: "The helicopter is coming close to us – it's chasing us." I looked out of the window and I could see the Apache getting closer. I told them all: "Don't be afraid – just say, Allahu Akbar [God is Great] and the name of the Imam Ali [son-in-law of the prophet and founder of the Shia faith]." I had told them not to be afraid but I was very frightened.'

Najla Abujahjah saw the same helicopter. 'It was getting lower and nearer, and I've learnt that this means the pilot is going to fire. I felt he was going to fire a missile but I didn't imagine the target would be so close to me. I heard a sound like "puff-puff", a very small sound. And I saw a missile flying from the Apache with a trail of smoke behind it.' In fact, the Israeli helicopter pilot fired two missiles; one was later discovered unexploded beside a neighbouring mosque, its steel cylinder, fins and nameplate still intact. Najla's videotape records what happened to the other rocket. Milliseconds after the ambulance cleared UN Checkpoint 1–23, the missile exploded through the back door, engulfing the vehicle in fire and smoke and hurling it 20 metres through the air into the living-room of a house.

All Fadila remembers was 'a great heat in my face, like a blazing fire. Somehow I was outside the ambulance and I found a big barrel of water and started to wash my face from the heat. It was all I could think of, despite the screaming and smoke, this terrible heat. It was as if someone was holding a flame in front of my eyes.'

Abbas Jiha recalls hurling himself from the door of the ambulance just before it crashed into the house. 'I was terrified. I couldn't believe it. It was the end of my world. I knew what must have happened to my family.' Najla, trembling with fear, was now videotaping the terrible aftermath of the Israeli missile attack. Wounded in the head and foot, Abbas Jiha stands in the road beside one of his dead daughters, weeping and shrieking 'God is Great' up into the sky, towards the helicopter. 'I raised my fists to the pilot and cried out, "My God, my God, my family has gone."'

Abbas found his son Mehdi alive. Then he saw two-month-old Mariam lying three metres from the ambulance. 'All her body had holes through it. Her head was full of metal.' Najla saw women and children 'coming out of the back of the ambulance, cowering and screaming and hiding. One man threw himself into the orchard then came out holding two children by the arms. One was a little girl who was wounded and barefoot but she was still trying to put her scarf back on. I saw a girl lying on the road with blood coming out of the top of her head. The driver was crying out, "My children have died, God have mercy on us." I saw another girl – she was Manar – and she had blood all over her, and she kept saying, "My sister's head has exploded."'

Still fearful that the helicopter would fire again – the pilot had clearly seen that his target was an ambulance – Najla ran towards the house to find a scene which she says will haunt her for the rest of her life. 'I couldn't get the doors open because the vehicle was wedged in the room. But there were three children inside who were clearly in the last seconds of their life. It was as if they were entombed. One of them – she was Hanin – collapsed on the broken window frame, her blood running in streams down the outside of the vehicle. In her last seconds she tried to look at me but she couldn't because dust covered her face. Another little girl was sitting in the lap of a dead woman, wailing and crying, "Aunty, Aunty." There was a third girl who had her face covered in blood; she was sitting up, turning her head from side to side. Another had a terrible wound to her head and neck and she collapsed.' As the children died one by one in front of her, Najla heard a strange scraping sound. 'The missile had set off the windscreen wipers and they were going back and forth against the broken glass, making this terrible noise. It will haunt me the rest of my days.'

Abbas Jiha, overwhelmed with grief, was tearing at the vehicle with his bare hands, along with UN Fijian troops from the checkpoint. 'I could see Hanin's back – she was cut through with holes like a mosquito net,' he remembers. 'Then I found my wife Mona. She was so terribly wounded, I couldn't recognise her face. I had lost her and three of my children.' Mona Jiha, nine-year-old Zeinab, five-year-old Hanin and the two-month-old baby Mariam were all dead. So was 60-year-old Nowkal and her 11-year-old niece

Hudu. The Israeli helicopter remained in the sky over UN Checkpoint 1–23 for another five minutes. Then it flew away.

Within hours the Israelis admitted they had targeted the ambulance but made two claims: that the vehicle was owned by a Hizballah member (which was untrue) and that it was destroyed because it had been carrying a Hizballah guerrilla (which was also untrue). 'If other individuals in the vehicle were hit during the attack,' an Israeli spokesman said, 'they had been used by the Hizballah as a cover for Hizballah activities.' There were no apologies. Yet international law demands the safeguarding of civilian lives even in the presence of 'individuals who do not come within the definition of civilians' (article 50, paragraph 3, of the 1949 Geneva Conventions' Protocol 1), and the claim that the vehicle had been targeted because it was believed to be owned by the Hizballah was in some ways even more extraordinary. How, the survivors asked themselves, could it be justifiable for the Israelis to slaughter the occupants of an ambulance just because they didn't like the suspected owner of the vehicle? And what kind of missile, they also asked, could home in on an ambulance, blasting it 60 feet through the air? If the Apache helicopter was American – as it most certainly was – who made the rocket that killed Nowkal, Mona and the four children, Zeinab, Hanin, Mariam and Hudu?

For days after the killings, the smashed ambulance lay in the wreckage of the house into which it had been blasted on 13 April. I passed it myself each day as I drove the frightening coast road south of Tyre, two Apache helicopters watching my movements as they did all vehicles on the highway. Within a week, the blood bath at Qana, in which 109 Lebanese refugees were massacred, had eclipsed this particular horror, eventually bringing Operation Grapes of Wrath to an ignominious end – and failing to win Shimon Peres' election. But there were many other incidents during the bombardment which bore a remarkable similarity to the ambulance attack. Close to the Jiyeh power station, south of Beirut, for example, another Israeli helicopter pilot had fired a missile at a car, killing a young woman who had just bought a sandwich from a local cafe. In west Beirut on 16 April, a missile decapitated a two-year-old girl. Two days later, yet another helicopter-fired missile was targeted at a block of apartments at Nabatieh, killing a family of nine, including a two-day-old baby.

What were these terrible weapons that were now being used so promiscuously in Lebanon? Who sold them to the Israelis? And – if it was an American company which had manufactured the missile – what conditions were attached to its sale? In the village of Mansouri, Abbas Jiha ruminated upon this same question. 'How would the people who made this missile feel if their children were killed as mine were?' he asked. 'These things are meant to be used against armies, not civilians.' Fadila al-Oglah was more resigned. 'The Americans will keep giving these weapons to the Israelis whatever we say,' she remarked one day in the same draughty two-room house she had fled last year. 'They don't care about us. We will continue to suffer.'

SHORTLY AFTER the Israeli bombardment ended, however, UN ordnance officers searching through the wreckage of the ambulance found an intriguing clue to the missile's identity. Among fragments of shrapnel and twisted steel, a young UN officer discovered a hunk of metal bearing most of a nameplate. It had come to rest a few inches from the bloodstained window frame where Hanin had died, and contained the logo 'AGM 114C' and a manufacturer's number: 04939. The UN officer knew AGM stood for 'Air-to-Ground Missile', and the 114 C coding identified the 5 ft 3ins projectile as a Hellfire anti-armour missile, jointly manufactured by Rockwell International and Martin Marietta. Rockwell – now taken over by Boeing – had its headquarters, according to Jane's Defence Weekly, at Satellite Boulevard, Duluth, in Georgia, about 20 minutes from Atlanta. Martin Marietta, now part of Lockheed, was in Orlando, Florida. Those who made the missile which killed four Lebanese children and two women now had an address. But how would the missile manufacturers respond to the blood bath inside the Mansouri ambulance?

The first question was how to send the missile fragment – the vital and only proof that the ambulance had been hit by a Hellfire – from Lebanon to the United States. It was not difficult to get it aboard an international flight from Beirut to Paris. But explaining to American security men that I wanted to carry it all the way to Washington was going to end in journalistic disaster. The hunk of shrapnel was no more a rocket than a piece of broken china constituted a plate, but the very word 'missile' would cause palpitations to any US agent in the aftermath of the TWA disaster off New York. In the end, a human-rights group offered to courier the shrapnel to its Washington office and, a few days later, after flying via New York, I picked up the Hellfire fragment in the heart of the capital whose alliance with Israel allows neither criticism nor restraint. The Crescent, a railroad train en route to New Orleans, would take me through the night down to Georgia where Bob Algarotti of Boeing had agreed to meet me to discuss the Hellfire at the very home of the missile.

I awoke next morning to see soft green countryside and clapboard houses sailing past the window of my carriage. How neat those little gardens were with their flowers and children's swings. Was I only 6000 miles away from southern Lebanon – or on a different planet? There were episcopalian churches and smart Georgian courthouses and towns called Carmelia and Magnolia flicking past, and a gunstore – in a land where every man has the right to bear arms – called Lock, Stock and Barrel. And so many flagstaffs that dawn morning I could see through my carriage window. And so many red, white and blue American flags snapping proudly from them. There hadn't been a war in these parts for 130 years.

I climbed down at Gainsville station where a taximan with one surviving tooth took me down Interstate 85 and the Old Peachtree Road where I saw a sign saying Duluth and then Satellite Boulevard and then – three miles further on – we turned into a campus of discreet two-storey buildings hidden behind tall trees and manicured lawns. 'Boeing Defence and Space Group,' it said on the sign at the gate.

It was to be a disturbing afternoon. A tiny green-painted model of the Hellfire stood on a shelf of the room in which Bob Algarotti of Boeing introduced me to two executives intimately involved in the production of the missile. They were highly intelligent men; both were former serving officers in Vietnam and both would later request anonymity – for their security, it seemed, although their concern about Boeing's reaction to the interview appeared to outweigh any concerns about the Hizballah.

I explained that I was interested in writing about the abilities of the missile – but also about its specific use in the Middle East. The executive to my right – whom I shall call the Colonel, for that was his rank in Vietnam – produced a glossy brochure which detailed the evolution of the Hellfire modular missile system, and placed it on the table between us. Page two carried a series of small illustrated cross-sections of the rocket and, following the dates 1982–1989, a coding of AGM 114 A, B, C. The piece of shrapnel – which, unbeknown to them was in my camera bag – was marked AGM 114 C. So the missile that killed Abbas Jiha's family, Nowkal and her niece was at least eight years old.

The Colonel listed those countries which had purchased either an early or later, improved category of the Hellfire – first on the list was Israel with both categories ('They take soldiering pretty seriously,' the Colonel remarked) but Egypt, South Africa and the United Arab Emirates were also included. Sweden and Norway had purchased an anti-ship version of the Hellfire. The British had category two. It was a popular product and the Colonel was keen to explain why. 'It's probably the most precise anti-armour weapon in the world,' he said. 'You can fire it through a basketball hoop at five miles and it would do it every time.' So the women and children in the ambulance, I thought to myself, had stood no chance.

I asked what checks Rockwell (the original missile company) carried out on how the Hellfire had been used by those nations which purchased it. They read the papers, both executives said. I asked about Israel. 'We do not get information from the Israelis about what they've done,' one of the men replied. 'They don't give much information.' It was time to produce the missile fragment. And as I knelt to extract it from my camera bag, I felt the electricity in the air behind me. I turned round and laid the shard of iron which had helped to kill the Lebanese in the centre of the table. I told all three men the date of its use, the location, the results and the Israeli explanation.

The Colonel picked it up first, turning it in his hand and muttering something about how it might be too small a fragment to identify. His colleague to my left said nothing, stared at the fragment and looked at me. Bob Algarotti, the public-relations man, picked it up, glanced at his colleagues, and said quietly: 'Yeah, well it's a Hellfire, we all know that.'

Then he said: 'I'm getting a little uncomfortable.' But the Colonel was angry. 'This is so far off base, it's ridiculous,' he said. I begged to disagree. They manufactured this missile. Did they not bear some responsibility for its use – at least to ensure that it was used responsibly by their clients? There then followed some very uncomfortable minutes. Algarotti complained that you couldn't blame a knife-maker if someone used the knife to murder someone else. Yes, I said, but this was not a knife. The Hellfire was an antipersonnel weapon. 'It's not!' the Colonel replied. 'It's an anti-armour weapon.' And then there was silence – because, of course, if the missile was an anti-armour weapon, it most surely was not an anti-ambulance weapon. 'Are you on some kind of crusade?' one of the executives asked.

I said I thought this an unfortunate remark – and Algarotti interrupted quietly to agree with me. We were dealing with the death of innocent people, I repeated, including four children. What was I looking for, one of the men asked? For some sign of compassion from them, I replied. One of the men in the room said: 'I, as a person – sure I have feelings, but as a Boeing company employee, all we do is make missiles.'

I agreed to lay down my pen while the three men discussed how they could frame some statement of their feelings. Both executives clearly felt deeply troubled about the events which I described; they were family men and wanted to express their horror at the deaths of innocents. But they didn't want Boeing involved and – equally obviously – they were frightened of criticising Israel. During the afternoon, one man at Boeing would be heard to say twice – in identical words, I observed in my notebook – 'Whatever you do, I don't want you to quote me as saying anything critical of Israel's policies.'

Then one of the executives made up his mind. 'Let me speak as a soldier, not as an employee of Boeing,' he said. 'No professional soldier is going to condone the killing of innocent people as targets. We're trained to preserve the peace . . . Of course, the Boeing company is troubled if its weapons are misused or targeted against, you know, innocent people. But we build weapons systems to US requirements, we get permission to sell to many different countries . . . we don't sell missiles that are intended for non-military targets . . .'

I pulled from my bag the photographs which Najla Abujahjah had taken of the victims. The executive to my left looked through them with an expression of horror. Then he said: 'I don't want these.' And he slid the pictures of the dead and wounded members of the Jiha family across the heavily polished table-top. The Colonel looked at them and gently returned them to me. We parted with handshakes; and I felt oddly sad for these men. They were decent, hard-working, loyal employees of Rockwell – now Boeing – and they had been shocked by the story of the ambulance. They wanted to express their compassion – and did so, up to a point – but were desperately anxious to avoid any offence to Boeing or to Israel. I told them to keep the Hellfire missile fragment. I was returning it to them. And as I left the room, I heard a voice behind me say: 'I don't think we'll put this one in the trophy room.'

AND THERE my journey might have ended were it not for a message from Bob Algarotti that I received two days later. It was, to say the least, confusing. His people, he said, had been studying the missile fragment. They thought it had been made in the late Eighties at the Orlando factory in Florida, by Lockheed Martin – at that time a rival company. But the story wasn't that simple. The 'fed log' number, partly damaged in the explosion, showed the figures to be 04939. 'And that – at least the last four [digits] – definitely indicated it's either got to be us or it's got to be Martin Marietta then.' This hardly seemed conclusive. If it was either Rockwell (now Boeing) or Martin Marietta (now Lockheed Martin), which of them made this killer-missile? Boeing – whose headquarters in Seattle refused to add to what I'd been told in Duluth – said it had not contacted Lockheed Martin about my enquiry.

But when I called Al Kamhi, Lockheed's director of communications – who, by chance, was on a business trip to London – he knew exactly what I was investigating. 'You talking about what you discussed with Rockwell?' he asked. '. . . I mean, I have no way of knowing what missile that was. I have no way of knowing if that missile ever came from where you say it came from . . . They [Boeing] can be as convinced as they want to be . . . as far as I'm concerned, I'm not going to start looking at missile fragments from . . . Their origin is totally unknown – I'm just not going to do that.'

'Can I let you have them anyway?' I asked. And our conversation became almost surreal:

Kamhi: 'No, I won't accept them.'
Fisk: 'You won't accept them?'
Kamhi: 'No.'
Fisk: 'Can you tell me why not, Sir? . . . I mean, this involves the death of four children and two women in an ambulance.'
Kamhi: 'I don't know that that missile has anything to do with it . . . I mean I can't comment on something I have no information on.'
Fisk: 'Well, I'm offering you the information so that you can check on it, Sir. Boeing do seem convinced that it was made by your people.'
Kamhi: 'And I'm not sure I understand – if it was or if it wasn't – what the point is.'

I told Kamhi that I wanted to know the response of the company that made the Hellfire to the events that took place when its missile was used. 'I have no comment on what took place,' he replied. 'I'm not even going to get into that arena . . . Our sales are made through foreign military sales . . . that's the way it's done, through the Pentagon.' I repeated that UN officers had found the missile in the ambulance, along with another close by which had failed to explode. There was no doubt about their provenance. Our conversation continued in an even more bizarre manner.

Kamhi: 'Well, frankly, the missile has nothing to do with the manufacturer.'
Fisk: 'But you made it.'
Kamhi: 'Well, we make a lot of things, too . . . our products are sold to allied nations.'
Fisk: 'Does that include Israel?'
Kamhi: 'I presume if Israel has Hellfire, then they purchase the Hellfires through legal channels and through legal means.'
Fisk: 'But I mean, do you care about the use to which your missiles are put by those people to whom you sell them? I mean, this is a very important point, Sir.'
Kamhi: 'I'm sorry – I'm not going to dignify that question with a response. It's a no-win question . . . I'm just not going to respond to that . . . the question you have asked is a 'have-you-stopped-beating-your-wife?' question. No matter how I respond to that question, we all of a sudden are the bad missile manufacturer. We make missiles. We make electronic systems. We make a variety of defence systems. And it is our hope that they're never used . . . We don't know that the missile was misused. A missile can miss . . .'

I explained to Kamhi that the Israelis agreed the ambulance was the target. Then they should respond to it, he said. But then, when I suggested that the US government was itself concerned about the use to which its country's weaponry was put by clients, Kamhi changed his tone, though only fractionally. 'We're always concerned when someone is hurt,' he said. 'As far as why the missile was used . . . there's no way we can control [sic] or understand why . . . We don't have any say in that . . . you know, every day over 600 people are shot in America. Not once do I know that anyone has gone back and questioned the bullet-maker.'

And so it went on, Kamhi ever more irritated. He didn't know if the ambulance was the intended target – and again I offered him my documentation with photographs of the missile part. 'I can't make the determination,' he replied impatiently. 'I wasn't the one pulling the trigger. Lockheed Martin was not the one that was there, firing the missile. Ultimately it has to come down to the responsibility of the user . . . It is not for us, the manufacturer, to go ahead and take action in a case like this.'

Kamhi's replies were hopelessly inadequate, even pathetic. But their message was clear. If an American missile was fired into an ambulance, those who made it would fiercely deny any blame. It was for Israel to explain. And when it did – agreeing that against all the rules of war, the Hellfire had deliberately been fired into an ambulance – America was silent. The equation was complete. Israel, it seems, can do what it wants.

Al Kamhi agreed to let me drop off at his London hotel a packet of news reports on the ambulance killings, along with the missile codings and photographs of the Hellfire fragment. So the next day, I took the Channel tunnel train from Paris to London with my package that included pictures of the missile part I had left in the United States. They travelled with me through the fresh spring countryside of Kent, through my own home town of Maidstone – it had been a long journey since I left the south-Lebanese village of Mansouri – and to the Britannia Hotel in Grosvenor Square where Al Kamhi was staying. He was not in, so I left the package with reception, receiving a promise that it would be handed to Mr Kamhi the moment he came back to the hotel.

Three days later, the same package – opened but resealed – arrived at *The Independent's* foreign desk in London: 'Return to Sender.'

Interview with Robert Fisk

Question *The story about the missile attack in Lebanon could have stopped with the news report, but you pushed on so that it became not just a story of that attack, those civilian deaths, but a story about humanity and armaments manufacture and moral responsibility. What made you decide to take this particular story so far?*

Fisk I always wanted to try and find the gun that fired the shell that landed somewhere else. It went back to the civil war in Lebanon, when a very good friend of mine was killed and I tried to find the artillery piece that fired the shell that did the killing. And then I wanted to try to find out where the gun was made and where the shell was made – and of course it's not easy in a civil war to do that.

So I had it in my mind ever since the early to mid-70s that I wanted to try to track down – from an actual incident – who made the gun, or the missile, or the airplane, or whatever. And when this happened [the shelling of the ambulance in Mansouri] I was on the road very close to the scene and I was outraged at what I saw. There was footage of the attack as you know and also terrible footage of the driver of the ambulance holding his dead son and shaking his fist at the Israeli helicopter pilot. And, with the help of a very sympathetic UN officer looking for evidence at the site, we did manage to get the full missile codings so I could actually track it back [to the US manufacturer].

When you did track it back, was it a difficult interview to set up?

I got the Washington office to call Boeing and give them the impression that I was coming to do an article about their wonderful Hellfire missile, because if they knew why I was coming then I wouldn't have got the interview. I was prepared to do a story about the missile as well and at the beginning of our conversation one of the executives produced a rather glorious brochure for the Hellfire. But after a while, as my questioning continued, the brochure was taken off the table.

So you had the idea of a confrontation on that issue in mind from the start?

Oh, yes, absolutely. Originally we were planning to get the whole thing on film. We were going to take cameras to Boeing and put the pictures of the children on the table, but that didn't happen. But the idea was the same. The idea was to see what responsibility they would take for the deaths of those children, because it seemed to me that the question of responsibility was everything. The thing is that if you can't get at the question of responsibility, it's always going to go on happening.

Your story provided an electrifying account of that moment anyway, when you laid out the missile fragment and the photographs. Did you feel the men in that boardroom knew what you were getting at – that broader question of responsibility?

Oh, yes, they knew, they knew exactly what I was talking about. One of them said to me 'this is about morality, isn't it?' and I said yes, it was. When I did a lecture on the subject after I wrote that story, I played the tape with the guy I talked to later – he was very hostile – and he sent back the package of photos I left for him to identify [marked Return to Sender]. And we played the tape and showed the film of the children being taken dead out of the ambulance. It was very powerful. I mean, if you can't go for the jugular with these huge, massive companies that make weapons then I'm not sure what you can do.

Looking back, what do you think about the impact of the story? The revelation that the missile had been manufactured in the US and allocated to US armed forces?

What was outrageous about that particular story was that only one American paper printed a version of it – cut back – and one other American paper in Chicago rang me up and said they were going to follow it up, but they didn't do it. The American press should be going for these people and saying, 'Look, hold on a second, what the hell happened here? This was *your* missile, what was it doing there?' And they didn't do it. The cosy relationship between power authority and the press in America prevents that and I think that that's what very depressing about it. You might say it's good journalism by me, but it didn't get anywhere. It did show Boeing that you could pursue them. But what I think should happen in situations like this is that these big companies should be sued in court for innocent deaths. I can only do it journalistically.

When you say it didn't get anywhere, what more of a role could a journalist play?

The answer to your question is that good journalism should produce a political response. And I don't think any longer that journalism – good or whatever – does do that. I mean Watergate got rid of Nixon, got the bad guy, didn't it? – it had a political response all right, an earthquake. But the result of my story was absolutely nothing. One would like to mobilise public opinion at this end too. Sometimes you can do it. The American women who've lost children in Iraq managed to embarrass Bush, didn't they? But, you see, that's Americans. It should be Arabs actually who should be mobilising about this, but the relationship with power in the United States through the oil nexus is obviously so close that they wouldn't do it. So you end up with just the little people again.

But telling the story starts a process, doesn't it? Heightens awareness, provokes debate?

I think I am quite influenced at present by the fact that writing my new book [*The Great War for Civilisation*] was very hard. And one of the things that came over to me was how much we as journalists had written and written and written about injustice. Look at the case on the West Bank. Still they're dividing up the Palestinians into these little bantustans. Still there is massive injustice after all the words we've written since 1948. And it makes no difference at all – the Israelis can get away with it.

What about the value of contributing to the debate? The process of education?

Education produces new generations. And new generations still have the power to change things. But individually as a journalist . . . and this is one of the reasons I was so depressed in writing my book. I went back through so many of the stories I'd written, and the wounded I'd seen, and at the end of the day it didn't change anything, it didn't correct the situation. I mean look, I went after the weapons of mass destruction story right from the start, before the war. I was in New York reporting from the United Nations – and it didn't make the slightest bit of difference. In they went. And when the war ended – or when the Americans reached Baghdad and said it had ended – I wrote in the paper that the real war between the occupying power and the insurgents was about to begin and I was laughed at. Now obviously I can't stop an invasion of Iraq, but the fact of the matter is that the result of our stories was that our readers knew something that others might not have known. And that was pretty much it.

You have just finished the book about your 30 years in the Middle East, revisiting all those war zones, and as you say it has been difficult and depressing . . .

The book might ultimately have a greater power to influence than the stories . . . I realised doing the book that I was very lucky to be alive, very lucky to be alive, particularly in the Iran Iraq war . . . and I realised too . . . I wondered why I'd done it. You see I'm 59 now and I came out here when I was 29 years old and full of my passion for journalism and love of life and so on. And when I was in Paris and Amsterdam for the book launching, I saw couples walking by in the street with their children, with a comparatively safe life, and I increasingly asked myself whether that shouldn't have been what I should have done. And I think I feel increasingly that I might have chosen a different form of career if I'd known what I was going to go through. I was saying to another interviewer, this morning actually, I think when you see so much suffering and so much blood, never mind the personal risk, I don't think you despair, but I think you come away with a very bleak and pessimistic view of the world you live in. I used to think that watching history was a privilege but now I think probably it was a curse. And the book is the story of a curse.

How do you feel about concerns that journalists are losing their freedom to operate, with a blanket of secrecy imposed over matters of public interest in the name of security?

You've got to break through the blanket – tell the story. The point is that there are always going to be leakers if you look for them, just like Watergate. There will always be leakers. And I think journalists have to work hard, and if journalists have the emotional desire to be close to power, to cosy up to it in this osmotic, parasitic way, then I think it's very difficult to disentangle journalists from those things.

It was Amira Hass, the courageous Israeli journalist, who used the phrase 'monitoring the centres of power' – about the responsibility of journalists. I had said to her that our job as foreign correspondents was to be the first witnesses to history and to write about it – and she said no, that I was wrong, our job was to monitor the centres of power and to challenge authority. I think what she said is the best definition of what journalism should be that I have heard. And by and large I don't think we do that. We probably do it a bit more now because of the lies governments suggested we should tell before the war, but I still don't see the great investigative journalists of America any more. There is some stuff coming out of America, the *New York Times* and so on – but it's got that sort of three-steps-forward-two-steps-back 'officials say' quality to it.

In a speech in Sydney in 2005 you talked about the dangerous situation in Iraq – how for the first time in covering all those wars you found yourself thinking about the risks.

Sixty-one journalists have been killed in Iraq. It's the world's most dangerous place for reporters and I don't know if it's still worth going through those risks. It's as simple as that. It may be necessary to go in from the side, to do stories from the side, so to speak, to find out what is going on with big power governments and the military and so on. You don't have to be there to get the stories. There are big stories about Iraq at the moment that are coming from Australia [bribes for Saddam, the release of new photos from Abu Ghraib]. They didn't come from Baghdad.

What advice would you offer to young people who might want to get into journalism?

I think the most important thing is that if you think you might want to be anything else apart from a journalist then don't be a journalist. You must really want to do it to do it well. I think you've got to form a good relationship with your editors – they've got to trust you, and they've got to give you backing. You've got to have a foreign editor who is fearless. Once you start to compromise, once you change a word, once you, for example, call the occupied territories the disputed territories, or a wall a barrier, or a settlement a neighbourhood . . . you're finished. You should never compromise in writing the truth.

You've talked about the difficulties and the sacrifices. Can you say what qualities you think have enabled you to keep at it?

You've got to be very tough. And you've got to be very tough with yourself. And you've got to make your decisions quickly. And you mustn't make mistakes. And you've got to be tough-skinned, and if you're going to write somewhere like the Middle East you've got to expect sticks and stones, sometimes quite literally.

You mention Amira Hass as a courageous journalist. What characterises the work of the journalists you admire?

They're tough. And they ask direct questions. And they don't let go when they've got their teeth into something. And they know that governments lie.

David Marr and Marian Wilkinson

Journalist and author David Marr was editor of the *National Times* and has worked for ABC TV's *Four Corners* and written for the *Bulletin* and the *Sydney Morning Herald*, to which he returned in 2005 after presenting ABC TV's *Media Watch* for three years. He is author of *The High Price of Heaven*, and the biographies *Barwick* and *Patrick White: A life*. He co-authored *Dark Victory* with Marian Wilkinson, following their extensive coverage of the Australian Government's standoff with refugees during the Tampa events, the 'children overboard' affair and the election campaign that brought the Howard government its third victory.

Marian Wilkinson is one of Australia's most highly esteemed journalists. Now national security editor of the *Sydney Morning Herald*, she has worked as deputy editor of the *Herald*, Washington correspondent of the *Herald* and the Melbourne *Age*, executive producer of ABC TV's *Four Corners* and senior reporter for the *Australian*. She is the author of *The Book of Leaks*, with fellow journalist Brian Toohey, *The Fixer*, an account of the life and career of Australian Labor Party figure Graham Richardson, and *Dark Victory* with David Marr.

THEY SHALL NOT LAND

David Marr and Marian Wilkinson

Sydney Morning Herald, October 20, 2001

THE call came for Captain Arne Rinnan about midnight on August 26. It had already been a hell of a night. Now it was going to get much worse. On the line was an official of Australia's Department of Immigration and Multicultural Affairs (DIMA) giving him the warnings given to people smugglers. The captain of the Tampa was being threatened with the huge penalties of the Migration Act unless he turned back to Indonesia. Those penalties included massive fines and the power to seize and sell ships.

For the past 12 hours, Rinnan had been engaged in a rescue operation working first with Australia and then with Indonesia to take 433 boatpeople on board his ship. But events during the night had taken a very nasty turn that led Rinnan to put the Tampa about and head for Christmas Island.

Until the midnight call from DIMA, the authorities had been playing it by the book. Communications between the Tampa and Australian officials over the previous hours had been courteous and professional. Suddenly Canberra was playing a different game. Australia was threatening the Tampa in the same way Coastwatch officers routinely try to halt the hulks used by people smugglers, boats flying no flags and acknowledging no owners. Canberra was acting ahead of its best advice. Once the lawyers started to look at the problem later in the morning, there was a shift of tactics. But the Government

did not pull back. Instead, at lunchtime, John Howard emerged from cabinet and said the human cargo on the Tampa 'will not be given permission to land in Australia or any Australian territories'.

Every aspect of the Tampa crisis was shaped by that declaration. Howard has been as good as his promise. This has made him one of the most popular prime ministers in the recent history of Australia. It helps that the minuses of his strategy are showing up abroad in Nauru, Oslo, New York, Geneva and Jakarta.

Back home it's all been pluses for the campaigning Prime Minister and his Government. Australia seems at last, and all on its own, to be defending its borders. Soren Jessen-Petersen, the assistant High Commissioner for Refugees and the UN's highest official handling the crisis, told the Herald that the UN had found countries to take many of those on the Tampa, but Australia refused this solution because it would have involved the asylum seekers first landing on Christmas Island. He also said those offers had since been withdrawn. It is almost inevitable many of the Tampa people will find themselves back in Australia. By going it alone in the Tampa crisis, Australia has used up its goodwill in the world over refugees.

Seven weeks into the crisis Australia finds itself in this position: we have deployed the SAS and the Navy, conducted a diplomatic quarrel with Norway, been snubbed by Indonesia and been rebuffed publicly and privately by the UN. We have been the target of press criticism around the world and praise from London tabloids. Very tough new migration laws have come into effect that will allow Australia to expel refugee boats.

Out in the Pacific, Australia is trying to establish a chain of holding camps. One is operating on Nauru, PNG has approved a second on Manus Island, and negotiations are continuing for camps on Kiribati, Fiji and Palau. So far all this has cost more than $103 million, with no end to that spending in sight.

Since the Tampa, six more boats have reached Australian waters. One of those boats has now been pushed out to sea from Ashmore Reef with a day-old child aboard. Yet Australia, by the standards of the world, has a very small problem with boat people. We are expecting maybe 5000 this year. Norway is planning for 16,000. The question is will Howard's dramatic message to refugees and people smugglers make any difference?

'We will do everything we can to defend the integrity of our borders consistent with our international obligations and the behaviour of a humane, decent country,' Howard told Alan Jones.

'On the one hand we want to defend our borders, rightly so; on the other hand, we are a decent people, we don't behave in a way that causes people to drown, and to die, we don't shoot people, we don't carry on in that fashion and it's probably because of that that we are seen by many around the world as a soft touch.'

A FEW facts to bear in mind about Norway: it has roughly the population of Sydney but is the fourth largest marine power in the world. Norway lives by the sea and international maritime law is crucial to its prosperity. The kingdom has a long, honourable record in search and rescue. Like Australia, Norway is a signatory to the UN Convention on the Law of the Sea which obliges ships to 'proceed with all possible speed to the rescue of persons in distress'.

At 1 pm on Sunday, August 26, Australian Search and Rescue (AusSAR) put out a general alert that a wooden ferry was drifting with a large number of passengers in the Indian Ocean north-west of Christmas Island. AusSAR had been keeping an eye on the boat for nearly 24 hours while trying, unsuccessfully, to alert its Indonesian counterpart to the problem. The stalled boat was in the Indonesian rescue zone. Rinnan answered the call and as he changed course for the boat, AusSAR asked him to co-ordinate further action with the Indonesians. Rinnan did so but he was in fact guided to the KM Palapa 1 nearly four hours later by an Australian Coastwatch plane.

For AusSAR, the issue throughout this night was the safety of the people on the Palapa 1 and the crew on the Tampa. But Canberra was in two minds here. It would later be said that the Palapa 1 was closer to Java than Christmas Island. This was not so. Rinnan found the Palapa 1 at a point in the ocean 75 nautical miles from Christmas Island and 246 nautical miles from the Indonesian port of Merak. On board were 433 men, women and children, all but 10 of whom identified as Afghans. They were undoubtedly on a people-smuggling operation but on past experience nearly all Afghans who reached Australia are accepted as refugees.

After two hours, with the empty Palapa 1 breaking up in the swell, the Tampa set off for Merak where permission to land these people had been given by the Indonesia Search and Rescue Authority. The Tampa expected the voyage to take 30 hours but after only about 90 minutes there was an alarming incident on the bridge.

A group of men appeared and confronted Rinnan. A few hours later Rinnan's lawyer told DIMA they described themselves as 'desperate people from a dangerous background and that they required him to take them to Christmas Island. They made it clear to him that there would be dire consequences for safety of ship, crew and passengers if he did not. He felt threatened.'

Rinnan is a very experienced ship's master with more than 40 years' service to Wallenius Wilhelmsen shipping. He now had on board his ship 355 men over the age of 16. They outnumbered his crew 13 to one and were threatening violence. Rinnan contacted AusSAR and spoke to the senior marine search officer on duty that night in Canberra. AusSAR has since confirmed Rinnan was advised the decision on what to do was his as master of the ship. Rinnan said he would head for the closest safe port, Christmas Island.

AusSAR is reported to have advised him to hold a position offshore once he arrived in the morning and await Australian Customs Service officers. Sometime after 9.40 pm, Rinnan turned the Tampa towards Australian waters.

That night, radio and newspapers had wind of the story and were checking details with Coastwatch and AusSAR. July and August had been a bad time for the Government on the immigration front but there had never before been a story quite like this: hundreds of boat people were being taken away from Australia when they demanded to be delivered to Christmas Island and the captain of the Norwegian freighter was complying. Again the Government was going to look as if it had lost control of illegal immigration.

NIGHT after night, an ashen Philip Ruddock, the Immigration Minister, had been appearing on television in these weeks to explain mass breakouts, suicides, nervous breakdowns, the presence of a catatonic boy and mass hunger strikes at the country's detention centres, including Villawood and Curtin.

Howard was calling on the Senate to pass legislation to limit even further the access of asylum seekers to the courts. The annual boat season was under way and to prepare for their arrival, Ruddock had announced new detention centres at HMAS Coonawarra in Darwin, the army camp at Singleton in NSW and at the El Alamein camp near Port Augusta in South Australia. Christmas Island was bursting: there would be 1000 asylum seekers there once those on the deck of the Tampa landed.

At some point after 9.40 on the night of August 26/27 someone made the decision that the Tampa was to be turned back to Indonesia by threatening the master with the full weight of the Migration Act. The Tampa was not to be thanked for rescuing the human cargo on the Palapa 1 but accused of facilitating their illegal voyage. Australia was taking the view that the Tampa was not on a search and rescue mission but conducting a people-smuggling operation.

The Migration Act doesn't use that colourful language. It talks about bringing 'non-citizens' into Australia without visas. The master of a vessel that brings them in is liable to a fine of $10,000. Anyone who facilitates the arrival of groups of five or more and who is 'reckless as to whether the people had, or have, a lawful right to come to Australia' can be imprisoned for 20 years and fined $220,000. Once the illegal passengers are taken into custody, the shipping line has to foot the bill for transporting, maintaining, detaining and deporting them. If necessary, the Government could get that money by seizing and selling the Tampa.

Who made the decision to threaten the Tampa is a mystery. Canberra knew what was going on out in the Indian Ocean because AusSAR, Customs and Ruddock's department (DIMA) were monitoring the situation all through the night. Ruddock has told the Herald no minister was involved: 'The decision that was taken was not a political decision.' But he is vague about the level it came from in his department. He states it was 'operational' but perhaps came from higher up the line.

'If the department tells you that matter went to the departmental head or the deputy head or was made at any other level, I would accept that advice was correct.' He insists this was standard procedure and his department was issuing 'the same warning we would issue to Indonesian sailors'.

But when Neville Nixon of DIMA's Sydney office picked up the phone about midnight, he was ringing to threaten the captain of a 45,000-tonne ship belonging to one of the most powerful shipping lines in the world, flying the flag of a great maritime power. That captain had just conducted a difficult rescue operation at Australia's request and now, feeling threatened by the presence of hundreds of hostile men on his ship, was heading for what he believed was the closest safe port, Christmas Island.

The phlegmatic Rinnan has never said publicly what he felt when he took Nixon's call. But we know what he did: he kept sailing and contacted Wallenius Wilhelmsen Lines. It was mid-afternoon Sunday in Norway but the line moved swiftly.

It contacted the Tampa's insurers who alerted their Sydney representative, James Neill, a solicitor employed by Aus Ship P&I in the northern beaches suburb of Newport.

He dealt with the crisis from bed. By 2 am he was on the phone to Nixon. The Tampa kept on course for Christmas Island.

The Norwegians were not familiar with Australia's Migration Act. They knew and operated under international law and the conventions that have grown up around sea rescues. In the weeks since this extraordinary night, the Norwegians and Australians have made many conflicting claims about the rules governing the fate of those who are rescued at sea. In 1981 the UNHCR proposed a principle that the rescued should disembark at 'the next convenient port of call'. Norway and Australia agree that's the working basis for solving these problems. But Norway disputes Australia's claim that the Indonesian port was 'next' and that Christmas Island, so very much closer, was not 'convenient' because the Tampa was too big to enter its harbour.

That to-and-fro had yet to develop. As the Tampa sailed towards Australian waters, Rinnan, backed by Wallenius Wilhelmsen Lines, was operating under the fundamental principle that it was for him as master of the ship to decide where, in this emergency situation, it was best to bring these people to land. The lawyers were already drafting a fax along these lines for Neville Nixon at DIMA: 'His view was that by far the safest course was to continue to Christmas Island.' The approach of Rinnan, the shipping line and their lawyers was exactly the same as that taken earlier in the night by AusSAR: it was for Rinnan to decide.

Canberra scrambled before breakfast. If the decision to threaten the Tampa was made by low-level DIMA bureaucrats, it didn't stay with them long. Before 9 am, Howard had convened a meeting of the National Security Committee of cabinet. Officials were meeting elsewhere. In the chair was the secretary to the Prime Minister's Department, Max Moore-Wilton. Their brief, in the words of the DIMA chief executive officer, Bill Farmer, was to prepare some very quick oral advice to ministers.

The Tampa was 17 nautical miles from Christmas Island and only five nautical miles from Australian territorial waters. The boat was buzzed by a Coastwatch Dash-8 which radioed Rinnan not to enter Australian waters but turn around and take the people to Merak. Rinnan kept going. Moore-Wilton ordered another call be made to Rinnan. Nixon told the Tampa's master 'the Australian Government at the highest level formally requests that you not approach Christmas Island'. Rinnan stopped the ship and agreed to hold his position just outside Australia's territorial waters.

Cabinet was now meeting. At some point in the morning, the Cabinet Office directed Bill Taylor, the administrator of Christmas Island, to close the port of Flying Fish Cove 'to ensure that boats from Christmas Island did not attempt to reach the MV Tampa'. It was to remain closed for days. At noon, Howard emerged to face a press scrum. The ground rule was: they shall not land. At this point, Howard must have felt he held all the cards. Norway had blinked. The Tampa was still on the high seas. His ministers and advisers were, in the words of DIMA's Farmer, 'focused on the necessity of securing arrangements for the Tampa to return whence it had come, that is, to continue on its voyage to Merak'.

But the strategy was already being undermined. Indonesia was turning its back on Australia. Norway was preparing a case to argue to the world that Australia was violating those conventions that safeguard lives on the high seas.

A FEW facts to bear in mind about Indonesia. Its attitude to asylum seekers is very like Australia's. It doesn't like them. It doesn't want them. Indonesia acted perfectly properly in giving Rinnan permission to land the human cargo from the Palapa 1 in Merak, but as events quickly proved, it was very happy to see those Afghans, and a few Sri Lankans and Pakistanis, disappear instead towards Australia.

At his 1 pm press conference on that first day of the crisis, Howard told journalists Australia was offering Indonesia 'financial assistance' to take the Tampa people back. This was the first payment Australia offered one of its neighbours to help solve the problem. Not the last. In Jakarta, Australian officials were insisting the boat people should go back to Indonesia. But Indonesia's view was that they'd already arrived in Australia.

A spokesman for Foreign Affairs Minister Alexander Downer told the Herald: 'From the outset, Indonesia expressed reluctance to receive illegal immigrants from third countries. Indonesia's view was the Tampa passengers were illegal in Indonesia, too.' That view never changed.

Both Australia and Norway knew by the end of that Monday, August 27, that the Tampa probably had nowhere to land the asylum seekers if Australia didn't take them on Christmas Island. Indonesia proved no more co-operative when Downer called on the ambassador on Tuesday morning. After the Foreign Minister Hassan Wirajuda returned to Jakarta from South-East Asia that night, the Indonesian ministers had met and, in the words of Downer's spokesman, 'reaffirmed their position that it was not Indonesia's problem'.

The news reached Canberra next morning as the Tampa crisis reached flashpoint. The drama of that day can't be understood unless it's realised that the men, women and children on the Tampa now faced not an overnight trip to Merak, but a long voyage with an uncertain destination on the open deck of a container ship. There was also the crew to worry about, but their fate was clearly not high on the Government's agenda.

Threats of violence to the crew had brought the Tampa to Australia. How would the crew fare at the hands of the unhappy passengers if the ship were now sent away? 'We are told they are not armed,' Howard told journalists at his first press conference. 'Do the Norwegians have guns or anything like that?' persisted one of the reporters. 'I don't know,' replied the Prime Minister. 'I think the captain always has something. But I just don't know. That's pure speculation on my part.'

TAMPA was still lying just outside Australian waters, in sight of Christmas Island and Flying Fish Cove still closed to all shipping. What Rinnan wanted most from the island was a doctor. He asked time and again in the first 36 hours after he arrived off the island. Promises were made by Howard and Ruddock in Parliament, in press conferences, and in radio interviews that the doctor would be sent. He never was.

How sick were the asylum seekers on the Tampa? For both Australia and Norway, this was an important legal question. Illness on board gave Rinnan, in international law, a far stronger case for crossing the line and entering Australian territorial waters. It was even a defence to minor people-smuggling charges under the Migration Act. But the legal usefulness of having sick people on board raised strong political doubts when the shipping line's solicitor, James Neill, told DIMA when the Tampa arrived off the island:

'The medical situation on board is critical. If it is not addressed immediately people w
die shortly.'

Sources in Oslo have now told the Herald the crew of the Tampa was in regular telephone contact with the Haukeland Hospital in Bergen, which specialises in rescue emergencies. The Norwegian doctors were most concerned about cases of dehydration on the Tampa and the predicament of a pregnant woman in pain whom the male crew could not examine.

From Bergen the doctors directed, as best they could, treatment using the basic medical supplies on board. They also instructed the chief officer how to check for faked symptoms. The crew reported to Oslo that things were going from bad to worse.

Why, if Rinnan was faking this, did he keep calling for a doctor? In a further fax late on the Monday, the shipping line's lawyer put first in a list of issues requiring resolution 'Health: avoidance of fatalities over the next 24–48 hours. Immediate relief is required in relation to food, medical supplies and shelter from the sun. Longer term in relation to chronic diarrhoea, dehydration, sanitation and shelter from the elements, cooking.' The following morning Tampa issued a medical distress signal. 'I don't think we can handle this situation any longer. Fifteen people have already lost consciousness and three of them no longer react to outside stimuli.'

All that day, medical help failed to appear from the island. At about 9 pm the Tampa issued a 'pan-pan' emergency call. This is a high priority call at sea, second only in urgency to a mayday. Canberra considered this and about midnight made a bizarre offer to Rinnan: if an empty lifeboat were sent, it would be filled with medical supplies and returned to the Tampa. But there would be no doctor. Rinnan rejected the offer.

Why this refusal to send a doctor? Again the explanation seems to be legal. The problem with having a civilian doctor moving back and forth to the ship was that he could bring home an appeal from one of his patients for refugee status. That would trigger the operation of the Migration Act. One person, at least, would have to be brought on shore and the rule of this operation was None Shall Land. That also appears to be the reason there was no more talk of Rinnan being a people smuggler: the charge would compel officials to bring on shore all the people he was accused of trying to spirit into the country.

Diplomatic notes had been passing between Norway and Australia for two days before Downer and his counterpart, Thorbjoern Jagland, finally spoke at 1.30 am on the Wednesday. Jagland insisted the Tampa be allowed to approach the island: 'People are dying on board.' Downer reiterated Australia's position that the Tampa's passengers would not land.

Both men were resolute. Later that morning, about 9.30, they spoke again. By this time, Downer must have known from his people in the Australian embassy in Jakarta that Indonesia was absolutely refusing to take the Tampa people back. Yet Downer continued to insist to Jagland that the Tampa could not enter Australian waters.

Lawyers in Oslo and in Canberra had been hard at work shoring up the positions of their governments. Australia's core contention was that nations have a fundamental right to close their territorial seas to protect their security. Norway's counterclaim was that Australia's security was not at stake: at issue here were the international rules of sea rescue. The Tampa had carried out a rescue at Australia's direction in accordance with Article 98 of the UN Convention on the Law of the Sea and was now a vessel in distress which Australia was obliged to assist under the Safety of Life at Sea Convention. 'It is therefore unacceptable that Australia does not allow the Tampa to go to the nearest Australian harbour.'

Downer's response was to threaten 'appropriate action' if the ship entered Australian waters. He had in fact been sent to make this call from a meeting in Howard's office at which Admiral Chris Barrie, head of Australia's armed forces, was present with Moore-Wilton, of the Prime Minister's Department. 'Appropriate action' was code for a military intervention. It was a very grave step. Australia was ready. SAS troops had arrived the day before on Christmas Island. They could secure the boat. Also on its way to the island was HMAS Arunta, which naval sources say would be powerful enough to tow the Tampa out to sea.

Norway was not deterred. A little after 11.30 am, Rinnan informed the Flying Fish Cove harbour master he was entering Australian waters: 'It is the only way we can see to get medical supplies on board.' Howard was told immediately. He rang the Norwegian prime minister but failed to persuade Stoltenberg that the Tampa should, even now, head for Indonesia. At noon, Lieutenant Gus Gilmore, the officer in charge of the SAS regiment, was ordered to board and secure the ship. He did this with 45 troops by 2 pm. Norwegian officials have told the Herald they cannot recall in recent memory a similar incident involving one of their ships. Jagland reported the armed occupation of the Tampa to the International Shipping Organisation and the UN.

AUSTRALIA'S strategy to this point had the full approval of the Labor Party. Immediately after the ship was occupied, Kim Beazley declared: 'This country and this Parliament do not need a carping Opposition.' But later that afternoon Labor baulked at Howard's Border Protection Bill. The electoral damage to Beazley for taking this late stand has been immense.

The bill did not enhance Australia's protection under international law. It didn't remove this country's name from any of the many conventions on the law of the sea to which Australia is a party. But the bill would allow the Government to tow the Tampa out to sea and keep it there without Wallenius Wilhelmsen Lines having any recourse in the Australian courts. This was, in fact, the second and essential arm of the military solution the Howard Government had chosen to pursue that morning: first the boat would be occupied by the SAS and then forced out to sea.

It was not the fate of the 433 people crammed on its decks, nor the very difficult position of the crew, nor the fact that by this time the Tampa had nowhere to sail to that stiffened the resolve of the Opposition. Labor objected to the way the legislation would exempt the Commonwealth officials involved in the operation against the Tampa from all legal liability, civil and criminal. Labor was unwilling to put public servants beyond the reach of the law.

John Howard was not perturbed. 'The law is often an unpredictable thing,' he told Parliament. 'It is in the national interest that the courts of Australia do not have the right to overturn something that rightly belongs to the determination of the Australian people, as expressed through their representatives in Parliament.' Nothing said or written about the Tampa crisis so perfectly captures the mood of the time: the law must not stand in the way when action is mandated by the popular will. Howard's actions were immensely popular.

But in the early hours of August 30, Labor rejected the Border Protection Bill and the Government had the Tampa on its hands. The SAS was on board but the legislative power to send the ship away never arrived. Rinnan was refusing to budge. Meanwhile, a doctor was at last treating the sick. There were ill people on the Tampa, but in the opinion of the SAS doctor none were so ill they now needed to be brought ashore.

Howard had succeeded on this point at least: after the chaos of the previous three days, and at extraordinary cost, not one of the people rescued by the Tampa had set foot on Australia.

A SAGA OF THE SEAS

SUNDAY AUGUST 26

5.30 pm: The Tampa rescues 433 from the Palapa 1 and sails for Java.

About 9.00 pm: Capt Rinnan is faced with 'dire consequences for safety of ship, crew and passengers' if he does not head for Christmas Island. Does so with permission from Australian Search and Rescue.

About midnight: Rinnan threatened with breaching the Migration Act unless he turns back to Indonesia. Rinnan contacts Oslo. Sails on.

MONDAY AUGUST 27

About 9 am: Tampa in international waters off Christmas Island. In Sydney and Oslo, lawyers work. In Canberra cabinet meets.

11.30: first call from the Tampa for medical help. 'People will die shortly.'

1 pm: Howard and Ruddock hold press conference: the Tampa 'will not be given permisson to land in Australia or any Australian territories.' Christmas Island harbour closed.

That night: Three Hercules shuttle SAS and supplies out to the island.

TUESDAY AUGUST 28

In the morning: Downer asks Indonesia through its Ambassador to take the Tampa people. Indonesia resists and that night refuses.

Afternoon: HMAS Arunta sails from Perth.

9 pm: Tampa makes pan-pan call: medical distress.

WEDNESDAY AUGUST 29

1.15 am: Norway's Foreign Minister, Thorbjoern Jagland, tells Downer Australia's attitude is contrary to international law.

8.45 am: Rinnan issues a second medical distress call.

9.30 am: Downer warns Jagland Australia will use force against the Tampa if it approaches Christmas Island.

11.30 am: Tampa enters Australian waters. Rinnan says: 'It is the only way we can see to get medical supplies on board.'

11.45 am: Operation Reflex. Admiral Barrie orders SAS to take control of Tampa. Howard warns Norwegian prime minister, Jens Stoltenberg.

12.45 pm: Australian troops board Tampa. Howard tells parliament: 'the ship is now under the control of the SAS.'

6.47 pm: Howard introduces the Border Protection Bill. Rejected by Senate.

ALL TIMES ARE AUST. EASTERN

Interview with David Marr

Question *The story we include here on the* Tampa *was one of many – culminating in the book* Dark Victory *– in which you chronicled the saga of Australia's standoff with the refugees. What are your thoughts looking back at this early story?*

Marr Now I see the gaps. This story was written a couple of months after these events and a couple of weeks before Australia went to the polls when John Howard won – with the *Tampa* wind behind him – his third term in office. We broke many details of the operation here, but ahead lay over a year's further research into every hour of these days. Grim as this first account made them seem, the full story was worse.

Since Tampa *you and Marian Wilkinson have regularly teamed up for stories that we call here 'going behind the givens'. What is your underlying purpose?*

Making sense of complex events; turning evidence into narrative; tracking power in Australia.

If journalism is the first draft of history what are the chances of a fair and balanced first draft when journalists are up against powerful official narratives backed by spin in a climate of secrecy?

Governments spin but they're also compelled to hold trials, inquiries and commissions. Buried in those proceedings is wonderful material which – with the help of leaks, independent experts and victims with their own stories to tell – we can use to write a first rough draft almost as history is happening.

How important is storytelling in all this?

Storytelling is crucial. It's how we make sense of the world. Facts don't mean much to any of us unless they build into a convincing story. The raw material of journalism has to be accurate, but the journalist's work isn't done until the story rings true.

Your features with Marian (e.g. on the Tampa, *the 'children overboard' affair, the Iraqi wheat bribes) are massively detailed, as was* Dark Victory. *Can you comment on the importance of detail for recreating events and telling stories?*

We love detail. We particularly value details compelled from witnesses and tested by lawyers before they even reach us. Transcripts are goldmines. Complex details don't necessarily produce complex narratives. Often the reverse: from a blizzard of detail comes the simple, true story.

Journalists have expressed concern about cutbacks in staff and budgets as the shareholders' bottom line looms larger. Is strong investigative work a dying art?

We're right to be concerned. Cash is being squeezed out of newspapers because shareholders continue to expect levels of profitability newspapers can no longer deliver. But here's the paradox: without journalism that digs deeper than press releases and stock market reports, people will have another reason for abandoning newspapers altogether.

What about the prospect of other forums providing a space for longer non-fiction pieces, e.g. magazines, online publications?

Magazines like the *New Yorker* have always done this. It's less a fresh trend than welcome survival. Of course, those magazines have to have deep pockets.

At a public forum you singled out as one of the best stories you'd ever read a feature in the New Yorker *about the 'sexing up' of the weapons of mass destruction issue, the suicide of David Kelly, etc. What made it so striking?*

John Cassidy's December 2003 report on the Kelly affair was without heroes. On an immense scale – about 16,000 words – he explored all the corners of the scandal. Everyone was human. Everyone was behaving badly. Through fine storytelling and an amazing grasp of detail, Cassidy showed beyond doubt that the British Government had done exactly what it was accused of doing: deliberately exaggerating the dangers posed by Iraq's weapons.

Are there journalists, writers, who have influenced you or whom you particular admire?

Too many. Some for style, some for tone, some for courage, some for obsessions, some for intelligence, some for intuition, some for expertise, some for breaking stories, some for storytelling. Even our heroes don't get it right all the time. But that's work and life.

Discussion question

The journalists' union, the Media Entertainment and Arts Alliance (MEAA), has voiced serious concerns about new laws and limitations affecting journalists in the post September 11 climate. What are some important areas of reporting and feature writing where a government clampdown 'in the national interest' might impact on public interest matters quite properly the domain of journalism?

Further reading

John Carey (ed.), *The Faber Book of Reportage*, Faber and Faber, 1987.

Robert Fisk, *The Great War for Civilisation: The conquest of the Middle East*, Fourth Estate, 2005.

Helen Garner, *Joe Cinque's Consolation: A true story of death, grief and the law*, Picador, 2004.

David Marr and Marian Wilkinson, *Dark Victory*, Allen & Unwin, 2003.

Adrienne Miller (ed.), *Esquire's Great Big Book of Great Writing*, Hearst Communications, 2003.

Matthew Ricketson, *Writing Feature Stories*, Allen & Unwin, 2004.

Writers on Writing, Collected Essays from the *New York Times*, Times Books, 2001.

Chapter 2

New Journalism and Its Legacy

Looking back and forward

Susie Eisenhuth

When the risk-taking, rule-breaking 'New Journalists' of the 1960s and 1970s are discussed (so dubbed by Tom Wolfe in 1973,[1] though critics chide his failure to more generously credit earlier writers like George Orwell and even Mark Twain), it's usually the boys who take centre stage. Think 'New Journalist' and the popular image that surfaces is of Hunter S. Thompson, Norman Mailer, Gay Talese, Truman Capote, Wolfe himself, flexing their literary muscles, kicking off the traditional shackles of objectivity and leaping headlong into their stories, firing off – at their wildest – a self-indulgent avalanche of words, flinging convention and punctuation to the winds.

Many a young journalist (this writer, for one), labouring under the short back and sides strictures of the day ('Lose the adjectives', 'Keep your sentences under 25 words'), could only gaze in wonderment at the typographical maelstrom whipped up by Wolfe, for example, at his tearaway best. ('There Goes (Varoom! Varoom! That Kandy-Kolored (Thphhhhhht!) Tangerine-Flake Streamline Baby (Rahghhht) Around the Bend . . .')[2]

Such show-stopping turns were by no means the norm as those early literary journalists staked their claim to the techniques of the novel – and the cachet attaching to the notion of 'literature'. But while the NJ boys were frequently lairising on centre stage, Joan Didion was, typically, huddled quietly in the wings. 'My only advantage as a reporter', she noted in the foreword to her early collection *Slouching Towards Bethlehem* – with the mix of diffidence and depth charge that has always been her trademark – 'is that I am so physically small, so temperamentally unobtrusive and so neurotically inarticulate that people tend to forget that my presence runs counter to their best interests'.[3]

In 2001 Susan Faludi reviewed *Political Fictions*, in which Didion, long a celebrated novelist, had returned to the essay writing of her early years, but in much stroppier mode. (Two years later Didion's extended piece *Fixed Ideas, America since 9.11*, a lacerating appraisal of the post September 11 American mindset, would give us a version of her style in which the cool detachment was altogether replaced by an infusion of slow-burning fury.)[4] Faludi noted that while Didion gained prominence in the New Journalism era, 'her first person approach had little in common with the sweaty showmanship of its chest-thumping bards'. Didion's style belonged 'more to noir than to hip', she said. 'She showed a generation of young American journalists how to make reporting moodily stylish, a personal expression.'[5]

Overwriting/paring it back

Another thing Didion showed them – and continues to demonstrate[6] – was the elegant economy of her style. Anyone who spends time with new writers knows the perils of overwriting, the way they often abandon their natural bent for the forthright and retreat instead into self-conscious writerly mode, producing complex sentences garlanded with adverbial tinsel and trailing dependent clauses as they head recklessly into their fourth or fifth line.

Jessica Mitford, who did a stint as a journalism teacher herself, recommended a bracing dose of Sir Arthur Quiller-Couch for writers who feel a spell of inspiration coming on. And the advice is still worth taking, even if it does date back to the professor's Cambridge lectures of 1913. 'Whenever you feel an impulse to perpetrate a piece of exceptionally fine writing', Sir Arthur cautioned, 'obey it – wholeheartedly – and delete it before sending your manuscript to press'.[7]

The key is in paring it back, getting rid of the 'clutter' referred to by William Zinsser, a deft wordspinner himself, whose books on writing are themselves a good read. Clutter, he tells us, is 'the ponderous euphemism that turns a slum into a depressed socio-economic area, a salesman into a marketing representative and garbage collectors into waste disposal personnel'. It is the official language of the corporation, 'of the Pentagon throwing dust into the eyes of the populace . . .'[8] Yet simplicity remains elusive in bureaucratic and academic writing, where impenetrable jargon thrives and the notion lingers that the more perversely obscure the text, the more likely it is to be packing intellectual wallop.

Excess words/telling details

Some fledgling journalists feel outraged when the Visigoths on the subs desk trash their finely honed prose. What would they know? Well, lest we forget Ernest Hemingway and his slash and burn campaign to achieve the pared-back prose for which he is celebrated. He rewrote the first section of *A Farewell to Arms* fifty times, he confessed, observing – with admirable economy – 'the first draft of anything is shit'.[9]

The trick is to trim back the flurries of excess words to make room for the details that will advance the narrative. Joan Didion tells a good story about the power of details in her early essay 'On Keeping a Notebook', where she's poring over notes she made in a bar some time before. There's a quote ('That woman Estelle is partly the reason why George Sharp and I are separated today') and some other jottings ('Dirty crepe-de-chine wrapper, hotel bar, Wilmington RR, 9.45 a.m. August Monday morning.')[10] As she studies the notes the bar scene comes back: the woman in the grubby wrap talking about her breakup, the long-suffering barkeep, the girl with her hem coming down. Finally she gives us the scene conjured up from those details:

> Here is what it is: the girl has been on the Eastern shore and now she is going back to the city, leaving the man beside her, and all she can see ahead are the viscous summer sidewalks and the 3 a.m. long-distance calls that will make her lie awake and then sleep drugged through all the steaming mornings left in august (1960? 1961?) Because she must go directly from the train to lunch in New York, she wishes that she had a safety pin for the hem of the plaid silk dress, and she also wishes that she could forget about the hem and the lunch and stay in the cool bar that smells of disinfectant and malt and make friends with the woman in the crepe-de-chine wrapper. She is afflicted by a little self pity, and she wants to compare Estelles.[11]

If you wanted a primer on the power of detail, 'Some Dreamers of the Golden Dream', the coolly elegant feature of the young Didion is hard to go past. Sparked by a domestic murder, her portrait of a claustrophobic marriage in a claustrophobic town still reads as a timeless human story about hopes and dreams, love and betrayal, its sense of place and time captured with the sharpness of acid-etched glass.

We know from the start, as she details the hot dry Santa Ana wind (how it 'whines through the eucalyptus windbreaks and works on the nerves'), that this ill wind will blow no one any good. 'It is the season of suicide and divorce and prickly dread, wherever the wind blows.' In the end, Lucille Miller is in jail and the man for whom she murdered her husband is marrying his children's pretty governess. The closing lines tap into the universal pain of love's labour's lost. And it's all in the detail: 'The bride wore a long white *peau de soie* dress and carried a shower bouquet of sweetheart roses with stephanotis streamers. A coronet of seed pearls held her illusion veil.'

Pulitzer Prize winning journalist and author Barry Siegel names Didion as one of his 'textbooks' in the 1970s:

> It's not like I wanted to write, or could write, like them, because they are so distinctive, but they inspire you to find your own voice . . . You look at [John] McPhee and you learn from him about intricate structure. You look at Joan Didion and you learn about the cadence and rhythm of sentences. With Tom Wolfe, his sophisticated use of point of view . . . skidding out of the narrator's voice and unfolding your story in the voice of the characters.[12]

'Literary journalism': bunging it on?

These days the fictional techniques explored by Wolfe and co – like unfolding the narrative scene by scene and peopling it with characters ('like a novel', as Wolfe put it, or like a play, or a movie, for that matter) are very much in the toolbag for feature writing, or 'literary journalism' as it's known at the more upmarket end of the spectrum. At its best literary journalism is about storytelling that re-creates a compelling narrative, celebrates detail, explores the perspective of the characters and taps into themes that are universal and thereby endure. Some journalists still tend to see the term as bunging it on a bit, but the fact is that the notion of literary journalism is gaining acceptance even in university English departments, which have traditionally disdained the reporting milieu that has nurtured so many novelists – the likes of Graham Greene and Ernest Hemingway, and in more recent times journalists turned non-fiction authors and novelists like Australians Robert Drewe and Geraldine Brooks, who won the 2006 Pulitzer Prize for fiction for her novel *March*, about the American civil war.

Writer Barry Siegel, who heads up a 'lit j.' course at the University of California at Irvine, has no problem with using the term. His program talks about 'non-fiction prose that has transcended the limits of daily journalism . . . prose that adopts the aims and techniques of the finest fiction . . . But I usually just say it's any really good non-fiction prose.'

At home with the techniques of fiction he nonetheless rejects absolutely the notion of imagining or otherwise fabricating quotes, inventing characters or blurring different sources into composites. Similar disquiet about softening the line makes journalists balk at the notion of 'creative' non-fiction – its title conveying a worrying whiff of illicit spoonbending. Clearly there is more than the odd pothole lurking at the intersection of literary journalism and creative non-fiction. Writer and journalist John Birmingham happily traverses all categories, his essay in this collection, like much of his work, highly personal and fiercely opinion driven. Yet on navigating the fact/fiction line he is unequivocal. 'You cannot make stuff up', he says. 'It is wrong. It is bad. You should get drummed out of the profession for doing so.'[13]

Reporting as the bedrock

Both writers point to the importance of extensive reporting. According to Birmingham, 'a thorough grounding in traditional techniques of reportage is vital, no matter what your intent as a writer'. For Siegel, 'reporting is the bedrock'. You need to be 'a prodigious and talented reporter' before you can become a writer of narrative journalism.[14]

The melancholy Utah trial story that won Siegel the Pulitzer – with its intriguing double narrative etching in the worlds of both the judge and the man he must, unwillingly, sentence – took that kind of prodigious reporting. It's a must, he says, if you want to transform reported events by re-creating them within a narrative. There were rooms full of documents, months of checking and collating, and hundreds of hours of interviewing, though he used minimal quotes. 'I rarely use direct quotes', he explains, 'because I'm trying to write a narrative, a non-fiction short story. So I want to stay in the narrative, rather than have characters step out of the story to talk to the reporter.'[15]

Siegel refers to the New Journalists as 'early literary journalists'. And certainly the emphasis on strong reporting is still as close to Tom Wolfe's heart as it was to his thesis in *The New Journalism*. Interviewed in 2001,[16] Wolfe said he had many enemies in New York literary circles 'just because I believe that anyone who writes – whether it is stories, novels, screenplays, even poetry – must have the journalistic bug, meaning the ability to do research. I think that one is a journalist first and then a writer.'

Joan Didion

Journalist and author Joan Didion has written five novels, including *Play It As It Lays* (1970), *Democracy* (1984) and *The Last Thing He Wanted* (1996). Her eight non-fiction books include *Slouching Towards Bethlehem* (1968), *The White Album* (1979), *Salvador* (1983), *Miami* (1987), *After Henry* (1992), *Political Fictions* (2001) and *Where I Was From* (2003). Her latest non-fiction work, *The Year of Magical Thinking*, was published in 2005 in New York and won the National Book Award for Non-Fiction.

SOME DREAMERS OF THE GOLDEN DREAM

Joan Didion
From *Slouching Towards Bethlehem* (1968)

This is a story about love and death in the golden land, and begins with the country. The San Bernardino Valley lies only an hour east of Los Angeles by the San Bernardino Freeway but is in certain ways an alien place: not the coastal California of the subtropical twilights and the soft westerlies off the Pacific but a harsher California, haunted by the Mojave just beyond the mountains, devastated by the hot dry Santa Ana wind that comes down through the passes at 100 miles an hour and whines through the eucalyptus windbreaks and works on the nerves. October is the bad month for the wind, the month when breathing is difficult and the hills blaze up spontaneously. There has been no rain since April. Every voice seems a scream. It is the season of suicide and divorce and prickly dread, wherever the wind blows.

The Mormons settled this ominous country, and then they abandoned it, but by the time they left, the first orange tree had been planted and for the next hundred years the San Bernardino Valley would draw a kind of people who imagined they might live among the talismanic fruit and prosper in the dry air, people who brought with them Midwestern ways of building and cooking and praying and who tried to graft those ways upon the land. The graft took in curious ways. This is the California where it is possible to live and die without ever eating an artichoke, without ever meeting a Catholic, or a Jew. This is the California where it is easy to Dial-A-Devotion, but hard to buy a book. This is the country in which a belief in the literal interpretation of Genesis has slipped imperceptibly into a belief in the literal interpretation of *Double Indemnity*, the country of the teased hair and the Capris and the girls for whom all life's promise comes down to a waltz-length white wedding dress and the birth of a Kimberly or a Sherry or a Debbi and a Tijuana divorce and a return to hairdressers' school. 'We were just crazy kids,' they say without regret, and look to the future. The future always looks good in the golden land, because no one remembers the past. Here is where the hot wind blows and the old ways do not seem relevant, where the divorce rate is double the national average and where one person in every thirty-eight lives in a trailer. Here is the last stop for all those who come from somewhere else, for all those who drifted away from the cold and the past and the old ways. Here is where they are trying to find a new life style, trying to find it in the only places they know to look: the movies and the newspapers. The case of Lucille Marie Maxwell Miller is a tabloid monument to that new life style.

Imagine Banyan Street first, because Banyan is where it happened. The way to Banyan is to drive west from San Bernardino out Foothill Boulevard, Route 66: past the Santa Fe switching yards, the Forty Winks Motel. Past the motel that is nineteen stucco tepees: 'SLEEP IN A WIGWAM – GET MORE FOR YOUR WAMPUM.' Past Fontana Drag City and the Fontana Church of the Nazarene and the Pit Stop A Go-Go; past Kaiser Steel, through Cucamonga, out to the Kapu Kai Restaurant-Bar and Coffee Shop, at the corner of Route 66 and Carnelian Avenue. Up Carnelian Avenue from the Kapu Kai, which means 'Forbidden Seas,' the subdivision flags whip in the harsh wind. ' HALF-ACRE RANCHES! SNACK BARS! TRAVERTINE ENTRIES! $95 DOWN.' It is the trail of an intention gone haywire, the flotsam of the New California. But after a while the signs thin out on Carnelian Avenue, and the houses are no longer the bright pastels of the Springtime Home owners but the faded bungalows of the people who grow a few grapes and keep a few chickens out here, and then the hill gets steeper and the road climbs and even the bungalows are few, and here – desolate, roughly surfaced, lined with eucalyptus and lemon groves – is Banyan Street.

Like so much of this country, Banyan suggests something curious and unnatural. The lemon groves are sunken, down a three- or four-foot retaining wall, so that one looks directly into their dense foliage, too lush, unsettlingly glossy, the greenery of nightmare; the fallen eucalyptus bark is too dusty, a place for snakes to breed. The stones look not like natural stones but like the rubble of some unmentioned upheaval. There are smudge pots, and a closed cistern. To one side of Banyan there is the flat valley, and to the other the San Bernardino Mountains, a dark mass looming too high, too fast, nine, ten, eleven thousand feet, right there above the lemon groves. At midnight on Banyan Street there is no light at all, and no sound except the wind in the eucalyptus and a muffled barking of dogs. There may be a kennel somewhere, or the dogs may be coyotes.

Banyan Street was the route Lucille Miller took home from the twenty-four-hour May-fair Market on the night of October 7, 1964, a night when the moon was dark and the wind was blowing and she was out of milk, and Banyan Street was where, at about 12:30 a.m., her 1964 Volkswagen came to a sudden stop, caught fire, and began to burn. For an hour and fifteen minutes Lucille Miller ran up and down Banyan calling for help, but no cars passed and no help came. At three o'clock that morning, when the fire had been put out and the California Highway Patrol officers were completing their report, Lucille Miller was still sobbing and incoherent, for her husband had been asleep in the Volkswa-gen. 'What will I tell the children, when there's nothing left, nothing left in the casket,' she cried to the friend called to comfort her. 'How can I tell them there's nothing left?'

In fact there was something left, and a week later it lay in the Draper Mortuary Chapel in a closed bronze coffin blanketed with pink carnations. Some 200 mourners heard Elder Robert E. Denton of the Seventh-Day Adventist Church of Ontario speak of 'the temper of fury that has broken out among us.' For Gordon Miller, he said, there would be 'no more death, no more heartaches, no more misunderstandings.' Elder Ansel Bristol mentioned the 'peculiar' grief of the hour. Elder Fred Jensen asked 'what shall it profit a man, if he shall gain the whole world, and lose his own soul?' A light rain fell, a blessing in a dry season, and a female vocalist sang 'Safe in the Arms of Jesus.' A tape recording of the service was made for the widow, who was being held without bail in the San Bernardino County Jail on a charge of first-degree murder.

Of course she came from somewhere else, came off the prairie in search of something she had seen in a movie or heard on the radio, for this is a Southern California story. She was born on January 17, 1930, in Winnipeg, Manitoba, the only child of Gordon and Lily Maxwell, both school-teachers and both dedicated to the Seventh-Day Adventist Church, whose members observe the Sabbath on Saturday, believe in an apocalyptic Second Coming, have a strong missionary tendency, and, if they are strict, do not smoke, drink, eat meat, use makeup, or wear jewelry, including wedding rings. By the time Lucille Maxwell enrolled at Walla Walla College in College Place, Washington, the Adventist school where her parents then taught, she was an eighteen-year-old possessed of unremarkable good looks and remarkable high spirits. 'Lucille wanted to see the world,' her father would say in retrospect, 'and I guess she found out.'

The high spirits did not seem to lend themselves to an extended course of study at Walla Walla College, and in the spring of 1949 Lucille Maxwell met and married Gordon ('Cork') Miller, a twenty-four-year-old graduate of Walla Walla and of the University of Oregon dental school, then stationed at Fort Lewis as a medical officer. 'Maybe you could say it was love at first sight,' Mr. Maxwell recalls. 'Before they were ever formally introduced, he sent Lucille a dozen and a half roses with a card that said even if she didn't come out on a date with him, he hoped she'd find the roses pretty anyway.' The Maxwells remember their daughter as a 'radiant' bride.

Unhappy marriages so resemble one another that we do not need to know too much about the course of this one. There may or may not have been trouble on Guam, where Cork and Lucille Miller lived while he finished his Army duty. There may or may not have been problems in the small Oregon town where he first set up private practice. There appears to have been some disappointment about their move to California: Cork Miller had told friends that he wanted to become a doctor, that he was unhappy as a dentist and planned to enter the Seventh-Day Adventist College of Medical Evangelists at Loma Linda, a few miles south of San Bernardino. Instead he bought a dental practice in the west end of San Bernardino County, and the family settled there, in a modest house on the kind of street where there are always tricycles and revolving credit and dreams about bigger houses, better streets. That was 1957. By the summer of 1964 they had achieved the bigger house on the better street and the familiar accoutrements of a family on its way up: the $30,000 a year, the three children for the Christmas card, the picture window, the family room, the newspaper photographs that showed 'Mrs. Gordon Miller, Ontario Heart Fund Chairman . . .' They were paying the familiar price for it. And they had reached the familiar season of divorce.

It might have been anyone's bad summer, anyone's siege of heat and nerves and migraine and money worries, but this one began particularly early and particularly badly. On April 24 an old friend, Elaine Hayton, died suddenly; Lucille Miller had seen her only the night before. During the month of May, Cork Miller was hospitalized briefly with a bleeding ulcer, and his usual reserve deepened into depression. He told his accountant that he was 'sick of looking at open mouths,' and threatened suicide. By July 8, the conventional tensions of love and money had reached the conventional impasse in the new house on the acre lot at 8488 Bella Vista, and Lucille Miller filed for divorce. Within a month, however, the Millers seemed reconciled. They saw a marriage counselor. They talked about a fourth child. It seemed that the marriage had reached the traditional truce, the point at which so many resign themselves to cutting both their losses and their hopes.

But the Millers' season of trouble was not to end that easily. October 7 began as a commonplace enough day, one of those days that sets the teeth on edge with its tedium, its small frustrations. The temperature reached 102° in San Bernardino that afternoon, and the Miller children were home from school because of Teachers' Institute. There was ironing to be dropped off. There was a trip to pick up a prescription for Nembutal, a trip to a self-service dry cleaner. In the early evening, an unpleasant accident with the Volkswagen: Cork Miller hit and killed a German shepherd, and afterward said that his head felt 'like it had a Mack truck on it.' It was something he often said. As of that evening Cork Miller was $63,479 in debt, including the $29,637 mortgage on the new house, a debt load which seemed oppressive to him. He was a man who wore his responsibilities uneasily, and complained of migraine headaches almost constantly.

He ate alone that night, from a TV tray in the living room. Later the Millers watched John Forsythe and Senta Berger in *See How They Run,* and when the movie ended, about eleven, Cork Miller suggested that they go out for milk. He wanted some hot chocolate. He took a blanket and pillow from the couch and climbed into the passenger seat of the Volkswagen. Lucille Miller remembers reaching over to lock his door as she backed down the driveway. By the time she left the Mayfair Market, and long before they reached Banyan Street, Cork Miller appeared to be asleep.

There is some confusion in Lucille Miller's mind about what happened between 12:30 a.m., when the fire broke out, and 1:50 a.m., when it was reported. She says that she was driving east on Banyan Street at about 35 m.p.h. when she felt the Volkswagen pull sharply to the right. The next thing she knew the car was on the embankment, quite near the edge of the retaining wall, and flames were shooting up behind her. She does not remember jumping out. She does remember prying up a stone with which she broke the window next to her husband, and then scrambling down the retaining wall to try to find a stick. 'I don't know how I was going to push him out,' she says. 'I just thought if I had a stick, I'd push him out.' She could not, and after a while she ran to the intersection of Banyan and Carnelian Avenue. There are no houses at that corner, and almost no traffic. After one car had passed without stopping, Lucille Miller ran back down Banyan toward the burning Volkswagen. She did not stop, but she slowed down, and in the flames she could see her husband. He was, she said, 'just black.'

At the first house up Sapphire Avenue, half a mile from the Volkswagen, Lucille Miller finally found help. There Mrs. Robert Swenson called the sheriff, and then, at Lucille Miller's request, she called Harold Lance, the Millers' lawyer and their close friend. When Harold Lance arrived he took Lucille Miller home to his wife, Joan. Twice Harold Lance and Lucille Miller returned to Banyan Street and talked to the Highway Patrol officers. A third time Harold Lance returned alone, and when he came back he said to Lucille Miller, 'O.K. . . . you don't talk any more.'

When Lucille Miller was arrested the next afternoon, Sandy Slagle was with her. Sandy Slagle was the intense, relentlessly loyal medical student who used to baby-sit for the Millers, and had been living as a member of the family since she graduated from high school in 1959. The Millers took her away from a difficult home situation, and she thinks of Lucille Miller not only as 'more or less a mother or a sister' but as 'the most wonderful character' she has ever known. On the night of the accident, Sandy Slagle was in her dormitory at Loma Linda University, but Lucille Miller called her early in the morning and asked her to come home. The doctor was there when Sandy Slagle arrived, giving Lucille Miller an injection of Nembutal. 'She was crying as she was going under,' Sandy Slagle recalls. 'Over and over she'd say, 'Sandy, all the hours I spent trying to save him and now what are they trying to *do* to me?'

At 1:30 that afternoon, Sergeant William Paterson and Detectives Charles Callahan and Joseph Karr of the Central Homicide Division arrived at 8488 Bella Vista. 'One of them appeared at the bedroom door,' Sandy Slagle remembers, 'and said to Lucille, "You've got ten minutes to get dressed or we'll take you as you are." She was in her nightgown, you know, so I tried to get her dressed.'

Sandy Slagle tells the story now as if by rote, and her eyes do not waver. 'So I had her panties and bra on her and they opened the door again, so I got some Capris on her, you know, and a scarf.' Her voice drops. 'And then they just took her.'

The arrest took place just twelve hours after the first report that there had been an accident on Banyan Street, a rapidity which would later prompt Lucille Miller's attorney to say that the entire case was an instance of trying to justify a reckless arrest. Actually what first caused the detectives who arrived on Banyan Street toward dawn that morning to give the accident more than routine attention were certain apparent physical inconsistencies. While Lucille Miller had said that she was driving about 35 m.p.h. when the car swerved to a stop, an examination of the cooling Volkswagen showed that it was in low gear, and that the parking rather than the driving lights were on. The front wheels, moreover, did not seem to be in exactly the position that Lucille Miller's description of the accident would suggest, and the right rear wheel was dug in deep, as if it had been spun in place. It seemed curious to the detectives, too, that a sudden stop from 35 m.p.h. – the same jolt which was presumed to have knocked over a gasoline can in the back seat and somehow started the fire – should have left two milk cartons upright on the back floor-board, and the remains of a Polaroid camera box lying apparently undisturbed on the back seat.

No one, however, could be expected to give a precise account of what did and did not happen in a moment of terror, and none of these inconsistencies seemed in themselves incontrovertible evidence of criminal intent. But they did interest the Sheriff's Office, as did Gordon Miller's apparent unconsciousness at the time of the accident, and the length of time it had taken Lucille Miller to get help. Something, moreover, struck the investigators as wrong about Harold Lance's attitude when he came back to Banyan Street the third time and found the investigation by no means over. 'The way Lance was acting,' the prosecuting attorney said later, 'they thought maybe they'd hit a nerve.'

And so it was that on the morning of October 8, even before the doctor had come to give Lucille Miller an injection to calm her, the San Bernardino County Sheriff's Office was trying to construct another version of what might have happened between 12:30 and 1:50 a.m. The hypothesis they would eventually present was based on the somewhat tortuous premise that Lucille Miller had undertaken a plan which failed: a plan to stop the car on the lonely road, spread gasoline over her presumably drugged husband, and, with a stick on the accelerator, gently 'walk' the Volkswagen over the embankment, where it would tumble four feet down the retaining wall into the lemon grove and almost certainly explode. If this happened, Lucille Miller might then have somehow negotiated the two miles up Carnelian to Bella Vista in time to be home when the accident was discovered. This plan went awry; according to the Sheriff's Office hypothesis, when the car would not go over the rise of the embankment. Lucille Miller might have panicked then – after she had killed the engine the third or fourth time, say, out there on the dark road with the gasoline already spread and the dogs baying and the wind blowing and the unspeakable apprehension that a pair of headlights would suddenly light up Banyan Street and expose her there – and set the fire herself.

Although this version accounted for some of the physical evidence – the car in low because it had been started from a dead stop, the parking lights on because she could not do what needed doing without some light, a rear wheel spun in repeated attempts to get the car over the embankment, the milk cartons upright because there had been no sudden stop – it did not seem on its own any more or less credible than Lucille Miller's own story. Moreover, some of the physical evidence did seem to support her story: a nail in a front tire, a nine-pound rock found in the car, presumably the one with which she had broken the window in an attempt to save her husband. Within a few days an autopsy had established that Gordon Miller was alive when he burned, which did not particularly help the State's case, and that he had enough Nembutal and Sandoptal in his blood to put the average person to sleep, which did: on the other hand Gordon Miller habitually took both Nembutal and Fiorinal (a common headache prescription which contains Sandoptal), and had been ill besides.

It was a spotty case, and to make it work at all the State was going to have to find a motive. There was talk of unhappiness, talk of another man. That kind of motive, during the next few weeks, was what they set out to establish. They set out to find it in accountants' ledgers and double-indemnity clauses and motel registers, set out to determine what might move a woman who believed in all the promises of the middle class – a woman who had been chairman of the Heart Fund and who always knew a reasonable little dressmaker and who had come out of the bleak wild of prairie fundamentalism to find what she imagined to be the good life – what should drive such a woman to sit on a street called Bella Vista and look out her new picture window into the empty California sun and calculate how to burn her husband alive in a Volkswagen. They found the wedge they wanted closer at hand than they might have at first expected, for, as testimony would reveal later at the trial, it seemed that in December of 1963 Lucille Miller had begun an affair with the husband of one of her friends, a man whose daughter called her 'Auntie Lucille', a man who might have seemed to have the gift for people and money and the good life that Cork Miller so noticeably lacked. The man was Arthwell Hayton, a well-known San Bernardino attorney and at one time a member of the district attorney's staff.

In some ways it was the conventional clandestine affair in a place like San Bernardino, a place where little is bright or graceful, where it is routine to misplace the future and easy to start looking for it in bed. Over the seven weeks that it would take to try Lucille Miller for murder, Assistant District Attorney Don A. Turner and defense attorney Edward P. Foley would between them unfold a curiously predictable story. There were the falsified motel registrations. There were the lunch dates, the afternoon drives in Arthwell Hayton's red Cadillac convertible. There were the interminable discussions of the wronged partners. There were the confidantes ('I knew everything,' Sandy Slagle would insist fiercely later. 'I knew every time, places, everything') and there were the words remembered from bad magazine stories ('Don't kiss me, it will trigger things,' Lucille Miller remembered telling Arthwell Hayton in the parking lot of Harold's Club in Fontana after lunch one day) and there were the notes, the sweet exchanges: 'Hi Sweetie Pie! You are my cup of tea!! Happy Birthday – you don't look a day over 29!! Your baby, Arthwell.'

And, toward the end, there was the acrimony. It was April 24, 1964, when Arthwell Hayton's wife, Elaine, died suddenly, and nothing good happened after that. Arthwell Hayton had taken his cruiser, Captain's Lady, over to Catalina that weekend; he called home at nine o'clock Friday night, but did not talk to his wife because Lucille Miller answered the telephone and said that Elaine was showering. The next morning the Haytons' daughter found her mother in bed, dead. The newspapers reported the death as accidental, perhaps the result of an allergy to hair spray. When Arthwell Hayton flew home from Catalina that weekend, Lucille Miller met him at the airport, but the finish had already been written.

It was in the breakup that the affair ceased to be in the conventional mode and began to resemble instead the novels of James M. Cain, the movies of the late 1930's, all the dreams in which violence and threats and blackmail are made to seem commonplaces of middle-class life. What was most startling about the case that the State of California was preparing against Lucille Miller was something that had nothing to do with law at all, something that never appeared in the eight-column afternoon headlines but was always there between them: the revelation that the dream was teaching the dreamers how to live. Here is Lucille Miller talking to her lover sometime in the early summer of 1964, after he had indicated that, on the advice of his minister, he did not intend to see her any more: 'First, I'm going to go to that dear pastor of yours and tell him a few things. . . . When I do tell him that, you won't be in the Redlands Church any more. . . . Look, Sonny Boy, if you think your reputation is going to be ruined, your life won't be worth two cents.' Here is Arthwell Hayton, to Lucille Miller: 'I'll go to Sheriff Frank Bland and tell him some things that I know about you until you'll wish you'd never heard of Arthwell Hayton.' For an affair between a Seventh-Day Adventist dentist's wife and a Seventh-Day Adventist personal-injury lawyer, it seems a curious kind of dialogue.

'Boy, I could get that little boy coming and going,' Lucille Miller later confided to Erwin Sprengle, a Riverside contractor who was a business partner of Arthwell Hayton's and a friend to both the lovers. (Friend or no, on this occasion he happened to have an induction coil attached to his telephone in order to tape Lucille Miller's call.) 'And he hasn't got one thing on me that he can prove. I mean, I've got concrete – he has nothing concrete.' In the same taped conversation with Erwin Sprengle, Lucille Miller mentioned a tape that she herself had surreptitiously made, months before, in Arthwell Hayton's car.

'I said to him, I said "Arthwell, I just feel like I'm being used." . . . He started sucking his thumb and he said "I love you. . . . This isn't something that happened yesterday. I'd marry you tomorrow if I could. I don't love Elaine." He'd love to hear that played back, wouldn't he?'

'Yeah,' drawled Sprengle's voice on the tape. 'That would be just a little incriminating, wouldn't it?'

'Just a little incriminating,' Lucille Miller agreed. 'It really is.'

Later on the tape, Sprengle asked where Cork Miller was.

'He took the children down to the church.'

'You didn't go?'

'No.'

'You're naughty.'

It was all, moreover, in the name of 'love'; everyone involved placed a magical faith in the efficacy of the very word. There was the significance that Lucille Miller saw in Arthwell's saying that he 'loved' her, that he did not 'love' Elaine. There was Arthwell insisting, later, at the trial, that he had never said it, that he may have 'whispered sweet nothings in her ear' (as her defense hinted that he had whispered in many ears), but he did not remember bestowing upon her the special seal, saying the word, declaring 'love.' There was the summer evening when Lucille Miller and Sandy Slagle followed Arthwell Hayton down to his new boat in its mooring at Newport Beach and untied the lines with Arthwell aboard, Arthwell and a girl with whom he later testified he was drinking hot chocolate and watching television. 'I did that on purpose,' Lucille Miller told Erwin Sprengle later, 'to save myself from letting my heart do something crazy.'

January 11, 1965, was a bright warm day in Southern California, the kind of day when Catalina floats on the Pacific horizon and the air smells of orange blossoms and it is a long way from the bleak and difficult East, a long way from the cold, a long way from the past. A woman in Hollywood staged an all-night sit-in on the hood of her car to prevent repossession by a finance company. A seventy-year-old pensioner drove his station wagon at five miles an hour past three Gardena poker parlors and emptied three pistols and a twelve-gauge shotgun through their windows, wounding twenty-nine people. 'Many young women become prostitutes just to have enough money to play cards,' he explained in a note. Mrs. Nick Adams said that she was 'not surprised' to hear her husband announce his divorce plans on the Les Crane Show, and, farther north, a sixteen-year-old jumped off the Golden Gate Bridge and lived.

And, in the San Bernardino County Courthouse, the Miller trial opened. The crowds were so bad that the glass courtroom doors were shattered in the crush, and from then on identification disks were issued to the first forty-three spectators in line. The line began forming at 6 a.m., and college girls camped at the courthouse all night, with stores of graham crackers and No-Cal.

All they were doing was picking a jury, those first few days, but the sensational nature of the case had already suggested itself. Early in December there had been an abortive first trial, a trial at which no evidence was ever presented because on the day the jury was seated the San Bernardino *Sun-Telegram* ran an 'inside' story quoting Assistant District Attorney Don Turner, the prosecutor, as saying, 'We are looking into the circumstances of Mrs. Hayton's death. In view of the current trial concerning the death of Dr. Miller, I do not feel I should comment on Mrs. Hayton's death.' It seemed that there had been barbiturates in Elaine Hayton's blood, and there had seemed some irregularity about the way she was dressed on that morning when she was found under the covers, dead. Any doubts about the death at the time, however, had never gotten as far as the Sheriff's Office. 'I guess somebody didn't want to rock the boat,' Turner said later. 'These were prominent people.'

Although all of that had not been in the *Sun-Telegram's* story, an immediate mistrial had been declared. Almost as immediately, there had been another development: Arthwell Hayton had asked newspapermen to an 11 a. m. Sunday morning press conference in his office. There had been television cameras, and flash bulbs popping. 'As you gentlemen may know,' Hayton had said, striking a note of stiff bonhomie, 'there are very often women who become amorous toward their doctor or lawyer. This does not mean on the physician's or lawyer's part that there is any romance toward the patient or client.'

'Would you deny that you were having an affair with Mrs. Miller?' a reporter had asked.

'I would deny that there was any romance on my part whatsoever.'

It was a distinction he would maintain through all the wearing weeks to come.

So they had come to see Arthwell, these crowds who now milled beneath the dusty palms outside the courthouse, and they had also come to see Lucille, who appeared as a slight, intermittently pretty woman, already pale from lack of sun, a woman who would turn thirty-five before the trial was over and whose tendency toward haggardness was beginning to show, a meticulous woman who insisted, against her lawyer's advice, on coming to court with her hair piled high and lacquered. 'I would've been happy if she'd come in with it hanging loose, but Lucille wouldn't do that,' her lawyer said. He was Edward P. Foley, a small, emotional Irish Catholic who several times wept in the courtroom. 'She has a great honesty, this woman,' he added, 'but this honesty about her appearance always worked against her.'

By the time the trial opened, Lucille Miller's appearance included maternity clothes, for an official examination on December 18 had revealed that she was then three and a half months pregnant, a fact which made picking a jury even more difficult than usual, for Turner was asking the death penalty. 'It's unfortunate but there it is,' he would say of the pregnancy to each juror in turn, and finally twelve were seated, seven of them women, the youngest forty-one, an assembly of the very peers – housewives, a machinist, a truck driver, a grocery-store manager, a filing clerk – above whom Lucille Miller had wanted so badly to rise.

That was the sin, more than the adultery, which tended to reinforce the one for which she was being tried. It was implicit in both the defense and the prosecution that Lucille Miller was an erring woman, a woman who perhaps wanted too much. But to the prosecution she was not merely a woman who would want a new house and want to go to parties and run up high telephone bills ($1152 in ten months), but a woman who would go so far as to murder her husband for his $80,000 in insurance, making it appear an accident in order to collect another $40,000 in double indemnity and straight accident policies. To Turner she was a woman who did not want simply her freedom and a reasonable alimony (she could have had that, the defense contended, by going through with her divorce suit), but wanted everything, a woman motivated by 'love and greed.' She was a 'manipulator.' She was a 'user of people.'

To Edward Foley, on the other hand, she was an impulsive woman who 'couldn't control her foolish little heart.' Where Turner skirted the pregnancy, Foley dwelt upon it, even calling the dead man's mother down from Washington to testify that her son had told her they were going to have another baby because Lucille felt that it would 'do much to weld our home again in the pleasant relations that we used to have.' Where the prosecution saw a 'calculator,' the defense saw a 'blabbermouth,' and in fact Lucille Miller did emerge as an ingenuous conversationalist. Just as, before her husband's death, she had confided in her friends about her love affair, so she chatted about it after his death, with the arresting sergeant. 'Of course Cork lived with it for years, you know,' her voice was heard to tell Sergeant Paterson on a tape made the morning after her arrest. 'After Elaine died, he pushed the panic button one night and just asked me right out, and that, I think, was when he really – the first time he really faced it.' When the sergeant asked why she had agreed to talk to him, against the specific instructions of her lawyers, Lucille Miller said airily, 'Oh, I've always been basically quite an honest person . . . I mean I can put a hat in the cupboard and say it cost ten dollars less, but basically I've always kind of just lived my life the way I wanted to, and if you don't like it you can take off.'

The prosecution hinted at men other than Arthwell, and even, over Foley's objections, managed to name one. The defense called Miller suicidal. The prosecution produced experts who said that the Volkswagen fire could not have been accidental. Foley produced witnesses who said that it could have been. Lucille's father, now a junior-high-school teacher in Oregon, quoted Isaiah to reporters: *'Every tongue that shall rise against thee in judgment thou shalt condemn.'* 'Lucille did wrong, her affair,' her mother said judiciously. 'With her it was love. But with some I guess it's just passion.' There was Debbie, the Millers' fourteen-year-old, testifying in a steady voice about how she and her mother had gone to a supermarket to buy the gasoline can the week before the accident. There was Sandy Slagle, in the courtroom every day, declaring that on at least one occasion Lucille Miller had prevented her husband not only from committing suicide but from committing suicide in such a way that it would appear an accident and ensure the double-indemnity payment. There was Wenche Berg, the pretty twenty-seven-year-old Norwegian governess to Arthwell Hayton's children, testifying that Arthwell had instructed her not to allow Lucille Miller to see or talk to the children.

Two months dragged by, and the headlines never stopped. Southern California's crime reporters were headquartered in San Bernardino for the duration: Howard Hertel from the *Times*, Jim Bennett and Eddy Jo Bernal from the *Herald-Examiner*. Two months in which the Miller trial was pushed off the *Examiner's* front page only by the Academy Award nominations and Stan Laurel's death. And finally, on March 2, after Turner had reiterated that it was a case of 'love and greed,' and Foley had protested that his client was being tried for adultery, the case went to the jury.

They brought in the verdict, guilty of murder in the first degree, at 4:50 p.m. on March 5. 'She didn't do it,' Debbie Miller cried, jumping up from the spectators' section. 'She didn't do it.' Sandy Slagle collapsed in her seat and began to scream. 'Sandy, for God's sake please don't,' Lucille Miller said in a voice that carried across the courtroom, and Sandy Slagle was momentarily subdued. But as the jurors left the courtroom she screamed again: 'You're murderers . . . Every last one of you is a murderer.' Sheriff's deputies moved in then, each wearing a string tie that read '1965 sheriff's rodeo,' and Lucille Miller's father, that sad-faced junior-high-school teacher who believed in the word of Christ and the dangers of wanting to see the world, blew her a kiss off his fingertips.

The California Institution for Women at Frontera, where Lucille Miller is now, lies down where Euclid Avenue turns into country road, not too many miles from where she once lived and shopped and organized the Heart Fund Ball. Cattle graze across the road, and Rainbirds sprinkle the alfalfa. Frontera has a softball field and tennis courts, and looks as if it might be a California junior college, except that the trees are not yet high enough to conceal the concertina wire around the top of the Cyclone fence. On visitors' day there are big cars in the parking area, big Buicks and Pontiacs that belong to grandparents and sisters and fathers (not many of them belong to husbands), and some of them have bumper stickers that say 'support your local police.'

A lot of California murderesses live here, a lot of girls who somehow misunderstood the promise. Don Turner put Sandra Garner here (and her husband in the gas chamber at San Quentin) after the 1959 desert killings known to crime reporters as 'the soda-pop murders'. Carole Tregoff is here, and has been ever since she was convicted of conspiring to murder Dr. Finch's wife in West Covina, which is not too far from San Bernardino. Carole Tregoff is in fact a nurse's aide in the prison hospital, and might have attended Lucille Miller had her baby been born at Frontera; Lucille Miller chose instead to have it outside, and paid for the guard who stood outside the delivery room in St. Bernardine's Hospital. Debbie Miller came to take the baby home from the hospital, in a white dress with pink ribbons, and Debbie was allowed to choose a name. She named the baby Kimi Kai. The children live with Harold and Joan Lance now, because Lucille Miller will probably spend ten years at Frontera. Don Turner waived his original request for the death penalty (it was generally agreed that he had demanded it only, in Edward Foley's words, 'to get anybody with the slightest trace of human kindness in their veins off the jury'), and settled for life imprisonment with the possibility of parole. Lucille Miller does not like it at Frontera, and has had trouble adjusting. 'She's going to have to learn humility,' Turner says. 'She's going to have to use her ability to charm, to manipulate.'

The new house is empty now, the house on the street with the sign that says

PRIVATE ROAD
BELLA VISTA
DEAD END

The Millers never did get it landscaped, and weeds grow up around the fieldstone siding. The television aerial has toppled on the roof, and a trash can is stuffed with the debris of family life: a cheap suitcase, a child's game called 'Lie Detector'. There is a sign on what would have been the lawn, and the sign reads 'ESTATE SALE'. Edward Foley is trying to get Lucille Miller's case appealed, but there have been delays. 'A trial always comes down to a matter of sympathy,' Foley says wearily now. 'I couldn't create sympathy for her.' Everyone is a little weary now, weary and resigned, everyone except Sandy Slagle, whose bitterness is still raw. She lives in an apartment near the medical school in Loma Linda, and studies reports of the case in *True Police Cases* and *Official Detective Stories*. 'I'd much rather we not talk about the Hayton business too much,' she tells visitors, and she keeps a tape recorder running. 'I'd rather talk about Lucille and what a wonderful person she is and how her rights were violated.' Harold Lance does not talk to visitors at all. 'We don't want to give away what we can sell,' he explains pleasantly; an attempt was made to sell Lucille Miller's personal story to *Life,* but *Life* did not want to buy it. In the district attorney's offices they are prosecuting other murders now, and do not see why the Miller trial attracted so much attention. 'It wasn't a very interesting murder as murders go,' Don Turner says laconically. Elaine Hayton's death is no longer under investigation. 'We know everything we want to know,' Turner says.

Arthwell Hayton's office is directly below Edward Foley's. Some people around San Bernardino say that Arthwell Hayton suffered; others say that he did not suffer at all. Perhaps he did not, for time past is not believed to have any bearing upon time present or future, out in the golden land where every day the world is born anew. In any case, on October 17, 1965, Arthwell Hayton married again, married his children's pretty governess, Wenche Berg, at a service in the Chapel of the Roses at a retirement village near Riverside. Later the newlyweds were feted at a reception for seventy-five in the dining room of Rose Garden Village. The bridegroom was in black tie, with a white carnation in his buttonhole. The bride wore a long white *peau de soie* dress and carried a shower bouquet of sweetheart roses with stephanotis streamers. A coronet of seed pearls held her illusion veil.

Barry Siegel

Pulitzer Prize winning journalist and author Barry Siegel was appointed as a roving national correspondent for the *Los Angeles Times* in 1980. A collection of the unconventional narratives he wrote in that role was published in *Shades of Gray* (1992). He has also written three novels and his non-fiction book *A Death in White Bear Lake*, published in 1990, was re-released in 2000. His stories for the *LA Times* have won many awards, including the 2002 Pulitzer for 'A Father's Pain, a Judge's Duty and a Justice Beyond Their Reach', published in the *Good Weekend* as 'One Moment of Weakness' on May 25, 2002.

A FATHER'S PAIN, A JUDGE'S DUTY AND A JUSTICE BEYOND THEIR REACH

Barry Siegel

Los Angeles Times, Sunday, December 30, 2001

SILVER SUMMIT, Utah – He sat in his chambers, unprepared for this. 'Just giving you a heads up,' his court administrator was saying. 'Paul Wayment hasn't reported in yet. They can't find him.'

Judge Robert Hilder felt uneasy. Wayment was supposed to start his jail sentence this morning.

The 52-year-old judge walked slowly to his Summit County district courtroom. The trial underway passed as a blur. More than once, clerks pulled him off the bench to give him updates on Wayment. Each time, in his chambers, he stared out windows at the jail, hoping to see Paul drive up. At the lunch break, he went into Park City to eat, alone with his thoughts.

He'd sentenced Wayment to jail even though the prosecutor didn't want this distraught father to serve time. Hilder felt he had to. Wayment's negligence caused his young son's death. There must be consequences, the judge ruled.

Now there were – more than he had intended.

On his way back from lunch, Hilder punched off the car radio, wanting to avoid the news. As always, his 6-year-old son's drawings and broken Lego toys covered the floor of his Ford Taurus. At the courthouse, he walked down a hallway that took him past the administrator's glass-walled office. She rose and waved him in. Concern, he saw, strained her face. He approached her door, bracing himself.

Had he driven Wayment to suicide? Hilder believed it possible. Just as he believed it possible that he'd caused his own father's suicide, 20 years before.

Although it includes the Park City ski resorts, Summit County is less the province of people than of rolling pastures and mountain forests. Only about 25,000 live in 1849 square miles. Only one judge – Hilder – hears criminal cases. Three lawyers comprise the county attorney's criminal division. Two private lawyers on a part-time retainer fill the public defender's role. When they heard of Gage Wayment's death, all of them knew it would come to them. They knew they'd soon have to make their own choices.

The first choice, though, had been Paul Wayment's.

There he stood last year on a radiant October morning, high in a remote forest. Before him spread the wild green abundance of Chalk Creek Basin, a rugged 8000-foot-high hunting ground where deer and elk and moose wander through dense stands of golden quaking aspens. Behind him, strapped in a car seat in his red Dodge pickup, sat his son Gage, his inseparable buddy, his most precious gift, his future hunting partner.

Paul Wayment felt more comfortable in these mountains than anywhere. At 38, he was an uncomplicated man, raised in small Utah towns, instructed in the Mormon faith, captivated by both hunting and the wilderness. When he worked, which wasn't always, it was in construction or on an assembly line. He found the inside of homes stifling. The same with any kind of social gathering, unless they held it outdoors, made it a picnic. He was fine with silence. He could sit for hours high on a ridge, watching the deer, studying the sky, searching for bald eagles. The mountains gave him solace and sanctuary, the mountains made him whole.

So did Gage. There had been a brief, troubled marriage, then a divorce. Now, for the time being, Paul had full custody. Gage was big for his age, a rambunctious 33-pound ball of energy who looked closer to 4. Father and son did everything together. Camping and boating as often as they could. Playing ball in the backyard, fixing things around the house, planting their vegetable garden. They'd roll around their neighbourhood, Paul pulling Gage in a wagon, giving away their extra produce. They'd hike down to a vacant field, Gage on Paul's shoulders, to see the cows and geese. They looked so happy, joined at the heart. You never saw one without the other. Gage's gregarious manner made Paul more outgoing. Mr. Mom, the neighbours called him. On days when she felt in need of a lift, one neighbour would sit on her porch just to watch them, just so she could smile inside.

Bringing his young son into the wilderness made sense to Wayment. There he could join together the two things he loved most. Yet on this morning, he had to choose between them.

Before him stood three deer, two does and a buck.

Behind him Gage slept in the pickup.

The deer began to move off, gliding into the forest. Wayment counted five of them now. He'd come to scout deer, preparation for a weekend hunting trip.

He turned toward Gage, then back to the deer. All around him, the quaking aspens seemed alive in the breeze, humming a faint prayer. 'In one brief monumental moment,' he would later say of this instant, 'I made the biggest and most painful mistake of my life.'

He took a step. He began to follow the deer.

He had left Gage asleep out here once before, but that time he'd strayed only 75 yards from the pickup. Now he was well beyond 75 yards, well beyond sight of Gage.

The deer disappeared over a ridge. Wayment crept after them. Minutes passed – just how many remains uncertain. Wayment walked a mile, maybe two.

While he walked, two hunters drove by his pickup. They saw Gage alone in his car seat, awake and watching them. What they saw bothered them, but they thought the dad must be nearby. They also feared being taken for kidnappers. So they drove on, deciding there was nothing they could do.

In the forest, Wayment began to have a bad feeling. He turned and hurried back to the pickup. Even from afar, he could see he was too late. The driver's side door was wide open. The car seat was empty. Gage had gotten out, Gage had wandered off.

Wayment plunged into a nearby pond, fighting a rising panic. Gage loved the water. That's where he'd go. For sure he's in the pond.

He wasn't, though. The pond was muddy, waist deep. Wayment thrashed about, reaching out, feeling nothing. He clambered out of the water. He raced up and down ridges, shouting Gage's name. He jumped into his pickup, roaring off in search of help. My son is missing, he gasped to the hunters he found. My son is gone.

Rather than duck responsibility, Wayment drowned in it. The first deputy sheriff to arrive found him writhing on the ground, crying and vomiting, his face caked with snot and pond mud. 'Just shoot me,' Wayment urged when the deputy asked what he could do for him. And minutes later: 'I should have never left him in the truck. That is the stupidest thing I've ever done in my life, and I should be skinned and shot for that.'

They kept someone by Wayment's side that evening, fearing what he'd do if left alone. Past midnight, a storm blew in as search crews gathered on the mountainside. Temperatures plummeted; the rain turned to sleet, then snow. At 3 a.m., Wayment sat in a search-and-rescue commander's Ford Explorer with two sheriff's detectives. He was calmer now, but no less aware.

'I'm responsible for his death if he is dead,' Wayment said. 'I'm responsible for his death. I don't think you can put it any other way. . . . I had custody of him. I was supposed to look out for him. He was under my care.'

Whispers and Suspicions

Impatient with the sound bite approach to journalism, Judge Hilder avoids television. For his news he reads the major newspapers on the Internet and listens to National Public Radio. Yet he could not help hearing about the missing boy on the mountain. At the Summit County Justice Center, 30 miles east of Salt Lake City, people he saw every day quickly became part of the organized search. The Wayments were a major topic of conversation.

Hilder's first response was as a parent, not a judge. In his second marriage now, he is father to six sons and one daughter, including two stepsons, the youngest 6 years old. Of the missing little boy, he thought, what a tragedy. He believed Gage had the slimmest of chances.

Then Hilder began to hear hints that this might be something other than an awful accident. In time, the hints became no easier to avoid than news of the search itself. After all, there was Wayment's ex-wife, Brenda, telling detectives and TV cameras that she believed Paul had hidden Gage in order to deny her custody.

As the search widened and more hours slipped by and the snow fell heavier, not just Brenda voiced suspicions. There were whispers about the Wayment family's 'marital problems.' There was talk of protective orders and a thick Division of Child and Family Services file. Those who hadn't seen Paul in the early hours wondered why he now appeared so stoic, so lacking in remorse. Some wondered why, with dogs and horses and computers and helicopters, they still couldn't find Gage. Many searchers came to believe that Gage was not in the forest at all. Many thought Paul Wayment guilty of foul play or deception.

When darkness fell Sunday night, four days after Gage disappeared, officials called off their search. Sheriff's deputies invited Wayment to their headquarters for a polygraph exam and what they promised would be 'a lengthy and detailed interview.' The lead detective believed they needed to investigate the 'ever-growing possibility that Gage had been abducted or hidden by his father.'

From the Bench, the Human Stories

It's an honest world when you're running, Robert Hilder believes. He can think clearly. So he jogs often, sometimes five or six miles a morning.

The Wayment affair now sometimes crept into his thoughts as he ran, but he made no conclusions. He couldn't, for he had to keep this matter at arm's length. He had to prepare himself to judge its meaning. What manner of story might he hear this time in his courtroom? If he felt some unease, he also felt anticipation. It was human stories like this that first drew him to the bench.

Hilder had always wanted to be a judge more than a practicing attorney. He was not at core committed to the adversary system, to the role of lawyer as advocate. He was much more interested in the narratives and issues heard in a courtroom. He liked to try to resolve them. He thought he was good at resolving them.

Sentencing, on the other hand, he found hard. There was always that horrible moment, after he heard the tremendous advocacy, the arguments, the pleas. Suddenly there was silence – and he had to decide. That was hell. That also was what he'd signed up for.

He didn't have a typical judge's background. For one thing, he'd never finished high school. He grew up in Australia, one of four siblings. His alcoholic father was abusive with his mother. By the time Hilder was 14 and more than 6 feet tall, he was intervening, getting his dad in headlocks. By 15, he'd left home.

For years, he found jobs where he could. He apprenticed on a farm. He laboured over pipelines in underground tunnels. He worked as a bartender and bouncer by night, a bank clerk by day. He was making his way, but at the age of 24, he thought his life empty. He had few friends and little social life beyond the bars where he drank.

Then, as he sat in his apartment one night, reading a book on Lenin and Stalin – one of many history volumes in his self-improvement program – there came a knock on the door. A reformed drinking buddy had sent two Mormon missionaries his way. At first Hilder listened only out of curiosity. The curiosity soon turned to interest. He admired these young men's commitment and asceticism, but what he embraced most was the sense of family they offered. They made him feel part of something.

Within two weeks, he'd joined the Church of Jesus Christ of Latter-day Saints; within six months, he was a Bible teacher and Sunday school president. He felt so needed.

Asked if he wanted to do missionary work, he readily agreed, setting off on a two-year tour of southern Australia.

There he grew close to the mission president, a lawyer from Salt Lake City. Hilder thought him an excellent role model. Far more so than his own father. When Hilder returned to Sydney from his mission, he found his dad in a halfway house, recently released from jail. He was 60 and looked pathetic. Once a successful wool and sheep-skin broker, he was living a drunken transient's life that took him to dry-out cells and psychiatric wards. Hilder had visited him as often as he could in these places. Yet it seemed as if his father wanted more from him – a rescue. He wrote Hilder letters, saying we need to make plans. I'm feeling stronger, he reported, as if to show he could be like his son. I'm reading the Book of Mormon, I'm meeting missionaries.

Hilder had hated his father for a time but had never deserted him. Now he could not think of a way to help him, for he'd met a woman on his Mormon mission, and they planned to move to the United States. Two weeks before he was to leave, Hilder got the call on a cold May morning: His father had hanged himself. This, Hilder believed, was his dad's response to hopelessness, to the prospect of his son leaving. At the funeral, an elderly aunt mentioned that his father had left a letter for him. Hilder never asked for it, never saw it. He was starting a new life. He just didn't want to know.

A month later in Utah's Mormon Temple, he married the woman from his mission. Ten months later came their first son. Hilder was 28, with a 10th-grade education. For a while, he made a living at day labour, then found a job as bookkeeper for a demolition company.

Desperate to do better, he took a high school equivalency test and then the college Scholastic Aptitude Test, scoring in the 99th percentile on both, a feat he credits to a lifetime of voracious reading. In January 1979, he was accepted at the University of Utah, from which he graduated 2 1/2 years later, a political science major with a nearly straight-A average. By the time he enrolled in the university's law school, he had three children. He earned his law degree at 35. Within 11 years, he was a Mormon bishop and managing partner at a Salt Lake City law firm.

That's when Utah's governor appointed Hilder, a Democrat in a very Republican state, to the bench. Eventually, he began sitting in Summit County, commuting from his Salt Lake City home. Over the last six years, he has earned the trust and warm regard of prosecutors and defence attorneys alike. Their testimonials on his behalf focus as much on his humanity as his legal acuity. They say there 'probably is no more decent person in the legal profession than Judge Hilder.' They call him 'one of the kindest, most compassionate, gentlest people to sit on the bench.' They think no jurist is 'more prepared, fair and understanding than Judge Hilder.'

That's not to say he's a pushover. He is seen as more complex than that. In one well-publicized case, Hilder sent a child molester to prison against all recommendations. Yet in another case, he spared a teenage boy who'd somehow accelerated his car into a crowd, killing two people. Hilder knew he should lock him up, but what he saw before him was a sweet kid he just couldn't send to jail.

Four days had passed now since Gage Wayment went missing. In Hilder's home, the news managed to filter through, as did images of Gage, for a house guest sometimes watched television. When would they find the body? When would this be Hilder's story to hear?

Rising Suspicions as the Search Goes On

The Utah Division of Child and Family Services did its best to quell the rising suspicions about Paul Wayment. For more than a decade, their own attention had been focused not on him but his ex-wife, Brenda, who had five children and two husbands before Paul, one husband after, and a 10-year history of domestic troubles. The agency director made this as plain as he could when he publicly confirmed that they'd intervened with the Wayment family, but only due to Brenda's alleged behaviour.

'We've had no allegations against him for any type of mistreatment,' Ken Patterson told reporters. It was Brenda, he said, who had been referred to the agency in the mid-1990s; it was from Brenda that all six children, including Gage, had been taken. In June, the court, pending a final hearing, had awarded Wayment sole custody of Gage. Subsequent visits by social workers to his home had been 'uneventful.'

The suspicions would not subside, however. Paul's sister Valerie Burke became convinced that authorities were dropping their search because they believed Paul had killed or hidden Gage. So even before the county withdrew Sunday evening, she made a public plea for volunteers to take their place.

By mid-morning Monday, about 150 citizens from across the state were swarming the snow-covered mountains above Coalville. Among them was James Wilkes, 35, the husky proprietor of a self-service pet wash shop in a Salt Lake City suburb.

He brought with him his dog Dino, a giant schnauzer. At the base camp, he met a shy muscular man who seemed consumed by pain. Paul Wayment introduced himself, tears welling in his eyes. He could not look at Wilkes. Instead, he offered a sandwich. Wilkes shared it with his dog as he sat in his pickup trying to warm up by the truck's heater. Then he climbed out and plunged into the forest.

It had started to snow, a foot deep in places. Wilkes lost the trail and his bearings. He slid into a gully. It began snowing harder. He couldn't tell north from south. Guessing, he started up a mountain. He stumbled. On his hands and knees, he crawled. Darkness fell. In time, he and Dino settled under a large sheltering pine tree. There he dug a hole, 2 feet by 4, and climbed in, his body wrapped around his dog. They each kept the other warm, the two covered by a blanket of broken branches.

It was the longest night Wilkes ever spent. He feared falling asleep, afraid he'd never wake up. Near 5 a.m., he rose and began to walk. Within minutes, Dino's nose went down. The schnauzer darted up a slope to the base of a pine tree. From below, Wilkes could see his dog licking a mound of snow. Then, as he approached, he saw two little feet.

By the time Wilkes reached the tree, Dino had cleaned off Gage's face. Six inches of snow covered the small body. Gage lay in a foetal position, his hands clenched, his eyes wide open. His pyjama legs were up to knees; his feet had worn through his thin booties. His throat was blue. In his eyes were frozen tears.

A Decision on the Charges

To those who wonder why he takes on the daunting role of judging others, Robert Hilder says: 'What am I going to do? Not do this job and instead let someone get up there and decide instead of me? Someone who sees it all in black and white? Some come in so sure. They don't see the complexity. I'm 52. What worries me is people who can't see the complexity.'

Watching the Wayment case unfold from afar, it was hard now for anyone to ignore the complexity. They had a body. They also had new suspicions. Some were asking how James Wilkes could have located Gage when hundreds of others had failed. Some wondered whether a conspiracy might be the explanation – a conspiracy between him and Paul Wayment.

Yet it still wasn't Hilder's turn. Maybe it never would be. The immediate issue – perhaps the toughest of all – was what, if anything, to charge.

That decision rested with Summit County Attorney, Robert Adkins. Like Hilder, his first response to news of a missing boy was as a parent. He knew the rugged terrain up there – he was a former hunter – and that gave him concern. Then he saw Brenda on TV, accusing Paul of hiding Gage. He hoped she was right; better that than a lost boy.

Adkins could feel Paul Wayment's anguish clear to his bones. In 1989, he'd lost his own 8-year-old son in an accident. The boy had been playing with his cousins across the street at his grandmother's house. Someone activated the automatic garage door, which lacked an auto-reverse. The door pinned Adkins' son, obstructing his breathing. He died 21 days later. Adkins, who'd been at work, at his desk, never forgave himself. Something had told him, go home. But he'd thought, I'll just finish up.

Now they had Gage Wayment's body.

Adkins knew that those investigating Wayment didn't believe he should be charged with a crime. The deputies and detectives had spent more time with him than anyone. They had also met with the family services staff, whose account convinced them that domestic abuse accusations against Wayment could not be substantiated. Brenda had twice sought protective orders against him, but the judge had dismissed one, and Brenda herself eventually moved to dismiss the other. To a man, the detectives felt Wayment had already suffered enough. To a man, they felt Wayment would already be punished for the rest of his life.

When Adkins received the sheriff's report, he tried to focus on the facts, not the mounting public furore. Wayment drove into the wilderness with Gage dressed lightly in pyjamas. He left Gage in a rugged, isolated area, with the pickup parked on a slant, which meant the car door could easily swing open, pulled by gravity. He was gone some unknowable length of time, anywhere from 30 to 90 minutes.

Certainly, it was not OK to do what Wayment did. Still, this was clearly a good man who had made a horrible mistake. He was a straight arrow, in fact, who didn't drink or use drugs. But for a stint in the Army, he'd lived at his mom's home until he met Brenda at age 34. He had no criminal history. Despite the headlines and whispers, Gage's death involved no conspiracies.

To Forgive and Empathize, or Condemn and Punish?

Adkins had never forgiven himself for failing to protect his own son. Now he had a chance to forgive another father. That was his inclination. Yet there were two other prosecutors in his office's criminal division, and they were of different minds.

For days, the three debated around a conference table. At times, voices rose. Adkins was most inclined toward leniency, David Brickey and Mary-Kathleen Wolsey toward exacting a severe punishment. Unable to sway his colleagues, wishing to give them their due, Adkins sought the advice of two consultants, who themselves couldn't agree.

In the end, Adkins had to make the call himself. Adkins struggled, wavered – and finally decided they must charge Wayment with something. If they didn't, they'd be saying it was OK, or at least not criminal, to leave children alone in a remote area.

Adkins didn't really want to punish Wayment, though. He chose one of the mildest recommendations, negligent homicide, a misdemeanour. He also decided he would not seek a jail sentence. He just couldn't argue for incarceration. Not in this situation, not where the man's son had died.

Robert Hilder learned of the prosecutor's choice when a detective appeared in his chambers one morning with a document that described the 'probable cause' for charging Wayment. Hilder glanced at the pages as the detective stood before him formally swearing to their truth. The judge kept his face blank, not saying or showing anything. What he saw distressed him, though.

It would have been so much easier if they hadn't charged Paul Wayment. They didn't have to. By filing, the prosecutors had handed their quandary to the judge.

There would be no right answer in this matter, he believed. In no way could he make a good decision when this came down. Sentencing would be the hardest. In fact, if Paul Wayment wasn't acquitted, sentencing would be impossible.

A Plea That Reflects the Defendant

Judge Hilder first saw Paul Wayment face to face at his arraignment on Jan. 9. At 6 feet, 2 inches and 205 pounds, Wayment was big and muscular, with strawberry blond hair and bulging shoulders. Although he showed no emotion, the judge knew his pain and shame must be unbearable. He thought Wayment a decent, stoic man.

Yet there Paul stood, not just being stoic but pleading not guilty. A guilty plea would not have surprised Hilder, given that Wayment had openly accepted responsibility. Instead, it looked as if his public defenders were digging in for a vigorous fight.

Hilder thought he understood. This didn't necessarily mean Wayment wasn't accepting responsibility. This meant he was deferring to counsel. The defence lawyers, in turn, were just doing their job.

As it happened, Hilder was only partly right. Paul Wayment's plea that day reflected something more complex than his attorney's natural reflexes. The plea reflected Wayment's own attitude.

From the beginning, Paul and his sister Valerie had talked of the consequences he faced. He felt he had to go to jail. He said it over and over. 'I know I'm going to jail.' It was almost as if he were willing it, Valerie thought, as if he wanted to pay a price.

Yet Wayment recoiled when the prosecutors finally did file charges. They were calling what he'd done 'criminal' negligence. Negligence he readily admitted, but he had a hard time with criminal. He felt they were saying he intentionally killed Gage. So he was adamant that he wouldn't plead guilty. Valerie sensed that it was somehow important for Paul's sanity that he not see himself as a criminal.

He was already tormented enough. There were terrible nightmares now, Paul waking up in a panic, reliving Gage's loss. He'd go out to his pickup in the middle of the night, trying to figure how Gage opened the car. He'd sit in the cab, locking and unlocking the door, asking, 'How could he get out?'

He'd regularly go up to the mountain, driving as far as he could in the winter snow, trying to reach where he'd lost Gage. Once he enlisted the help of James Wilkes, who'd served as honoured pallbearer at Gage's funeral. They rented snowmobiles and plunged deep into the frozen wilderness but had to turn back when one of the vehicles caught fire.

Paul wrote a letter to Gage: So strong so sweet an angel, a warrior, my dreams with you had only begun. If I could only be with you again. To hold you again . . . to kiss your tiny face. . . . Oh how I love you. . . . You were my most precious gift, heaven sent. . . .

Valerie and Paul talked openly in these days about suicide. She'd ask whether he thought about hurting himself. He would always reassure her. He couldn't do that, he pointed out, because then he'd never see Gage. Since he died so young, Gage went to the highest level of the Mormon heavenly kingdom. If Paul killed himself, he'd never get to that level, never rejoin his son. 'So don't worry,' he told Valerie. 'I won't kill myself. This is my test. I have to live through this.'

His test only intensified in the days after his arraignment. The public debate about Wayment expanded steadily, consuming much of Utah. There he was in newspaper articles and on TV news broadcasts, a magnifying glass put to his past domestic troubles, to his spotty employment record, to his love for hunting. People wrote letters to the editor, called radio talk shows, sent Internet messages, rendered verdicts on Web site polls. Those opposed to guns and hunting were heard from, and those horrified or victimized by child abuse. It was as parents, particularly, that so many spoke out – parents who could imagine themselves in Wayment's place and parents who could not. There were those who shuddered, thinking of their own past lapses. There were many more who thundered, unable to accept Wayment's failing.

Wayment cringed at the attention. He withdrew ever deeper into his stoicism. He hesitated to leave his house. He phoned his sister Valerie, in a monotone asking what was in the newspapers that day. One morning, it was Brenda's sister, publicly accusing him once again of domestic violence. He couldn't bear that. Nor could he bear being called a killer.

'Why do they hate me?' he asked Valerie.

In an e-mail to a friend, she wrote: 'I'm wondering if it will stop once he kills himself.'

Legal Manoeuvring Takes Its Toll

The fevered public discourse about Paul Wayment reached even into Judge Hilder's bedroom. Because his daughter had changed the station on his alarm clock radio, there were two mornings when he awoke to talk show conversations. In both, he heard rabid voices declaring that the death penalty was not a sufficient punishment for this man.

Then, in late March, came an evidentiary hearing. Again a stoic Paul Wayment stood before Robert Hilder, saying little, visibly uncomfortable in a coat and tie. Three detectives took the stand, offering detailed accounts of what transpired in the days after Gage went missing. The lawyers followed, rising to argue over what photos of Gage and statements by Paul could be admitted at trial. Listening, Hilder for the first time gained direct exposure to this distraught father's grief and his ex-wife's suspicions. Nothing he heard persuaded him that this case involved anything more than a tragic mistake.

That was not, however, how the Summit County chief criminal prosecutor, David Brickey, saw matters. He saw in Paul Wayment a neglectful father. Brickey had a son himself, a 10-month-old. He couldn't forget Gage, couldn't forget that this little boy had been a real person.

Like Hilder, Brickey loves stories. What he must do in the courtroom, he believes, is tell the better story. He learned that much when he attended a prosecutors' school in South Carolina. There Brickey took a course on child abusers. The class taught him you always want to use any information that suggests the parent isn't a perfect person. He came back to Utah promoting the fact that prosecutors don't use 'prior bad acts' nearly enough. He started planting that idea with his boss, Summit County Atty. Robert Adkins. Let's try to use prior bad acts to our advantage.

In the Wayment case, Brickey believed there were 'prior bad acts' in Paul's domestic problems. He believed this despite the fact that Adkins saw nothing in the family services file they could use at trial. They weren't going to wade into that history, Adkins had resolved. They definitely weren't going to call Brenda's other children to the stand.

Adkins hadn't shared that decision with Wayment's attorneys, though. In fact, for bargaining purposes, he'd argued in court that the family history should be admissible. Brickey took that thought further in his own talks with the defense attorneys. He meant to use whatever he could, he told Glen Cook and Julie George. If you don't plea bargain, he warned them, if you go to trial, we will seek to establish that Paul has done this before.

Cook and George, unsure where Hilder might land, saw no alternative: If Brickey was going to fling accusations, they'd have to respond, they'd have to disprove. That meant bringing in Brenda, bringing in the kids, bringing in the whole juvenile file.

Outrage and frustration consumed Wayment when his lawyers told him what might be coming. 'All that stuff isn't true,' he shouted. 'Just look at the documents. I don't understand why you have to disprove anything. I don't want the kids involved. I don't want Brenda involved.'

While they debated, they heard again from David Brickey. One Friday afternoon, he called Julie George to say he might also charge Paul Wayment with witness tampering. Wayment, it turned out, had contacted James Wilkes. He'd asked Wilkes if they could try again to visit where Gage died. Wilkes had balked, for he had a lawyer now, a lawyer who'd ordered him not to talk with Paul, not to fuel suspicions about their connection. They'd talked anyway, among other things about the coming trial. Wilkes' lawyer had alerted Brickey. The prosecutor paid Wilkes a visit – and brought a tape recorder.

Clutching her phone, Julie George swore at Brickey, screaming and threatening, reminding that Wilkes wasn't even a subpoenaed witness. Then she called Wayment. This latest development stunned him. He began to cry.

Refusing to plead guilty – in his mind, refusing to say he intentionally, criminally harmed Gage – was the strand of sanity Wayment had been clinging to for months. Now he let go, now he conceded.

Julie George's phone rang three days later. 'I need to take a plea,' Wayment told her. 'I want it over. I can't take any more.'

During the course of two hours and three calls, they argued and anguished. It was no use. Wayment spoke in a monotone. 'I can't put my family through this anymore,' he said. 'This is hurting too many people. Nobody else should be hurt by this except me.'

Wayment quit going to church. He quit talking to Julie George. Using directions provided by a sheriff's detective, he started weekly pilgrimages to the spot where Gage had died. He brought Gage's toys with him, he carved their names in a tree, he built a memorial. There he sat for hours on end, reading the Bible.

He Knew He Had to Land Somewhere

To say that Paul Wayment made a tragic mistake did not, in Judge Hilder's view, mean there was no culpable negligence. That's what bothered him as Wayment stood before him on June 5. Once again this man looked so stoic. Rather than admitting guilt, he was entering a no contest plea, which meant he was only conceding the state could prove its case. In exchange, the prosecutors were not seeking a jail sentence.

Hilder couldn't help wonder: If this was what it came down to, then why were they all here?

I understand your deal, he told those gathered before him. But I'm not bound by it. I retain the right to impose jail or any other penalty.

Hilder pondered for days about Paul Wayment, often while jogging through the dense stand of sycamores that shaded his urban Salt Lake City neighbourhood. Influenced by his tenure on the bench, he'd strayed from his Mormon faith in the last two years. After looking at so many good but fallible human beings, it was hard to live with any religion certain it had all the answers. The truth was, Hilder's role as a judge had caused him to question the nature of God, and particularly the certainty of the Mormon faith.

Yet he finally had to land somewhere.

For Paul Wayment, he decided, there's got to be a consequence. Wayment was not a monster; Wayment was no more or less than any man. All the same, he'd exposed Gage to significant risk. He'd caused Gage to wander through the forest, terrified and suffering.

There was no need for deterrence here, and no need for punishment. There was need for society to make a statement, for society to say, this is wrong. There was also need for rehabilitation. Hilder felt Wayment must pay some kind of penance, or he would never be able to put this behind him.

Was this a court's job, to worry about atonement? Hilder thought it was. Of course, he had to be careful not to step over a line. He wasn't a priest; he didn't want to play God.

And yet: In a way, a judge was a god.

'God.'

Hilder would later speak that word out loud, reflecting on the Wayment case. Then he'd say, 'I shudder at how that will look on paper. But it's true.'

An Admission; an Acceptance of Fate

When his sentencing hearing began on the morning of July 17, Paul Wayment seemed not just stoic but hollow, as if he weren't there. Rising first, Summit County Atty. Robert Adkins talked of how 'difficult' this case was, of how much 'sympathy and empathy' his office had for the defendant. Then came defence attorney Glen Cook, arguing that Paul's 'punishment will continue until he and Gage are together again.' Finally Paul Wayment spoke, in an expressionless monotone:

If I could change places with my son, I would give up my life without question. But I can't. The life that I now live in is the hell that I alone created. The pain is incomprehensible. . . . The word 'sorry' does not even begin to express the feelings I now live with. . . . I admit full responsibility for my actions and will accept whatever punishment you deem appropriate.

Soon enough came the horrible moment that Hilder thought such hell. Silence fell in the packed courtroom. Even those lawyers and defendants there for other matters stopped conferring and turned to the bench. As Hilder began to speak, Paul Wayment remained impassive while around him his relatives blinked back tears. Paul's sister Valerie Burke thought the judge seemed so soft-spoken, so kind, so determined to explain his decision to Paul. She also thought the judge seemed full of heartache.

He'd planned to give Wayment a 90-day sentence, a quarter of the possible one-year maximum. But after hearing the arguments – and seeing that the probation department also opposed jail – he chose to reduce the penalty and require a mental evaluation, followed by counselling if recommended. 'The pre-sentence report . . . ,' Robert Hilder began, 'says that nobody associated with this case believes serving jail time will serve a useful purpose. The problem . . . is that none of these people have to make the decision. The decision comes here. . . . The court understands that there is nothing it can do that would be a greater punishment to Mr. Wayment than the suffering he's going to endure daily for the rest of his life. But the court cannot fully accept the argument that there shouldn't be some further consequence. . . . The court rules there must be a consequence.'

Moments later, Hilder imposed a 30-day jail sentence and invited Wayment to pick the date when it would start. Paul and his attorney Glen Cook conferred privately for 90 seconds. Then Cook said, 'Thank you for the courtesy, judge. Tomorrow morning.'

At the defence table, Julie George hugged Paul. Of the coming jail time, Wayment said, 'It's three hots [hot meals] and a cot.' George offered to walk him to his car, as she'd done before to buffer him from reporters. 'You don't have to anymore,' he said, patting her on the back. 'It's over.'

Robert Hilder did not rise from the bench this morning feeling he had made the right decision. He did not walk out thinking, I got it right. He walked out thinking, I did the best I could.

A Father's Final Choice

The questions still haunt about Paul Wayment's final choice, for they can't be answered. Why did neighbours see him outside planting flowers just days before? Why had he just gotten a new hunting license, a new truck, a new job? All people know is that Paul, as he left his sentencing hearing, said he was 'going to the ridge.' No one stopped him, for he always went up the mountain for comfort. Valerie told him, 'Phone me when you get home.'

Around nightfall, she started calling his house. By midnight, she was scared. In bed, in the middle of the night, she heard his voice speaking to her. Valerie. That gave her a warm feeling, a sense that Paul was home, Paul was OK. She fell back asleep.

Only in the early morning did she learn he still hadn't returned. Maybe he stayed for sunrise, she told herself. But in her heart, she knew.

So did Julie George. 'I have my four-wheel drive,' she told colleagues at 9:45 a.m. 'I'm going to go look for him.'

They found his body on a sloping ridge next to a pair of binoculars, a Pepsi Big Gulp and a Winchester .243 hunting rifle. He'd picked a spot, surrounded by quaking aspens, that provided a view of the hills where they'd searched for Gage. Julie George imagined his final afternoon. He'd sat with the binoculars, surveying where Gage died. At sunset – he would have waited for his beloved dusk – he'd put down the binoculars and picked up the rifle.

By the time Valerie Burke arrived on the ridge, a news media helicopter was hovering overhead. Julie George and others rushed to cover Paul's body, not wanting his mother to see it on TV. But the helicopter kept blowing the cover off.

At the courthouse that afternoon, Hilder sat dazed in his chambers. Tears filled his eyes. For a moment, he fixed on the far wall. There hung an aboriginal bark painting, an image of a shearing shed in the Australian outback. That was a memory; he'd worked in just such a shed in his teens. Hilder wanted nothing more now than to call his wife, Jan. When he reached her, she offered to come be with him. 'I don't think that would help,' he said. 'I have to go on the bench.'

What consumed him as he walked into the courtroom was his father's suicide. He'd never stopped wondering what he could have done. Suicides made their own decisions, he realized, and his father was never a happy man. Could he have prevented his death, though? He'd left his father's farewell letter unclaimed, not wanting to know what it might say.

This time, with Wayment, he did want to know. He didn't want to fight off his sense of responsibility.

On the witness stand, a water rights expert was testifying. Only occasionally did Hilder listen. Mostly, his eyes were on the legal pad beside his right hand. Judges never do such things, but he felt compelled to compose a public statement. He wanted to let people know why he sentenced Paul Wayment to jail. Blame me for this, he would tell them. Blame me if you will. But not because I didn't think about it.

Hilder picked up a pen and began. The first sentence he scratched out. The rest came without struggle or revision.

> It is a judge's worst nightmare that his or her actions may lead to unforeseen and tragic human consequences. The death of Paul Wayment is such a tragedy. . . . As hard as it is for me to contemplate any contribution of mine to Mr. Wayment's death, his family and the public have a right to know how I feel as a person and as a judge. As Paul Wayment's fellow man, I am devastated, I hurt deeply. . . . Having suffered through my father's suicide over 20 years ago, I know the survivors' anguish. . . . As a judge, however, my sworn duty is to all who appear before me. . . . If the jail sentence I imposed was a factor, large or small, in Mr. Wayment's decision, I regret that result with all my heart, but I cannot change my decision. . . . For the rest of my career I will remember Paul Wayment and try to never lose sight of the human consequences as I discharge my responsibilities.

There Is Much Anguish Now

Among those besides Robert Hilder whose choices affected Paul Wayment in his final months – the lawyers, detectives, journalists, relatives, hunters and friends – there is much anguish now. Many berate themselves. Many look to themselves when talking of responsibility.

It was Hilder, though, who faced the greatest barrage of criticism immediately after Wayment's death. A few particularly harassing letters prompted the county to provide temporary protection. Where once there were calls for accountability and consequences, now there was outrage at the judge who provided just that. People assailed Hilder, demanding his resignation or dismissal, charging him with 'a pathetic lack of wisdom,' declaring him 'directly responsible for the death of Paul Wayment.'

Soon enough, there came an even greater wave of support for Hilder from lawyers, pundits, hundreds of citizens and – over and over – Wayment's sister Valerie Burke. 'I don't believe the 30-day sentence caused Paul to kill himself,' she told reporters. 'I think the judge was compassionate. Our family understands where the judge was coming from, and we don't blame him at all. He had to do what he felt was right.'

Hilder can only shake his head at that phrase, 'what he felt was right.' He takes comfort from all the support but is no more certain now than before of making correct decisions. This latest experience, above all, has made him look even harder at the role of the judge.

He reflects on what the law accomplishes, what the law can't accomplish. He loves the law but does not worship it. He believes it does not have the answer to everything. In matters full of ambiguity, he suggests, there may be no good solution. 'Black and white answers are not always what's needed,' he says. 'But sometimes they're the only answer.'

He says something else as well: 'It's not a bad thing to have Paul Wayment's face forever part of my life.'

Interview with Barry Siegel

Question *Were you always drawn to particular sorts of stories?*

Siegel I just simply gravitated towards the stories where the people were facing ambiguous moral issues, where characters had to choose and act in situations where there were no clear right or wrong answers. Instinctively as a writer, it struck me as being rich material for storytelling . . . and it's universal. This is what life is and this is what we all do.

What I am doing is looking for certain elements. Is there a narrative arc? Is this a situation that is just an interesting situation, or am I going to unfold a tale with a beginning, a middle and an end? Are there interesting characters here? Are they wrestling with an issue that matters? If those elements are there, I don't know exactly what the story is, but I know there is a story that I will be able to tell.

Where do you look for those sorts of stories?

I am always scanning the horizon, often coming after the dust has settled. And actually I like it better, though it rubs against the grain of the newspaper's own instincts. I can sit here and in an instant see all the stories moving on all the wire services that day. And I can go to the websites of individual small papers and see the stories that might not even make the regional or national wires. I also subscribe to a lot of the specialised journals, legal journals, medical journals because in them you will find cases that have to do with moral issues.

And this particular story about the trial in Utah?

In this instance I happened to see a short Associated Press wire service story out of Salt Lake City the day Paul Wayment went up into the hills and killed himself after he lost his son in the woods. That story was big in Utah but didn't go wide. I asked the librarian at the *Times* to get me the back stories and the first one on the pile was the wire service story that had run the day before, [when] Judge Hilder was sentencing Paul Wayment. And it quotes the judge explaining why he was putting him in jail. He said choices have consequences, actions have consequences in this world. Well, I froze. I mean literally a chill went down my back, because Judge Hilder was talking about Paul Wayment's choice to leave his son. As he said those words he couldn't know that within hours those words would also apply to himself. And I immediately thought, parallel narratives. Two wrongs, two choices, two consequences. I realised this story was the epitome of the theme that I have been exploring in one way or another in my entire writing life – the need to make a choice. The judge has to make a black-and-white choice in a shades-of-grey situation. So I had to do the story.

And it went ahead from there?

You can't do an intimate story like this by reporting around the subject. The only way I could do it was if I could gain access to Judge Hilder. This seemed very unlikely. So I wrote him a letter introducing myself, described my previous writing, why I was interested, how deeply moved I was by the statement he issued, and that I wanted to really explore this. So he knew it wasn't sound-bite journalism. I get a lot of praise for my article, and thank you everyone, but you know what? You need someone. Judge Hilder is an open, thoughtful, articulate person. We all look for that kind of character and I was just very fortunate that Judge Hilder felt compelled to go deep like that.

Can you tell us about your approach to the interviews?

I flew in to start reporting on this story on the afternoon of September 10, 2001. So I researched this story entirely in the shadow of 9/11. I couldn't get out of Utah if I wanted to at that point. So I spent 9/11 in the living room of the house of Valerie Burke, Paul Wayment's sister – alternately talking to her about her kid brother, and checking the reports on the TV news. I probably spent about as much time with Valerie Burke as Judge Hilder . . . she is the way I can get close to Paul Wayment, who is not alive any more. I also interviewed the District Attorney, the lawyers involved, the prosecutor, the investigators and others. I ended up spending a couple of weeks in Utah – but I spent many more hours on the phone with Hilder afterwards. I don't have a count. We talked and talked and talked. I would have spent tens and tens of hours.

There must have been many documents involved as well.

A story like this, you'd be amazed how much of your story rests in documents. I had all the police reports. I had all the transcripts of interviews with Paul Wayment up on the mountain in the first hours after he lost Gage. I had the pre-sentencing report that the probation people wrote about Wayment, the whole child welfare report. I had all the letters from the neighbours, that's how I knew about him and Gage in the neighbourhood.

I came home in September and didn't finish till the end of December, but much of that time had to do with reading through many, many documents, cataloguing, indexing, correlating, And much of the material in the story was drawn from the documents and the correlations.

The sense of place is very strong in this story.

Sense of place means an enormous amount to me – be it the novel or the stories, the non-fiction book, or the journalism. I am using these stories always as windows. If they work they work because they are about more than just themselves. First of all they are windows into human nature. But the other thing they are is they're windows into a way of life – a part of the country. That is always what I am after in every piece. To me that is not an incidental adornment, it is a fundamental element of what the story is doing if it is working right.

What about the importance of seeking out details?

I always say God is in the details. Actually, I think I have revised that; particularly with longer writing projects I have come to feel that God is in the structure. But I am always looking for details. First of all there is just the sense of the authenticity of a felt life, of a real world, you want to create that sense of three-dimensional authenticity. But you pick the right details they tell a story. They are resonant, they have meaning, they reveal. They reveal character. They reveal where we are. And they do it in a show-not-tell way. And so I am always writing down details that I notice, but also, when I am interviewing, people tend to talk abstractly and generally, so I'm always trying to get them to be precise and to tell me the detail. Now where were you sitting? And what was he wearing? And what kind of facial expression? And where was the ray of sun? And I tell people, you are my eyes and ears – help me with this.

The structure you came up with for this story is very interesting.

I struggled with this story at the start and finally it was a structural decision that made it work. When I came back to start to write it, I started with an opening scene with the judge. But then I realised – this guy, he's not what I would call a 'through character' I can follow – a 'through point of view character'. Because I can open with the scene of him in his courtroom, but then the story turns into being all about Paul Wayment and Judge Hilder comes into the story at the end when he sentences him to jail.

You need to ride a particular point-of-view character through. So I turned it around and started opening with Paul Wayment . . . and I started to make the beginning with him up on the hill, about to make his choice to follow the deer. I started writing . . . and I look up and I have written a richly detailed 8000 words. And I am still on the mountain on the first weekend. And it is all about Paul Wayment. Jeesus Christ!

So I look at the chronology – even if I don't intend to follow a straight chronology, I make a chronology – and I see there were about three hearings before we got to the pivotal sentencing hearing. Now I had jumped over those because they were procedural. But as I stared at my chronology, what's the critical thing about all three of them? Judge Hilder is sitting on the bench in each one of those scenes. Then I realised, you don't have to get bogged down in what is going on legally in these hearings, but it's a way to get Hilder on the stage all through the narrative. And once you get him on the stage you can have him looking down at

Paul Wayment, but then you can go off in his mind as he thinks about his father's suicide, or his doubts about the Mormon church, or his doubts about God, or his role as a judge making decisions.

One other thing I realised . . . he had told me he was the only judge sitting on the criminal bench in Summit County, which means he would have known from day one that this case was coming to him. All of a sudden I saw what my story was: Judge Hilder sitting there and watching this case approach and knowing all the time that he is going to have to make a decision . . . a black-and-white decision in a shades-of-grey area which he is already troubled by in his life. I tell my students, it's not that God is in the structure – structure *is* story. When you decide what your structure is, you are deciding what the story is.

Journalism is often about conveying information in black-and-white ways . . .

What I have always fought for and believed strongly is that you can tell a complex ambiguous shades-of-grey story and you can tell it with compelling clarity without simplifying or dumbing it down. What I struggle against is reducing it to black and white. What I want is the nuance and the complexity. And certainly you want it because it is more reflective of true life, it weighs more true . . . but I would argue that it is more compelling. When you simplify it you lose what makes it compelling. When I came into this field I was a Lit major and interested in writing non-fiction that adopted the techniques and aims of the finest fiction – and you are not going to find much fine fiction that doesn't incorporate ambiguity.

Journalists complain that there are fewer and fewer outlets for a long read that can explore those shades of grey.

Well, it's been shrinking since the 1960s. If you look back at all the new journalism that was coming out in those days, it all appeared originally in places like *Esquire, Harpers,* the *Atlantic,* the *New Yorker.* That was the world I was drawn into and it did tend to evaporate. It's expensive to do literary journalism. It takes a lot of time and the support and investment isn't there. You still find them from time to time, particularly compelling pieces. But the most prominent and growing and vital example of narrative non-fiction now is in the book world. If you look at the *New York Times* bestseller list you will usually have three, four or five examples of really good narrative non-fiction.

What about the importance of reporting experience?

For me reporting is the bedrock of the writing. You can't do the narrative writing without being able to first get it into your notebook. You have to be able to get those details, get that fact, get those scenes. This sort of writing actually takes more reporting, not less. You need to be a prodigious and talented reporter before you even have the opportunity to become a writer of narrative journalism.

One of the things you notice about this story is that there are so few direct quotes, despite the extensive interviews. Can you talk about your choice to go that way?

I rarely use direct quotes because I'm trying to write a narrative, a non-fiction short story. So I want to stay in the narrative, rather than have characters step out of the story to talk to the reporter. That kind of 'he said' direct quote is the stuff of standard newspaper writing. It distances the reader from the story that's unfolding . . . I try instead to 'mine' what people tell me in my many hours of interviewing, using their words in ways that let me form a third-person point-of-view narrative or interior monologue.

What about choosing particular scenes for your stories?

Sometimes you just need a slice of life or a scene. Structure becomes more and more important the longer the story goes. You need a long piece to have that forward motion, through time. You need the narrative line to arrive someplace. The analogy I always have is that you are building a house and you have to frame it out first and then you can decide are you going to put shutters on, what kind of tile roofing, the trim, and stuff like that. Our program [at UC Irvine] is based on the mantra that writing is rewriting. In our workshops you turn in a rough, lousy working draft and then you get to the real work. There is overriding anxiety when we have a blank page and 3000 documents. So somehow you have to get over that hump, get that frame up. You can still move your pieces around, but now you can start to make it into poetry.

What about the ethical dimension in this sort of story?

The truth is that literary journalism is a very complex moral endeavour here. You have a covenant with your readers and there is a covenant with your subjects in a way that you might not have in regular journalism. Because you do say 'Let me in', you ask for intimate access into their lives and you are seeking and encouraging and using your skills to bring about the most extraordinarily vulnerable revelations. And so you have a double covenant and it's a balancing act and it always is.

Let me tell you why that is easier here [with the judge] than in other circumstances . . . it's easier because of who he is. He is an educated, thoughtful, cultured, aware judge. I am not taking advantage of him, not manipulating him into a revelation which he doesn't understand the consequences of. But you often are, and that's where it really gets difficult, because you can talk somebody into it, but you can't protect them. What I say is, you are right, there may be consequences here that aren't so good and I can't control how people respond to a story. But I say I would sure like to go there because this is important to the story. And then, yes, if they go there with you, yes, you worry about every semi-colon and the nuance of every word . . .

Is there a line beyond which you can't really pass with non-fiction?

You can't make it up. You think like a narrative writer, use the same techniques, the same aims. By techniques I mean things like narrative arc, point of view, interior monologue, dialogue, scene-by-scene. By aims I mean the high aims of literature that are telling us not just to report about this thing. You are trying to get at the same matters of the human heart that the finest fiction gets at, you are trying to get those resonant multiple meanings. Let's face it . . . you can't be objective. Just the act of imposing a narrative on messy life creates a certain kind of meaning. This is storytelling that is always going to be subjective. And that's allowed. But you cannot make it up. Scenes can't be made up and dialogue can't be made up. You can't make it up, period. It is the incredible amount of reporting that gives you the licence to write the scenes.

What do you say about the approach where you use real dialogue, but perhaps give it to composite characters?

That used to happen in New Journalism a lot. Joseph Mitchell wrote 'Old Mr Flood', which is a famous piece from the *New Yorker* and it was a composite. John Hershey did that once. There was also Janet Malcolm who got into trouble for taking quotes from different interviews and putting them into different scenes. Composites are not allowed. You have great freedom to use literary techniques, but what is happening in the story has to happen.

What do you think it is that makes some stories endure?

It has to do with those underlying currents, it's the universality. If you are writing about event x that happened now, that is not going to matter, but if you are writing about the underlying issues of the human heart, those don't change. And as long as your story fundamentally resonates to the more universal elements, the story endures. That is why you are always looking for – the kind of story that stays current. Most newspaper journalism is predicated on the idea that its value is that you got it into the paper today. But I am never going to get it into the paper today. I'm always coming late and then taking a long time, so I have to pick a story that has that kind of lasting meaning, no matter what.

Discussion question

Some literary journalism aims to reduce, or eliminate, direct quotes so that the resulting narrative – though based on interviews – is more like a short story than a conventional feature. Does the technique risk reducing the importance of the people whose story it is, with the writers appropriating their words and voices to create characters for 'their' story?

Further reading

Truman Capote, *In Cold Blood*, orig. published Random House, 1965.

Kevin Kerrane and Ben Yagoda, *The Art of Fact: A historical anthology of literary journalism*, Scribner, 1997.

Stephen King, *On Writing: A memoir*, Hodder & Stoughton, 2000.

Robert Love (ed.), *The Best of Rolling Stone: 25 years of journalism on the edge*, Straight Arrow, 1993.

Writers on Writing, Collected Essays from the *New York Times*, Times Books, 2001.

William Zinsser, *On Writing Well*, Harper Collins, 1994.

Chapter 3
Profiles

Talking to people/beyond celebrity flimflam

Susie Eisenhuth

Journalist and broadcaster Tony Squires remembers having fun interviewing Australian actor Colin Friels and writing up the profile. And it comes across. Two gabby blokes yarning away over a beer, the larrikin style of the piece in tune with its larrikin subject, who clearly prefers talking about Aussie Rules football than British theatre.

At the time, Squires recalls, he hadn't written a profile for a while and he wasn't too thrilled at the prospect of trying to make something interesting out of a routine celebrity profile based on the opening of a new play. And with good reason. New play, new book, new movie, new TV show, new recording – each week the media grows ever more paunchy on a sugary diet of PR-driven promotional guff. The era of celebrity journalism has spawned a plague of paper-thin profiles, a fluffy variant on the in-depth profile, in which instead of insights into the interviewee, we are often treated to breathless revelations about the reporters themselves, who we don't know and – if their repartee proves daggy – don't wish to.

In or out of the story

It's an old debate, whether to get into the story with your subject. New writers are quite properly urged to exercise caution. The slippery slope of self-indulgence beckons (and you better be sure that you're interesting enough to hog the spotlight). But getting into the story is fine if it adds an element to the narrative. With Squires that element is an agreeably laid-back tone. As a columnist he uses humour a lot. So why not import it here? There is, after all, an old saying in journalism: 'Write funny, make money.'

Noting Friels' habit of re-shaping his sentences ('I loved the feeling of it. It was the feeling of it I loved.'), Squires has a bit of a play with the device himself. ('Right now I'm loving the way Friels shapes his sentences. It's the way he shapes his sentences I'm loving.') He goes on to imagine lively conversations in the Friels household, but confesses to feeling tremulous (and who wouldn't?) at even invoking the name of Friels' famously forbidding spouse, actor Judy Davis:

> I haven't got the whole image worked out yet. For example, I'm not sure how his wife, Judy Davis, is reacting in this fantasy scene. I'm too intimidated by the great actress to include her, even in make-believe.[1]

Award-winning *Good Weekend* writer Greg Bearup knows how to use the first person judiciously. In fact he provides a lesson in restrained first person in his richly detailed profile of the eccentric Sydney judge Roddy Meagher, a rare glimpse behind the fusty façade of the law's highest office. Bearup ventures only briefly into the story, dropping the odd baleful remark about Roddy's dog Diddi.

'The man is as odd as the dog is mad', he mutters at their first encounter, moving on to a description of Meagher himself – all bejewelled necklaces, rings and purple beret. The brief bits of business with the spoiled, badly behaved dog pay off neatly in the closer, as Bearup farewells the spoiled, badly behaved judge, whose mix of winning ways and jaw-dropping political incorrectness he has deftly skewered. 'Like his dog, he bites occasionally I think, looking back at the man in the dopey hat. Maybe he needed better discipline as a puppy, but it's too late for that.'

Details, quotes, anecdotes

Bearup's piece showcases the benefits to be gained when journalists apply their bower bird's eye to the collection of small, striking details. The opening scene-setter neatly illustrates the dictum that details, quotes and anecdotes are the best tools in the profile writer's arsenal:

> An unhinged alsatian slobbers about the room searching for somewhere to eat the cow shank he has between his teeth. He settles on a couch next to *The Complete Letters of Oscar Wilde*. His master is sitting at the kitchen table blowing

> kisses to the dog above the strains of Schubert on the radio. 'Diddi is a lovely dog. He bites people occasionally but that's okay.'

Then there's the quick visual take on the judge: 'His is a face fashioned by a diet of red wine and cheese. His hair has been dyed a shade of kelpie red . . . ' Less is more when it comes to personal detail. As Stephen King says in his book *On Writing*, which is full of useful tips for both fiction and non-fiction writers:

> If I tell you that Carrie White is a high school outcast with a bad complexion and a fashion-victim wardrobe, I think you can do the rest, can't you? I don't need to give you a pimple-by-pimple, skirt-by-skirt rundown. We all remember one or more high school losers, after all; if I describe mine, it freezes out yours, and I lose a little bit of the bond of understanding I want to forge between us. Description begins in the writer's imagination, but should finish in the reader's.[2]

On the other hand, the *Australian*'s Susan Chenery made a great decision when she singled out one physical attribute in her 2004 profile of Maggie Smith, giving us a defining image of the consummately British actor in her superb intro:

> The voice, oh my god, the voice, the voice. It soars through a closed door, slides down a flight of stairs and sort of slaps you round the face as you enter the building. It is full of bruised fruit, boiled sweets and bags of broken bones; imperious, commanding, arch; it kind of caresses words, goes all the way around them before spitting them out to lie in little broken pieces on the floor. It is so quintessentially and exaggeratedly the thespian voice of the British theatre that you are tempted to think it is a deliberate parody. Except that you have read so many formidable things about its owner that you wouldn't dare to laugh.[3]

Ethics and intrusiveness

Experience helps a lot when it comes to profiles, especially on the ethical issues, which start with questions about who to profile, and why, and continue through to how the treatment will affect the subject. In the midst of his profile on Colin Friels, Tony Squires inserts a warning. 'This picture of Friels', he says, 'could be completely wrong too, since we've met only twice, both times over a tape recorder – the Reverse Intimacyatron'.

He is being funny, but it is a warning worth considering. At best, the profile can only be a snapshot of the person, and it doesn't hurt to allude to the limitations of the process itself, as when Squires refers directly to the phony intimacy of a tape recorder on the table between strangers.

Profile writing is inevitably intrusive – and there's always the risk of commodifying people for no good reason. Several controversial profiles later, former *Good Weekend* writer David Leser is well aware of the moral ambiguities to be navigated. 'Why do we want to know about this person?' he asks in the foreword to his collection *The Whites of Their Eyes,* where he acknowledges the hurt feelings that can be a by-product, and the blistering rage – as in the case of talkback radio's Alan Jones – that can stalk you later. Knowing the terrain, he is always 'seized by the same apprehensions':

> How far do I need to go in unravelling their lives in the public interest? What is the public interest? . . . Should my obligations be first and foremost to my editor? Or my readers? Or my subject? Or myself?[4]

Not that Leser's measured profile writing style even remotely approaches the blitzkrieg tactics of a writer like Antonella Gambotto, whose stylish, but wincingly – paint-strippingly – caustic portraits of public figures (notably rock singer Nick Cave) are collected in two aptly titled volumes, *Lunch of Blood* (1994) and *Instinct for the Kill* (1997). Cave famously penned a song called *Scum* about Gambotto and fellow journo Mat Snow in retaliation.

Seduction and betrayal

Leser concedes there is 'more than a kernel of truth' in the much quoted barb of writer Janet Malcolm that a journalist is 'a kind of confidence man, preying on people's vanity, ignorance or loneliness, gaining their trust and betraying them without remorse'.[5] Malcolm, it must be noted, is no stranger to ethical potholes herself, a fact gleefully seized upon by the media when she herself was dragged through the courts by one of her interview subjects, psychoanalyst Jeffrey Masson,[6] claiming betrayal. The protracted case was lost in 1994, but Malcolm was hung out to dry during the lengthy proceedings over her own merciless style and cavalier attitude to fudging quotes. Yet her con-man accusation, recycled by critics of journalism ever since, stands as a reminder that questions need to be asked. Why am I here? Am I being up-front about that? What impact will my presence have?

Greg Bearup makes the point that caution must be exercised in relation to people who are without media experience, or naïve, as opposed to public figures with access to well-oiled PR machinery. And on the question of seduction, sweet-talking sources into compliance? There is 'no journalist in the history of the profession' who is not guilty of it, he says. 'Newsrooms are full of journalists with their heads below their desks, out of earshot of colleagues, saying "Look mate, we just want to tell your side of the story".'[7]

Greg Bearup

Greg Bearup started as a cadet at the *Armidale Express* in country New South Wales and worked at the *Inverell Times* and the *Newcastle Herald* before joining the *Sydney Morning Herald*, where he specialised in crime reporting. After moving to the newspaper's *Good Weekend* magazine in 2000 he won a Walkley Award for feature writing in 2001 for 'Death Surrounds Her', a revelatory murder follow-up that led to the arrest of his subject, Belinda van Krevel. He also won a Walkley for Social Equity Journalism in 2003 for his controversial feature on New South Wales prisons, 'Inside No-one Can Hear You Scream'.

THE BEAK WORE BEADS

Greg Bearup

Sydney Morning Herald, May 4, 2002

An unhinged alsatian slobbers about the room searching for somewhere to eat the cow shank he has between his teeth. He settles on a couch next to *The Complete Letters of Oscar Wilde*. His master is sitting at the kitchen table blowing kisses to the dog above the strains of Schubert on the radio. 'Diddi is a lovely dog. He bites people occasionally, but that's okay.'

The man is as odd as the dog is mad. Skinny arms poke from the sleeves of an extra large T-shirt. His fingers and wrists are bejewelled with '70s chunky gold rings and bracelets. Strands of exotic beads hang beneath his jowly neck. His is a face fashioned by a diet of red wine and cheese. His hair has been dyed a shade of kelpie red, but the grey still pokes through at the roots. Luckily, on most of his public appearances he wears a wig, for the man at the table is an eminent judge.

The eccentric, amusing and sometimes outrageous presence of Roderick Pitt Meagher, 70, has loomed large in Sydney's legal circles for almost 50 years. Almost everyone seems to have a Meagher story. He is said to possess one of the finest legal minds in the country. At the University of Sydney he won the university medal for arts (Greek and Latin) and law. He was admitted to the bar in 1960 and went on to become a QC and president of the NSW Bar Society, where he mounted a spirited campaign against any reform. He now sits on the NSW Supreme Court's appeals court, after being appointed a judge in 1989.

But outside those circles, it's not for his contribution to the law that Meagher is best known. For someone who has stated throughout his career that judges should steer away from controversy, Meagher himself seems to have embraced it with unusual vigour. Unlike most of Australia's beaks, unknown unless you're appearing before them, Meagher is often in the news – sometimes for his Wildean wit, sometimes for his art collection and, not infrequently, for his unashamedly out-of-step utterances about women, Aborigines, single mothers and lesbians. In after-dinner speeches to the chaps at the

NSW Bar Association, or in the crusty confines of the Australia Club, he is given to railing against 'political correctness' and the appointment of 'Abos' and 'hairy-legged lesbians' to all sorts of official positions on positive discrimination grounds.

He has also lambasted prominent republicans, calling the late Patrick White (his cousin) 'an old curmudgeon with a tea-cosy on his head' while Tom Keneally, he said, 'thinks too little and talks too much'. He has publicly lamented the passing of the glorious days of the law when its corridors were trod by 'dusty conveyancers and staid trustees', supplanted by one where 'our corridors are thronged with unmarried mothers and abused children, people who are stoned, or were hatched in bottles, or have been raped or cloned'.

He has even blasted his fellow judges.

He once accused Justice Michael Kirby of 'xenophobic rodomontade' over a judgment he delivered while the pair sat on the same bench. The case involved a Macedonian who had exaggerated his work injuries in a compensation case. Kirby argued that while in the Australian tradition a stiff upper lip was admired, in Macedonia a degree of exaggeration might be acceptable. Meagher demurred. Alexander the Great was well known as an honest and honourable Macedonian, he said, and there was no evidence that those who came after were any different.

In 1998, he tried – unsuccessfully – to jail John Laws for contempt, after Laws solicited an interview with a juror. He also drew fire from the then NSW police minister Paul Whelan when he ruled in a case that the word 'f . . . ' was not offensive when used by a policeman in a station.

The Aboriginal magistrate Pat O'Shane last year threatened to refer him to the Judicial Commission, saying that for 25 years he had been making 'sexist, racist and homophobic' statements. When contacted to comment for this story, she said, 'I know nothing good about him', and would say no more.

Legal columnist Richard Ackland has for years lampooned him in columns in *The Australian Financial Review*, *The Sydney Morning Herald* and the law journal *Justinian*. Commenting recently on Senator Bill Heffernan's pursuit of Michael Kirby, Ackland wrote in jest: 'God knows where it might lead if [Heffernan] ever sniffs out Justice Roddy Meagher's purple satin undies.' Meagher countered that he was a man of silk.

The judge has recently returned from Europe when we sit down to talk in his country 'shack' – an enormous, light and open Glenn Murcutt-designed house overlooking the valleys of Bowral in the NSW Southern Highlands. Meagher had wanted to go to Libya, which has one of the finest collections of Greek and Roman antiquities, 'but September 11 rooted all that' and he had to content himself with Italy.

Art is his great love. In the room, half-empty bottles sit on the kitchen bench, the morning toast is unmoved by midday, the windows need cleaning, and yet you barely notice because all you look at is the magnificent array of art. Meagher collects carpets, antiquities, Persian rugs and antiques, too – but paintings are his real love. Thousands of them. In his house in Darling Point, there's hardly a spare space on the walls. ('Is that a Matisse?' I ask, as we pass a drawing. 'Yes,' he says. 'I have two others, but I just can't remember where they are.') Works of art spill out from his chambers in the NSW Supreme Court. (When Michael Kirby, an openly gay judge, was on the Court of Appeal, Meagher hung several sexually explicit Whiteley women on the wall opposite Kirby's door.) Included in his vast collection are Vuillard, Picasso, E. Phillips Fox, Lloyd Rees, Ian Fairweather and 17 paintings by his favourite Australian artist, Grace Cossington Smith.

Any leftover spot is crammed with books. Strewn around the lounge room at Bowral are biographies of Darwin, Hitler and Stalin, art books and a beautiful bound volume containing photographs of paintings by his late wife, Penny.

He's explaining his reading habits as his dog gnaws at my boot under the table. 'Stop it, Diddi. Don't worry,' he says to me as the dog backs away, growling, 'he has bitten lots of eminent people. He has a long and distinguished list of victims.'

Meagher speaks with a slight lisp and the accent is old landed-gentry Australian, still clinging to England. Not that his family were part of the squattocracy, but they were wealthy. He grew up in Temora in south-western NSW. His family owned a string of department stores in the country and in Melbourne – they sold out to Grace Bros in the '70s.

He was sent to St Ignatius College (Riverview) at an early age and then went to St John's College at Sydney University – the most conservative of Catholic upbringings.

As children, he and his siblings were encouraged to explore life, to do what they wished. His sister is an archaeologist living in London. One of his brothers, Chris, was a bullfighter in Spain for five years. 'Roddy was a very different child,' says the retired matador, now a Sydney lawyer. 'I remember once trying to get him to kick a ball with me. He refused because he was busy drafting a letter to the Portuguese government over some aspect of their foreign policy that he disagreed with. He was 10 at the time, and they replied.'

Propped against the wall in Bowral is a framed newspaper poster, 'Are Judges Out of Touch?' The particular story was not sparked by him, but his wife liked it and had it framed. Sitting amid this opulence, it seems a fair question. 'I don't think so,' he drawls. 'For one thing, the advantage of the bar is that it brings you into very rude contact with rapists and murderers and Christ knows what.' But isn't that a very 'us and them' relationship? 'I should hope so,' he deadpans.

The truth is that Meagher's dealings as a barrister were with the pointy end of town – in intellectual property and equity law. Not too many known rapists and murderers sat on the leather couch in his chambers. His has been a rather narrow world of boarding school, the bar, the bench: rarely has he had to deal with anyone outside that privileged circle. Perhaps it's why he has so much trouble in seeing his critics' arguments. He can't see that attacking the appointment of 'hairy-legged lesbians' may be offensive to women who may have got there solely on merit, or demean their achievements, or at the very least make their sexuality an issue rather than an irrelevancy. Similarly, while the term 'Abo' might have been common parlance in Temora in the '50s, it is as offensive to many Aborigines as the term nigger is to African Americans. I put this view to him and he shrugs it aside. 'I don't think my comments really matter at all, in the end.'

Asked if he thinks women in general could be offended by some of the things he says, he replies, 'I find that most extraordinary. I know that the poor things are illogical but they can't be as illogical as that. I love women.'

Richard Ackland, Meagher's perpetual tormentor, says that the judge's views are rooted in a deep conservatism, but that it comes with an interesting twist – he champions the belief that others, too, should be able to say what they think. Meagher, he argues, is an old-style libertarian. 'A lot of what he says is Roddy simply being naughty – his comments come from his immense dislike of political correctness. Yet, over the years he has often said to me that while he disagrees with what I have written about him, he defends my right to say whatever I like about him. He's not the type to run off to the defamation lawyers. That's not how Roddy operates – he doesn't think people, whatever their views, should be gagged.'

While Meagher tends to ruffle feathers and make enemies with his public utterances, he seems to be held in quite different regard by those who know him personally or work with him. Talk to his former and present staff and, while none of them agrees with his views, they insist they are fond of the man.

He has employed both women and gay men as his juniors.

Richard Weinstein, a Sydney barrister, says that when he told his lecturers at Sydney University that he was going to work for Roddy Meagher, they were aghast: 'People who have never met him think he is a dog. Within a very short time, he became one of my favourite people in the world.'

'He is one of the most open-minded and tolerant people I have ever met,' says Edwina McLachlan, a Sydney lawyer who worked as his associate for many years. McLachlan went to work for him straight from university, a firebrand, Doc Marten-wearing feminist; she says Meagher soon won her over personally, but never to his opinions. 'He spouts these stupid reactionary views, but underneath he's a big softy. He was always willing to listen to another point, to help and mentor people.'

'He's a larrikin with a classical education.

'I think he enjoys stirring the possum just to see the reaction. I remember marching into his office and saying, "Roddy, stop offending people", and he would just look at me with this stupid look and say, "Whom am I offending?"'

Back at the Bowral house, Meagher has cleared a space for lunch. He's eating a piece of bread smeared with Persian fetta, when he puts it down to make a point. 'The bar desperately needs more women barristers.' Why? 'Well, there are so many bad ones that people may say that women can't be good barristers and are hopeless by nature – but that is not so. It's a pity the able people don't come.'

Before long, we seem to be back on the subject of the law and lesbians. 'What I object to is this modernism, this desire to make lawyers socially and politically correct. We had got to the stage where the reformists were urging that we should employ someone because they were a lesbian.' Had it actually reached that stage? 'No, but it was tending to that direction.' He launches into his oft-quoted spiel on representation (referring to the statistic that 10 per cent of the population are gay and lesbian): if 10 per cent of the population are drug addicts, should that mean that 10 per cent of the bench take to heroin? He says that the bench, and all other areas, 'should be representative of talent'.

It would be easy to dismiss Meagher as just some dotty old conservative, but underneath the wit and bluster is a pithy lawyer. He has co-authored two important legal texts, *Equity, Doctrines and Remedies* and *Jacob's on Trusts*, which sit on the shelves of most lawyers and law students in the land. He has mentored many of Sydney's leading male and female silks.

His judgments are sharp and short (all written in longhand). Where many judges write 40- or 50-page judgments, Meagher often writes only two. Critics say it's because he is lazy. (One of the jobs of his tipstaffs and associates is to kick him should he fall asleep in court.) Others say his great skill lies in getting swiftly to the point of complex legal argument.

The supposed arch-conservative is often more on the side of the common man than the establishment, his supporters argue, and often dissents with his fellow judges to rule this way.

Jerrold Cripps sat on the Court of Appeal with him before going on to head the NSW Land and Environment Court. Cripps says that Meagher delivered some environmentally aware judgments. 'He is immensely intelligent and broad-minded and great company,' Cripps says. 'And a wonderful judge.' But Cripps agrees he can be infuriating. 'The tradition has been to call judges Mr Justice. A few years ago, when more women were coming to the bench, my suggestion was just to drop the Mr and that we all be called Justice. Roddy seriously held the view that the women should be called Mr Justice, because that was tradition.'

Years ago, another barrister recalls, when Meagher was a QC, a junior barrister sought his opinion in a complex legal matter. The clients wanted to see him in person and the junior led seven suited men into his chambers where they tried to find seats among the Portuguese cannons and Chinese pots. 'Gentlemen,' Meagher said, without any chitchat. 'The answer to your question is no.' The men stood up, shook his hand and left. Meagher turned to the junior and asked, 'Who exactly were those men?' 'Roddy,' the junior explained, 'that was the board of BHP.'

Another favourite anecdote has Meagher coming down in a lift with two silks who were discussing their prestige cars – one a Mercedes, the other a BMW. One turned to the dishevelled man beside them and asked, 'What kind of car do you drive, Roddy?' 'It's brown, I think,' Meagher replied.

But Cripps and other friends say that Meagher sometimes doesn't know when to pull back on a joke, or not to tell it at all.

'He can be a little insensitive without knowing it.' When he was on the bench in the John Laws contempt case, he ridiculed the educational qualifications of a Laws assistant. He prickles slightly when I put this to him. 'The woman said she got first-class honours in English or English literature,' he says. 'What she'd written in her affidavit was so far from being English, it was just unintelligible gibberish. When her counsel read this out, I made some impolite remark about the standard of English, in which she was supposed to have some expertise. I can't see anything wrong with that.' Several people who witnessed the event in court that day, however, described it as an appalling and unnecessary humiliation from the bench.

Meagher takes me for a walk around his garden – it is rambling, unplanned and overplanted. Diddi is in tow. Each time the dog comes to a thistle, it flies into a rage, barking and poking the weed with its nose, snarling at anyone who comes near, and finally ripping it from the earth. 'Roddy, that dog is mad,' I say. 'He has a few issues, Greg, but he's not mad.'

We settle into a conversation about what reforms, if any, he would like to see. He has a few, mainly in the area of criminal law, none of a liberal agenda.

'I would like to make it perfectly plain that if a person wakes in the middle of the night to find a robber in their house, then they should have the right to shoot them. Particularly if it is a woman who is in danger of being raped. Why shouldn't she just shoot the brute? Whenever I mention this to my friends, they say it is because she is a woman and she would probably miss. Since I am not a misogynist, I do not agree with that.'

He takes me past some sculptures, upright chunks of welded iron. 'That one is called Harlot,' he says, pointing to a mass of tractor parts. 'No, what's the biblical name? Strumpet.' He moves back to law reforms and mentions a case where a man waited for a 12-year-old schoolgirl to get off a bus, then raped and strangled her and threw the body in a dam. 'Why should he live? I would cheerfully hang him.' The return of the death penalty for the worst crimes is a public debate we should be having, he says. 'And I think that most people would agree with me on that.'

As we head back into the house, he is telling me that while he needs beautiful things around him, he has no personal vanity. This from a man who, in his old age, has taken to wearing leather pants and vests. I ask him about his dyed hair: 'I get the local barber to do it. I don't want to frighten people.' The hair, like the common hatred of Diddi, is a great joke among his friends. 'He doesn't go to the local barber to do it – that's the problem,' a friend tells me. 'He does it himself in the sink in his chambers, believing he is saving money. Several times he's had to be reminded that it's not a great look for a judge to have brown dye running from his wig, down his neck and into his gown.'

His 30-year-old daughter, Sarah, rubs her hands with glee at the prospect of deflating some of the Meagher myth. 'For some reason, he inspires this hero worship,' she says. 'He likes to see himself as some quirky individual.' She laughs when I tell her that he doesn't read the newspapers, or care what is written about him. 'Yeah, sure. I will get this phone call from him saying "You should read the paper today." "Why?" I will ask. "Because I am in it."'

They are close, but she, too, cannot understand some of his public tirades against women. 'He really loves women and they love him – I think he does all this [stirring] just to be the centre of attention. He treated Mum like gold. He's found it very hard to live without her. Since Mum died, there's been a string of women wanting to take him out – some of them not much older than me. I've had to chase them off.'

His wife, Penny, died of cancer in 1995. 'I miss her dreadfully,' Roddy says. 'I was always bursting with the desire to tell her some little bit of gossip or news or something.'

She was an artist and, after she died, Meagher had her paintings photographed and bound into a book to distribute to their friends. A colleague describes it as 'Roddy's love poem to Penny'.

'She and I were married on July 3, 1962, and she gave me 30 years of unalloyed bliss,' he writes in the foreword to the book. 'She was the gentlest person I have ever met and her art reflects her gentleness.'

Have you thought about remarrying? 'Yes, but not with any great enthusiasm.

'I had a dreadfully happy marriage and I don't think it is possible to repeat that. I've had no intimate relationships since then.'

We talk for a while longer, meandering around his garden in the afternoon sun. When it's time to go, he waddles to my car with the assistance of his stick. He has to put Diddi in the back of his Toyota Camry because he attacks people getting into cars. I shake hands and leave with Diddi in a rage in the back of the car and Meagher smirking, leaning on his cane. Like his dog, he bites occasionally, I think, looking back at the man in the dopey hat. Maybe he needed better discipline as a puppy, but it's too late for that.

Interview with Greg Bearup

Question *What makes a good profile, for you as a reader?*

Bearup I like to feel I have got to know the subject. That doesn't mean you get to know everything they have done in life, but you get the essence of the person. I remember years ago reading Frank Robson's profile on the now dead lawyer John Marsden. When I met Marsden he was exactly how Frank had described him. There was a scene in Robson's article where Marsden is cruising past The Wall, a gay pick-up spot in Sydney, and describing the talent on offer. It captured Marsden in a few short sentences.

How do you choose a good subject for a profile?

I read lots and follow the news. A few years ago I read a small article in one of the tabloids about tourist buses stopping at Bethany, Joh Bjelke-Petersen's farm in Queensland. Joh had basically gone broke and was partially reliant on pensioners calling in for tea and scones to keep the wolves at bay. It provided the perfect platform for a profile on the retired premier.

The number one priority for me when looking for a subject is that they have an interesting story and have led an interesting life. Generally I hate celebrity profiles and I try to avoid them – although the pressure to produce celebrity crap is forever mounting.

My favourite profiles are of flawed characters and I am always on the look-out for these people. I have made a career out of shonky Greek publishers, female murderers, renegade senators, sexist judges, dubious PNG coffee planters and a poet who tried to shoot Arthur Calwell.

I find that these people shine a light on the best and worst of human behaviour. An interesting character with a story to tell makes the profile easier to write. I pity those poor buggers who are dispatched every few years to do Janette Howard.

Paper-thin and predictable profiles are the order of the day in our celebrity-ridden culture. With PR and image control so rife is there a good argument for celebrity profiles?

There are few good arguments for celebrity profiles but editors and publishers seem to know them all. Having said that you will occasionally read a well-written and revealing celebrity profile, such as Jack Marx's searing profile on Russell Crowe. The trick is, I think, not to get sucked into the formula. Try and avoid doing a profile on someone promoting a book or film or album. Try and take them out of the hotel room. Try and do it on your terms, or not at all. I have done a couple of celebrity profiles that worked – one was of Slim Dusty and the other on John Farnham – and the only reason they worked was that I went on the road with them. If I'd have interviewed them at their homes or in an office I think it would have been a disaster.

What do you see as the best preparation for a profile?

Obviously the best preparation is to read as much as you can about the subject and to talk to as many people as you can who know them – it will help you with your questions and the flow of the interview.

How much time do you like to spend with subjects for a long profile? Is it important to have a number of conversations in different settings?

As much time as I can get. If I am doing a profile I would like to have at least two long, face-to-face interviews with them. My technique is to let them ramble in the first interview and see where it leads. I have often got my best stuff letting people hang themselves. The second interview is saved for all the hard questions.

I often find it is best to interview people in their environment. If it is a farmer, take them for a drive in their Toyota or a musician with their instrument.

It is often good to get people in different locations. A businessman may be stiff and hard in his office, but relaxed and willing in his backyard with a beer. The more time you spend with a subject, the better the result. I also find during an interview it is best to tape everything, even if you have good shorthand. It leaves you time to make observations.

Also, if you are doing a job and a photographer is with you, or the photographer is sent out separately, talk to them about what they saw. The photographers are very visual and will notice things that you don't as you concentrate on what they are saying.

Your interview with Roddy Meagher is richly detailed. Can you say something about the importance of observational detail?

I had several interviews with Roddy at his various locations. The article is richly detailed because the houses were rich in detail. Roddy had wonderful art and books and I would get him to describe them to me. If he was distracted by a phone call or left the room I would take the time to walk around and write down what was there. The things in his life told much about the man himself.

I also got Roddy to show me around his garden, which is a place he felt relaxed. It gave me some good quotes.

There is also a strong sense of place in your stories. How important is that?

I like to take the reader with me to the places I have been to meet the people I have met. Setting a sense of place is very important, I think, in grabbing the reader's attention and holding them until the end of the story. You want them there with you in the room.

Given the close-up focus, is there a dimension to profile writing that makes ethical considerations an issue? Is it sometimes a tricky balancing act to stay on the safe side of intrusiveness?

The golden rule with profiles is that it is your profile and not their profile. You are writing for your readers, not your subject. There are always ethical considerations in journalism and profile writing is no different. My attitude is that you need to collect everything you can, when you have the chance, and then make the ethical decisions about what to run when you are sitting in front of your computer.

Don't worry about being intrusive, that is your job.

What do you think of the 'seduction and betrayal' accusation sometimes levelled at journalists – perhaps not being as honest about their motivation as they are about their need to know?

It is true, seduction is part of the job – there is no way around it. Newsrooms are full of journalists with their heads below their desks, out of earshot of colleagues, saying 'Look mate, we just want to tell your side of the story'. There is no journalist in the history of the profession who is not guilty of this and in some ways the profession cannot operate without it.

Roddy Meagher's often outrageous public statements had earned him a lot of disapproval. Was it hard to separate yourself from that on approach? Can preconceptions be a problem?

Roddy had expressed some pretty unsavoury views over the years and had been widely criticised for them. However, I had spoken to many people who knew him well. Many of those people hated his views but loved the man. And that is how I found him. I disagreed with much of what he said, but found him utterly charming, which made him a great subject to profile.

Much of the public criticism of Roddy was completely valid and he needed to be taken to task for it – but it didn't need to condemn him.

Everyone has preconceptions, especially about public figures. Your views about your subject may change several times during the research for the article. It is your job to gather as much as you can and look at the entire picture before deciding how you will write it.

What about the issue of writers getting into the story themselves? Sometimes reporters seem to have more to say about themselves than the subject.

I am very wary of writing myself into a story. Be very wary of this as it often fails. The subject should be more interesting than the writer – if not, you have chosen the wrong subject.

How do you handle it when people trust you and tell you things about themselves that you know they shouldn't – i.e. you know they aren't going to look good for them on paper?

This is one of the most difficult aspects of feature writing and everyone has to make their own judgements. My general rule is that if they are people in the public eye who know how the media operate, like politicians or public figures, then everything they tell you, unless they specify, is on the record. It becomes more difficult with people who are a bit naïve. My general rule here is not to embarrass these people or make them out to be idiots.

I recently did an article on a female drover. The woman took me aside and said that her husband was a womaniser. She didn't want to see these exact words in print, but she didn't want me to make a hero of her husband. She wanted it known that all was not good. This is how I handled it:

> And what about Billy, how has all this time apart affected your relationship? She stops to light a smoke. 'It's not all roses,' she says, after a bit. 'Love it to be, and could tell lies to make it sound like it is, but it is not. There's too many people know the truth.'
>
> She goes to the caravan and pulls out a copy of *The Land* newspaper, where Billy is quoted talking about droving. 'He just never thanks me. He doesn't respect me for what I do or as a human being. I am just always here, like the good old faithful dog.'
>
> Billy, she says, does what he likes, when he likes and with whom he likes. She hasn't heard from him since a couple of days after he left the camp three weeks ago.

Tony Squires

Broadcaster and journalist Tony Squires began his twenty years in newspapers at the *Newcastle Herald*. He later worked as a reporter for the *Australian* and the *Sydney Morning Herald*, where he also became a columnist. Moving into television he presented the sports entertainment program *The Fat* on ABC TV, *110 percent Tony Squires* on Channel 7 and *Inside the Arena* on Foxtel/Austar. He hosts the drive program on dmg radio Vega in Sydney and Melbourne. He is also co-author – with comics Mikey Robins and Steve Abbott – of *Big Man's World*.

GOOD SPORT

Tony Squires

Sydney Morning Herald, May 4, 2002

'I loved boxing,' says Colin Friels. The actor. 'I loved the feeling of it. It was the feeling of it I loved.'

Right now, I'm loving the way Friels shapes his sentences. It's the way he shapes his sentences I'm loving. And reshapes. He does a lot of that with words: turns them around and repeats, like a square dance.

Is he doing it for emphasis, to get things in the right order, to stall while he conjures up the next image? Is it because he enjoys the wordplay? Has he been reading *Green Eggs and Ham*? We'll go with all of the above.

I have this image of Friels in his harbourside house, throwing back big reds and throwing up big ideas. He'd be loving the journey of the conversation, caring little about its destination. I haven't got the whole image worked out yet. For example, I'm not sure how his wife, Judy Davis, is reacting in this fantasy scene. I'm too intimidated by the great actress to include her, even in make-believe.

This picture of Friels could be completely wrong, too, since we've met only twice, both times over a tape recorder – the Reverse Intimacyatron. The thing is, it's good that Friels finds words and ideas intoxicating, since he's starring in a complete wordathon for the Sydney Theatre Company.

His character is Werner Heisenberg and the play is *Copenhagen* by Michael Frayn. In it, three extremely intelligent people bucket on about science, the Bomb, life, death, betrayal, loyalty, love, loss and place. There's not one car chase in it. It's an egghead thriller and a brilliant read. More of that soon.

But first, boxing.

'The biggest crushing defeat in my life was that I couldn't be a boxer,' says Friels, who is talking to me in a break from rehearsals. 'Oh, I looked great, I was pretty. A mate of mine said, "Frielsy, you look great, there's only two things you can't do". "What's that?" "Take one and throw one".'

Friels dreamt of Madison Square Garden, of being able to throw a punch. He went to TV Ringside at Melbourne's Festival Hall on Monday nights in the '60s with his old man, a builder who looked after a couple of young fighters.

Friels was born in Glasgow, raised in Australia and left school to cart bricks around before getting into the National Institute of Dramatic Art (NIDA).

You might know him from a stack of films such as *Malcolm* or from television as the crumpled cop Frank Holloway in *Water Rats*. You might know him from hundreds of theatre performances. Or you might know him as the bloke bellowing for the Swans at the SCG.

It's that bloke who's talking now. If missing out on stepping into the ring to get his face Tysonned into a new and less interesting shape was a life blow for Friels, he rates delivering a speech at the Swans jersey presentation night as a highlight.

'For some reason they asked me,' he says, ever the underseller. 'I think they actually wanted the missus to do it, but she couldn't. So I rang [Swans chairman] Richard Colless and he said, "Could you?" I said, "You probably don't want me; no-one will know who I am." He said, "No, that's true, but that doesn't matter." '

You and I both know Friels and I should be talking serious theatre, not sport, but don't underestimate how passionate he is about the subject and how reluctant I am to move on from such topics. He's reliving the five weeks he had before the presentation night to come up with 15 minutes of inspirational gold for his team. And he's right – addressing your team is a big moment. Naturally, the five weeks dissolved into hours, the ideas had only clattered around in his head and none had been poured onto the safety of a page.

'The day before, the missus says "Have you written that speech yet?" I said, no, it hasn't come to me yet. So I was sweating. Three o'clock that afternoon . . . we had to be at Star City at seven . . . it came to me and I wrote brrrrrrrrrrr [this is the sound of furious writing, apparently] eight pages. I was so nervous. But they all liked it, you know.

'And you wouldn't guess who I'm sitting with – on one side is Ron Barassi and the other side is Bob Skilton.'

These are legendary football players of the past. This is Friels who's over-excited. Friels, who could get a seat next to just about anyone. Come on, he's won a Logie. Friels, who sat next to Judy Davis at the Golden Globes when she won an award for her performance as Judy Garland. And who probably sits next to her at dinner most nights, now that I think of it. Yet he's star-struck at the footy. I love that. That I love.

Friels recalls seeing Skilton, whose captaincy record Paul Kelly claimed in March, being introduced to the crowd at Festival Hall after he'd won his third Brownlow Medal. He had a couple of black eyes from a collision in that Saturday's game.

'But there he was [at the Swans event], he was this beautiful little man. Beautiful man. He was gorgeous.'

But they don't have to be gorgeous to get his approval.

'You look at footy players now and think, he's not a footballer, he's a modeler. Doesn't look like a footballer. That's why you see Barry Hall and you think: footballer.

'This whole thing about sportsmen having to be role models . . . One of them goes out and has a few beers and somebody's in their face and they have a go at 'em. It's as though this kid's done something bad. I mean, that's what f—ing young men do. Nothing wrong with that. That's just pathetic. I don't want a f—king role model, I don't want kids to have role models: they'll choose their own, thanks. Which is why you watch certain footy players on television and they can't even be themselves. You poor bastards. They're just kids.'

Michael Frayn, *Copenhagen*'s author, penned *Noises Off*, the very funny play revealing the backstage goings-on in a disintegrating theatrical production. It's a modern farce. *Copenhagen* is no *Noises Off*. They are similar in the way that Danny DeVito and Arnold Schwarzenegger were similar in *Twins*.

Copenhagen is about a meeting during World War II between two of the world's leading physicists, Werner Heisenberg and Niels Bohr, and Bohr's wife, Margrethe.

The men worked together on a number of principles in quantum mechanics in the 1920s. Heisenberg was called upon to work on a nuclear bomb for Hitler and, in 1941, made his precipitous visit to the Bohrs. All this rests in fact.

What happened at that meeting, however, is largely speculation. All that is known is that the relationship between Heisenberg and Bohr was all but destroyed. Enter *Copenhagen* with a lot of questions: was Heisenberg fishing for Bohr's knowledge of the Allies' nuclear progress? Did he want to save the planet or help destroy it?

There's no point trying to simplify this play. It's a sinewy, complex bit of work but, as Friels says, the science isn't the point, it's the chemistry between the characters. Friels was surprised when the STC's artistic director, Robyn Nevin, handed him the script.

'I took it home, had a look and thought, Christ, they must have given me the wrong play. It's an incredibly theatrical piece, in the best sense of the word.

'It's a joy to work on it. How tragic a figure Heisenberg was. And the questions they were dealing with – life and death. They did drop the bomb on Hiroshima. The war was over, the Germans had submitted. They did drop the bomb. And they dropped it on Nagasaki, too. Huge questions Bohr had to answer for himself. And did Heisenberg really stymie Hitler's attempts to get the bomb or did he just not do the actual calculations?

'I reckon in 50 years, people will still be doing the play. It's really smart and I reckon theatre's got to have that content. Of course it does. That's why it's so great to work on, as an actor. It really does test you. And there's no time to do silly acting in the play. Just doing the play, you've got no time to do any stupid acting.'

Stupid acting?

'You know, when you can see someone acting . . . it's very embarrassing. Just get on with it, just present it clearly. Hate watching acting . . . showing off. Can't stand it.'

One of the themes that resonates through *Copenhagen* is a sense of place. There's a great slab of dialogue from Heisenberg about unquestioning love of country: 'Yes, and it would be another easy mistake to make, to think that one loved one's country less because it happened to be in the wrong.'

Friels nods and takes up the dialogue, which he's obviously learnt better than he's letting on.

'As he says, "Germany's where I was born, it's what made me what I am. It's all the faces of my childhood, all the hands that lifted me up when I fell" . . . all that stuff. 'It's what I am. I can't love it any less because it's wrong. So I have to decide what I think about it.'

'Which is what's wrong in Australia – we can never get off on the right foot to have the right debate. What's happening with refugees, what's happening with indigenous people, what's happening to the environment.

'[People stymie debate by saying] "Oh, it's just as bad in America" or "Oh, that's un-Australian" or "Oh, you can't say that, it's racist." So you never get off on the right foot. The debate never starts: 'Well, what are we about as a country? What do we love?' Friels believes that helping to create a sense of place is the best way actors, sportspeople and musicians can give to their communities.

'Sense of place is fantastic in this play,' he says.

'I think all great art, all that stuff, comes out of a deep sense of place. Aboriginal people have it so strongly. It's a fantastic thing to have. If you haven't got it, you're f—ed.'

Friels very nearly lost all contact with place a few years ago. He had life-saving surgery for the pancreatic cancer that was attacking him.'I really should be dead. The way the director looks at me sometimes I think I am. Got no f—ing rehearsal technique.

'Was I good at being ill? Yeah, I wasn't bad. I wasn't as good as I'd like to have been. There were a couple of times I got a bit sorry for myself. You've just got to get on with it. It's much easier for the patient than the person looking after them. Caring is really hard. And you can't be Saint Joan, you can't be perfect.

'My missus, she was great looking after me, but she wasn't putting up with any shit either.'

Surprise me.

The return to health meant a return to work – as simple as that. Because Friels sees himself as simply a working actor.

'It's a bit like . . . I'm sure if Paul Kelly or Tony Lockett was sitting on the bench . . . you've gotta have a game. Just get in and kick the footy about, that's all it is. If you don't do it, you die. Your guts just sort of go all soft.'

And is he good at choosing the life-affirming projects?

'No, I'm hopeless. I haven't got a career instinct in my life, I wouldn't have a clue. If you like it, you do it.

'At my age now – I'm getting old and all that – if work doesn't come, I don't sweat. F— it. I've got kids, life, all sorts of stuff. There's plenty to do in life. But I love, I love work. I love working, when you are working on something good, I love it. Love it. I do.

'I'm no good at [acting] tricks. I work out things a year after the play's finished. I know what directors need sometimes and I can't give it to them and I see them getting disheartened.

'All I've learned over the years is: you shit yourself, but don't panic. Just don't panic. If it's not gonna work, OK, you're f—ed, but just keep going, just keep going. Have patience and don't panic, don't lose it.'

I could be being fooled, but I reckon Friels is an honest man. I reckon he's a good man.

He has a final go at the undersell.

'I can't see that there's an audience in Sydney for this play. I'm glad they're putting it on and I hope they get an audience, but I don't see it. Especially in Sydney.' He points to a sleek motor boat sliding across the harbour. 'That's what Sydney wants.'

I'm caught up in the spirit of all this beautiful self-deprecation: 'Sorry about my interviewing technique, I'm out of practice.'

'I'm hopeless at it, too,' he says. 'It doesn't matter. Write what you want.'

Discussion question

The movie *Capote* raised questions about whether Truman Capote exploited the murderers he interviewed for *In Cold Blood*, perhaps falsely implying he was helping them fight the death penalty. Was 'helping' part of his responsibility? If there is an important truth to be told, does the end justify the means in terms of getting at the facts?

Further reading

David Leser, *Dames and Divas: 21 remarkable women*, ACP Publishing, 2006.
David Leser, *The Whites of Their Eyes*, Allen & Unwin, 1999.
Life Stories (profiles from *New Yorker*), Random House, 2000.
Janet Malcolm, *The Journalist and the Murderer*, Bloomsbury, 1991.
Gail Sedorkin and Judy McGregor, *Interviewing: A guide for journalists and writers*, Allen & Unwin, 2002.
Ruth Wilson, *A Big Ask: Interviews with interviewers*, New Holland, 2000.

Chapter 4

Investigations

'Muckraking' with honour

Susie Eisenhuth

American journalist Carl Bernstein, whose Watergate investigation for the *Washington Post* with Bob Woodward made him one of the best known reporters in the world, said he was reminded about the basics of reporting when he first read Jessica Mitford's article 'Let Us Now Appraise Famous Writers'. Fresh from doing over the greedy funeral vendors of America in her bestselling book, *The American Way of Death*,[1] Mitford had spied another ripoff in the unlikely promises made to aspiring writers in the ads featuring the Famous Writers School and its illustrious board of authors, including columnist and publisher Bennett Cerf.

An amusing raconteur and writer and a rebel from her upper-crust British background, Mitford liked to park herself squarely in her stories, using humour to deflate the pretentious and lampoon the corrupt. Not that her humour was universally admired. Her enthusiasm for dishing it to the Establishment made her a target of the US House Un-American Activities Committee in the McCarthy era.

When the Famous Writers story was published in *Atlantic* magazine in 1970, *Time* magazine dubbed Mitford 'Queen of the Muckrakers', and consumer watchdogs and government committees launched inquiries. What got Bernstein was that she had done the story with no big media backing, armed only with 'a sturdy pair of legs, a winsome manner, an unfailing ear and an instinct for the jugular'.[2] Bernstein reckoned he'd been easily outgunned by the doughty British writer, having done a series on fly-by-night academies himself. Now, his series seemed 'leaden, sodden, lugubrious'. Why hadn't he added details about the shonky proprietor's office, 'an oasis of Astroturf and citrus tree atria and whirlpool baths'. Why had he been so 'unselective' about quotes, letting his sources 'filibuster to the point where only the most dedicated reader could plough through the propaganda'. And why, he groaned, 'had I left myself out?'

Here is Mitford, who unabashedly used her pukka origins as an entrée to the smart literary set she was circling, meeting with Cerf:

> Bennett Cerf received me most cordially in his wonderfully posh office at Random House . . . 'May I call you Jessica?' he said at one point. 'I don't see why not, *Mortuary Management* always does.' We had a good laugh over that.

There were other tactics too, Bernstein grumbled, where Mitford's common sense had come up trumps. He had spent months tracking down dropouts and graduates from the schools he was investigating. Mitford put an ad in the paper and scored swags of anecdotes from disgruntled Famous Writers School students. Another strategy she would later urge on would-be reporters was to check the small provincial newspapers for ideas and scour the inside information on tap in trade journals and in-house publications. She was, of course, an avid reader of *Mortuary Management*, *Casket and Sunnyside* and *The Journal of Creative Ideas for Cemeteries* as she prepared her rout of the American funeral industry.

Investigative journalism? That's just reporting

The way *Sydney Morning Herald* journalist and novelist Malcolm Knox tells the story, his 2004 exposé of Norma Khouri, the author of *Forbidden Love*, offers the same salutary lesson in getting back to basics. Asked about winning the national Walkley Award for Investigative Journalism, he referred to the comment of his *Herald* colleague, multi award-winning investigator Gerard Ryle. What Ryle – 'as one of the best of them' – had said was that investigative journalists 'just do what any other journalist does, which is checking and checking and asking more and more questions. Applying the same basic skills, but going further – and going again, and again, and again.'[3]

The Khouri story began with a vague tipoff that led Knox to a group in Jordan campaigning against so-called 'honour crimes'. They were suspicious of Khouri, who had falsely claimed they had endorsed her book. Knox kept the story on the back burner, but ongoing checks over time nurtured his hunch that Khouri was not, as she claimed, a fearful single woman who had fled her homeland after the honour killing of her friend.

When he first phoned Khouri to ask about a US connection, she claimed he was just picking up on a paper trail deliberately laid down to help her escape from Jordan. And the story might have ended there, because Knox's request to travel to Jordan and Chicago was knocked back by the *Herald,* no surprise at a time when concern for the shareholders' bottom line has led to cutbacks in newsroom resources that have stymied much time-consuming investigative work.

After the knockback, Knox only took up the Khouri story again when an opportunity arose to pursue it in his own time. On holidays in Chicago, he took to the streets armed with a photo of Khouri and a list of possible family connections. Fruitless hours of door-knocking later he struck paydirt when a man looked at the photo of Khouri and nodded. Yes, indeed, that was his sister Norma, who had been out of touch for a couple of years. And then – in one of those moments memoirs are made of – he added that the family didn't really miss Norma, or her husband, but they did miss her children. ('Riiiight', Knox recalls stammering.)

It's a great yarn, the story of Khouri's elaborate con (and it wasn't her first, as we learned when journalists around the world followed up the story). But it's also a great yarn about the dogged persistence good storytelling requires, especially when journalists are facing off with often powerful interests intent on stalling, muddying the waters and/or the journalist's reputation, locking down access.

It's also a good example of what veteran ABC investigative reporter Chris Masters calls 'bottom-up reporting'. After former deputy FBI chief Mark Felt revealed in 2005 that he was 'Deep Throat', the high-level source for the Watergate story, Masters was asked to comment on Felt's dramatic tales of secret signals and assignations with the *Washington Post* reporters. He replied that he wasn't big on deserted car parks and pot plant signals on balconies. 'One of the things that bothers me is too many people – members of the public and even journalists – think that life is a movie and that it's all about finding a Deep Throat in a car park and a lot of trade-craft that goes on alongside it.' The truth is simpler: 'It's about the facts; it's about assaying the facts.'[4]

His 'bottom-up' approach means breaking into the story at ground level and speaking to as many sources as possible. At a later stage you go to a higher level and say, 'Look, this is what I think is going on; do you know anything about this?' If you just go to high-level sources 'they might not know what's going on down there in the bowels of the story'. Or worse, 'they may have some reason to steer you in another direction'. As for anonymous sources, 'if you read a newspaper article and it says "A source told me this" then you'll grade that intelligence, you'll probably give it a lower value . . . But let's say you speak to nine or ten anonymous sources and they're all pretty much backing up the story – then you'll give that story greater credibility. That's why investigative journalism takes time.'

And determination. Getting it right on complex issues is demanding enough at a time when costly and restrictive FOI barriers have been beefed up and 'commercial in confidence' labels are routinely slapped on public interest matters. The threat of litigation is commonly used to shut down uncomfortable inquiries. And the real thing can be a nightmare, as Chris Masters attests after a career dogged by protracted legal wrangles. 'What can't be marked on the calendar is the cost to the home front of all the bad temper and unrelenting depression that accompanies oppressive litigation, the curse of investigative journalism.'[5]

Michael Southwell lived with similar threats and pressure as he pursued his investigation into community health fears about Alcoa in Western Australia (see chapter 1). 'As I got into the story the pressure was just incredible', Southwell recalls. 'Alcoa and the government had such a symbiotic relationship and they put enormous pressure on the paper, and the paper instead of standing up to them put enormous pressure on me. In the end I was spending hours and hours sitting there checking and checking, every single word. The pressure was huge because I knew if I made even the smallest mistake, if I showed just one chink in my armour, they'd jump on it and use it to distract the attention away from the story itself.'[6]

Not that fact finding was meant to be easy, as the legendary independent American journalist I. F. (Izzy) Stone liked to remind his colleagues.[7] Famed for his many exposés of high-level official cover-ups, Stone frequently observed that his best stories came from tireless scanning of the public record, never mind those leaky official sources and their coercive agendas.

'I think it is good advice', says Masters.[8] 'However, I don't advise reporters to stop cultivating highly placed sources – more, don't allow yourself to completely rely on them . . . Reporters who feel that once they have a contact book stocked with secret numbers they can relax are making a big mistake. The highly placed sources also have a way of cultivating us.'

Stone is perhaps best remembered for his nose-thumbing remark that 'Every government is run by liars and nothing they say is to be believed'. And a sense of humour remains an important resource for journalists soldiering away in the investigative trenches amid fusillades from powerful opponents. Carl Bernstein noted a similar trait in Jessica Mitford's approach, singling out the important lesson to be drawn from her work: 'Use common sense. Write well. Make a joyful noise – after all, journalism can be fun. Hallelulah.'

Jessica Mitford

Dubbed 'Queen of the Muckrakers' by *Time* magazine, a title she cheerfully embraced, Jessica Mitford (1917–1996) rebelled against her aristocratic British family and lived in the United States, where she gained prominence as a civil rights activist and a target of the House Un-American Activities Committee during the McCarthy era. In 1960 she published her autobiography *Hons and Rebels*. Her career in investigative journalism was launched when she turned a magazine article on the American funeral industry into a major bestseller, *The American Way of Death* (1973). Her other books include *Kind and Usual Punishment: The prison business* (1973), *The Making of a Muckraker* (1979) and *The American Way of Birth* (1992).

LET US NOW APPRAISE FAMOUS WRITERS

Jessica Mitford

Atlantic, July 1970

Beware of the scribes who like to go about in long robes, and love salutations in the market places . . . and the places of honor at feasts; who devour widows' houses . . . (Luke 20: 46, 47)

In recent years I have become aware of fifteen Famous Faces looking me straight in the eye from the pages of innumerable magazines, newspapers, fold-out advertisements, sometimes in black-and-white, sometimes in living color, sometimes posed in a group around a table, sometimes shown singly, pipe in hand in book-lined study or strolling through a woodsy countryside: the Guiding Faculty of the Famous Writers School.*

Here is Bennett Cerf, most famous of them all, his kindly, humorous face aglow with sincerity, speaking to us in the first person from a mini-billboard tucked into our Sunday newspaper: 'If you want to write, my colleagues and I would like to test your writing aptitude. We'll help you find out whether you can be trained to become a successful writer.' And Faith Baldwin, looking up from her typewriter with an expression of ardent concern for that vast, unfulfilled sisterhood of nonwriters: 'It's a shame more women don't take up writing. Writing can be an ideal profession for women . . . Beyond the thrill of that first sale, writing brings intangible rewards.' J. D. Ratcliff, billed in ads as 'one of America's highest-paid free-lance authors,' thinks it's a shame too: 'I can't understand why more beginners don't take the short road to publication by writing articles for magazines and newspapers. It's a wonderful life.'

* The Guiding Faculty of the Famous Writers School are: Faith Baldwin, John Caples, Bruce Catton, Bennett Cerf, Mignon G. Eberhart, Paul Engle, Bergen Evans, Clifton Fadiman, Rudolf Flesch, Phyllis McGinley, J. D. Ratcliff, Rod Serling, Max Shulman, Red Smith, Mark Wiseman.

The short road is attained, the ads imply, via the aptitude test which Bennett Cerf and his colleagues would like you to take so they may 'grade it free of charge.' If you are one of the fortunate ones who do well on the test, you may 'enrol for professional training.' After that, your future is virtually assured, for the ads promise that 'Fifteen Famous Writers will teach you to write successfully at home.'

Those offers are motivated, the ads make clear, by a degree of altruism not often found in those at the top of the ladder. The Fifteen have never forgotten the tough times – the 'sheer blood, sweat and rejection slips,' as J. D. Ratcliff puts it – through which they suffered as beginning writers; and now they want to extend a helping hand to those still at the bottom rung. 'When I look back, I can't help thinking of all the time and agony I would have saved if I could have found a real "pro" to work with me,' says Ratcliff.

How can Bennett Cerf – Chairman of the Board of Random House, columnist, television personality – and his renowned colleagues find time to grade all the thousands of aptitude tests that must come pouring in, and on top of that fulfill their pledge to 'teach you to write successfully at home'? What are the standards for admission to the school? How many graduates actually find their way into the 'huge market that will pay well for pieces of almost any length' which, says J. D. Ratcliff, exists for the beginning writer? What are the 'secrets of success' that the Famous Fifteen say they have 'poured into a set of specially created textbooks'? And how much does it cost to be initiated into these secrets?

My mild curiosity about these matters might never have been satisfied had I not learned, coincidentally, about two candidates for the professional training offered by the Famous Writers who passed the aptitude test with flying colors: a seventy-two-year-old foreign-born widow living on Social Security, and a fictitious character named Louella Mae Burns.

The adventures of these two impelled me to talk to Bennett Cerf and other members of the Guiding Faculty, to interview former students, to examine the 'set of specially created text-books' (and the annual stockholders' reports, which proved in some ways more instructive), and eventually to visit the school's headquarters in Westport, Connecticut.

An Oakland lawyer told me about the seventy-two-year-old widow. She had come to him in some distress: a salesman had charmed his way into her home and at the end of his sales pitch had relieved her of $200 (her entire bank account) as down payment on a $900 contract, the balance of which would be paid off in monthly installments. A familiar story, for like all urban communities, ours is fertile ground for roving commission salesmen skilled in unloading on the unwary housewife anything from vacuum cleaners to deep freezers to encyclopedias to grave plots, at vastly inflated prices. The unusual aspect of this old lady's tale was the merchandise she had been sold. No sooner had the salesman left than she thought the better of it, and when the lessons arrived she returned them unopened.

To her pleas to be released from the contract, the Famous Writers replied: 'Please understand that you are involved in a legal and binding contract,' and added that the school's policy requires a doctor's certificate attesting to the ill health of a student before she is permitted to withdraw.

There was a short, sharp struggle. The lawyer wrote an angry letter to the school demanding prompt return of the $200 'fraudulently taken' from the widow, and got an equally stiff refusal in reply. He then asked the old lady to write out in her own words a description of the salesman's visit. She produced a garbled, semi-literate account, which he forwarded to the school with the comment 'This is the lady whom your salesman found to be "very qualified" to take your writing course. I wonder if Mr. Cerf is aware of the cruel deceptions to which he lends his name?' At the bottom of his letter, the lawyer wrote the magic words 'Carbon copies to Bennett Cerf and to Consumer Frauds Division, U.S. Attorney's Office.' Presto! The school suddenly caved in and returned the money in full.

Louella Mae Burns, the other successful candidate, is the brainchild of Robert Byrne and his wife. I met her in the pages of Byrne's informative and often hilarious book *Writing Rackets* (Lyle Stuart, 1969, $3.95), which treats of the lures held out to would-be writers by high-priced correspondence schools, phony agents who demand a fee for reading manuscripts, the 'vanity' presses that will publish your book for a price.

Mrs. Byrne set out to discover at how low a level of talent one might be accepted as a candidate for 'professional training' by the Famous Writers. Assuming the personality of a sixty-three-year-old widow of little education, she tackled the aptitude test.

The crux of the test is the essay, in which the applicant is invited to 'tell of an experience you have had at some time in your life.' Here Louella Mae outdid herself: 'I think I can truthfully say to the best of my knowledge that the following is truly the most arresting experience I have ever under undergone. My husband, Fred, and I, had only been married but a short time . . .' Continuing in this vein, she describes 'one beautiful cloudless day in springtime' and 'a flock of people who started merging along the sidewalk . . . When out of the blue came a honking and cars and motorcycles and policemen. It was really something! Everybody started shouting and waving and we finally essayed to see the reason of all this. In a sleek black limousine we saw real close Mr. Calvin Coolidge, the President Himself! It was truly an unforgettable experience and one which I shall surely long remember.'

This effort drew a two-and-a-half-page typewritten letter from Donald T. Clark, registrar of Famous Writers School, which read in part: 'Dear Mrs. Burns, Congratulations! The enclosed Test unquestionably qualifies you for enrolment . . . only a fraction of our students receive higher grades . . . In our opinion, you have a basic writing aptitude which justifies professional training.' And the clincher: 'You couldn't consider breaking into writing at a better time than today. Everything indicates that the demand for good prose is growing much faster than the supply of trained talent. Just consider how a single article can cause a magazine's newsstand sales to soar; how a novel can bring hundreds of thousands in movie rights . . .'

There is something spooky about this exchange, for I later found out that letters to successful applicants are written not by a 'registrar' but by copywriters in the Madison Avenue office of the school's advertising department. Here we have Donald T. Clark's ghost writer in earnest correspondence with ghost Louella Mae Burns.

Perhaps these two applicants are not typical of the student body. What of students who show genuine promise, those capable of 'mastering the basic skills' and achieving a level of professional competence? Will they, as the school suggests, find their way into 'glamorous careers' and be 'launched on a secure future' as writers?

Robert Byrne gives a gloomy account of the true state of the market for 'good prose' and 'trained talent.' He says that of all lines of work free-lance writing is one of the most precarious and worst paid (as who should know better than Bennett Cerf & Co.?) He cites a survey of the country's top twenty-six magazines. Of 79,812 unsolicited article manuscripts, fewer than a thousand were accepted. Unsolicited fiction manuscripts fared far worse. Of 182,505 submitted, only 560 were accepted. Furthermore, a study based on the earnings of established writers, members of the Authors League with published books to their credit, shows that the average free-lance earns just over $3,000 a year – an income which, Byrne points out, 'very nearly qualifies him for emergency welfare assistance.'

What have the Famous Fifteen to say for themselves about all this? Precious little, it turns out. Most of those with whom I spoke were quick to disavow any responsibility for the school's day to day operating methods and were unable to answer the most rudimentary questions: qualifications for admission, teacher-student ratio, cost of the course. They seemed astonished, even pained to think people might be naïve enough to take the advertising at face value.

'If anyone thinks we've got time to look at the aptitude tests that come in they're out of their mind!' said Bennett Cerf. And Phyllis McGinley: 'I'm only a figurehead. I thought a person had to be qualified to take the course, but since I never see any of the applications or the lessons, I don't know. Of course, somebody with a real gift for writing wouldn't have to be taught to write.'

One of the FWS brochures says, 'On a short story or novel you have at hand the professional counsel of Faith Baldwin . . . all these eminent authors in effect are looking over your shoulder as you learn.' Doesn't that mean in plain English, I asked Miss Baldwin, that she will personally counsel students? 'Oh, that's just one of those things about advertising; most advertisements are somewhat misleading,' she replied. 'Anyone with common sense would know that the fifteen of us are much too busy to read the manuscripts the students send in.'

Famous Writer Mark Wiseman, himself an ad man, explained the alluring promises of 'financial success and independence,' the 'secure future as a writer,' held out in the school's advertising. 'That's just a fault of our civilization,' he said. 'You have to over-persuade people, make it all look optimistic, not mention obstacles and hurdles. That's true of all advertising.' Why does the school send out fleets of salesmen instead of handling all applications by mail? 'If we didn't have salesmen, not nearly as many sales would be made. It's impossible, you see, to explain it all by mail, or answer questions people may have about the course.' (It seems strange that while the school is able to impart the techniques requisite to become a best-selling author by mail, it cannot explain the details of its course to prospects and answer their questions in the same fashion; but perhaps that is just another fault of our civilization.)

Professor Paul Engle, a poet who directed the Writers' Workshop at the University of Iowa, is the only professional educator among the fifteen. But like his colleagues he pleads ignorance of the basics. The school's admissions policy, its teaching methods and selling techniques are a closed book to him. 'I'm the least informed of all people,' he said. 'I only go there once in a great while. There's a distinction between the *Guiding* Faculty, which doesn't do very much, and the *Teaching* Faculty, which actually works with the students – who've spent really quite a lot of money on the course!' Professor Engle has only met once with the Guiding Faculty, to pose for a publicity photograph: 'It was no meeting in the sense of gathering for the exchange of useful ideas. But I think the school is not so much interested in the work done by the Guiding Faculty as in the prestige of the names. When Bennett Cerf was on *What's My Line* his name was a household word!'

How did Professor Engle become a member of the Guiding Faculty in the first place? 'That fascinated *me!*' he said. 'I got a letter from a man named Gordon Carroll, asking me to come to Westport the next time I was in New York. So I did go and see him. He asked me if I would join the Guiding Faculty. I said, 'What do I guide?' We talked awhile, and I said well it seems all right, so I signed on.' How could it come about that the Oakland widow and Louella Mae Burns were judged 'highly qualified' to enrol? 'I'm not trying to weasel out, or evade your questions, but I'm so very far away from all that.'

Bennett Cerf received me most cordially in his wonderfully posh office at Random House. Each of us was (I think, in retrospect) bent on putting the other thoroughly at ease. 'May I call you Jessica?' he said at one point. 'I don't see why not, *Mortuary Management* always does.' We had a good laugh over that. He told me that the school was first organized in the late fifties (it opened for business in February, 1961) as an offshoot of the immensely profitable Famous Artists correspondence school, after which it was closely modeled. Prime movers in recruiting Famous Writers for the Guiding Faculty were the late Albert Dorne, an illustrator and president of Famous Artists; Gordon Carroll, sometime editor of *Coronet* and *Reader's Digest*; and Mr. Cerf. 'We approached representative writers, the best we could get in each field: fiction, advertising, sportswriting, television. The idea was to give the school some prestige.'

Like his colleagues on the Guiding Faculty, Mr. Cerf does no teaching, takes no hand in recruiting instructors or establishing standards for the teaching program, does not pass on advertising copy except that which purports to quote him, does not supervise the school's business practices: 'I know *nothing* about the business and selling end and I care *less*. I've nothing to do with how the school is run, I can't put that too strongly to you. But it's been run extremely cleanly. I mean that from my heart, Jessica.' What then, is his guiding role? 'I go up there once or twice a year to talk to the staff.' The Guiding Faculty, he said, helped to write the original textbooks. His own contribution to these was a section on how to prepare a manuscript for publication: 'I spent about a week talking into a tape machine about how a manuscript is turned into a book – practical advice about double-spacing the typescript, how it is turned into galleys, through every stage until publication.' How many books by FWS students had Random House published? 'Oh, come on, you must be pulling my leg – no person of any sophistication whose book we'd publish would have to take a mail order course to learn how to write.'

However, the school does serve an extremely valuable purpose, he said, in teaching history professors, chemistry professors, lawyers, and businessmen to write intelligibly. I was curious to know why a professor would take a correspondence course in preference to writing classes available in the English department of his own university – who are all these professors? Mr. Cerf did not know their names, nor at which colleges they are presently teaching.

While Mr. Cerf is by no means uncritical of some aspects of mail order selling, he philosophically accepts them as inevitable in the cold-blooded world of big business – so different, one gathers, from his own cultured world of letters. 'I think mail order selling has several built-in deficiencies,' he said. 'The crux of it is a very hard sales pitch, an appeal to the gullible. Of course, once somebody has signed a contract with Famous Writers he can't get out of it, but that's true with every business in the country.' Noticing that I was writing this down, he said in alarm, 'For God's sake, don't quote me on that "gullible" business – you'll have all the mail order houses in the country down on my neck!' 'Then would you like to paraphrase it?' I asked, suddenly getting very firm. 'Well – you could say in general I don't like the hard sell, yet it's the basis of all American business.' 'Sorry, I don't call that a paraphrase, I shall have to use both of them,' I said in a positively governessy tone of voice. 'Anyway why do you lend your name to this hard-sell proposition?' Bennett Cert (with his melting grin): 'Frankly, if you must know, I'm an awful ham – I love to see my name in the papers.'

On the delicate question of their compensation, the Famous ones are understandably reticent. 'That's a private matter,' Bennett Cerf said, 'but it's quite generous and we were given stock in the company, which has enhanced a great deal.' I asked Phyllis McGinley about a report in *Business Week* some years ago that in addition to their substantial stock holdings each member of the Guiding Faculty received 1.6 percent of the school's annual gross revenue, which then amounted to $4,400 apiece. 'Oh? Well, I may have a price on my soul, but it's not *that* low, we get a lot more than that!' she answered gaily.

With one accord the Famous Writers urged me to seek answers to questions about advertising policy, enrolment figures, costs, and the like from the director of the school, Mr. John Lawrence, former president of William Morrow publishing company. Mr. Lawrence invited me to Westport so that I could see the school in operation, and meet Mr. Gordon Carroll, who is now serving as director of International Famous Writers schools.

The Famous Schools are housed in a row of boxlike buildings at the edge of Westport ('It's Westport's leading industry,' a former resident told me), which look from the outside like a small modern factory. Inside, everything reflects expansion and progress. The spacious reception rooms are decorated with the works of Famous Artists, the parent school, and Famous Photographers, organized in 1964.

The success story, and something of the *modus operandi*, can be read at a glance in the annual shareholders' reports and the daily stock market quotations. (The schools have gone public and are now listed on the New York Stock Exchange as FAS International.)

Tuition revenue for the schools zoomed from $7,000,000 in 1960 to $48,000,000 in 1969. During this period, the price per share of common stock rose from $5 to $40. (It has fallen sharply, however, in recent months.)

The schools' interest in selling as compared with teaching is reflected more accurately in the corporate balance sheets than in the brochures sent to prospective students. In 1966 (the last time this revealing breakdown was given), when total tuition revenue was $28,000,000, $10,800,000 was spent on 'advertising and selling' compared with $48,000,000 on 'cost of grading and materials.'

The Famous Schools have picked up many another property along the way: they now own the Evelyn Wood Speed Reading Course, Welcome Wagon, International Accountants Society (also a correspondence school), Linguaphone Institute, Computer College Selection Service. Their empire extends to Japan, Australia, Sweden, France, Germany and Switzerland, Austria. An invasion of Great Britain is planned (the report warns) as soon as the English prove themselves worthy of it by stabilizing their currency situation. In the 'market testing stage' are plans for a Famous Musicians School, Business Courses for Women, a Writing for Young Readers Course.

Summarizing these accomplishments, the shareholders' report states: 'We are in the vanguard of education throughout the world, the acknowledged leaders in independent study and an innovator in all types of learning. We will continue to think boldly, to act with wisdom and daring, to be simultaneously visionary and effective.' The schools, mindful of 'the deepening of the worldwide crisis in education,' are casting predatory looks in the direction of 'the total educational establishment, both academic and industrial.' The shareholders' report observes sententiously, 'As grave times produce great men to cope with them, so do they produce great ideas.'

From Messrs. Lawrence and Carroll I learned these salient facts about Famous Writers School:

The cost of the course (never mentioned in the advertising, nor in the letters to successful applicants, revealed only by the salesman at the point where the prospect is ready to sign the contract): $785, if the student makes a one-time payment. But only about 10 percent pay in a lump sum. The cost to the 90 percent who make time payments, including interest, is about $900, or roughly twenty times the cost of extension and correspondence courses offered by universities.

Current enrolment is 65,000, of which three-quarters are enrolled in the fiction course, the balance in nonfiction, advertising, business writing. Almost 2,000 veterans are taking the course at the taxpayer's expense through the GI Bill. Teaching faculty: 55, for a ratio of 1,181 4/5 students per instructor.

There are 800 salesmen deployed throughout the country (for a ratio of 14 3/5 for every instructor) working on a straight commission basis. I asked about the salesmen's kits: might I have one? 'You'd need a dray horse to carry it!' Mr. Carroll assured me. He added that they are currently experimenting with a movie of the school, prepared by Famous Writer Rod Serling, to show in prospects' homes.

I was surprised to learn that despite the fact the schools are accredited by such public agencies as the Veterans Administration and the National Home Study Council, they preserve considerable secrecy about some sectors of their operation. Included in the 'confidential' category, which school personnel told me could not be divulged, are:

The amount of commission paid to salesmen.

Breakdown of the $22,000,000 'sales and advertising' item in the shareholders' report as between sales commissions and advertising budget.

Breakdown of the $48,000,000 income from tuition fees as between Writers, Artists, Photographers.

Terms of the schools' contract with Guiding Faculty members.

If Bennett Cerf and his colleagues haven't time to grade the aptitude tests, who has? Their stand-ins are two full-timers and some forty pieceworkers, mostly housewives, who 'help you find out whether you can be trained to become a successful writer' in the privacy of their homes. There are no standards for admission to FWS, one of the full-timers explained. 'It's not the same thing as a grade on a college theme. The test is designed to indicate your *potential* as a writer, not your present ability.' Only about 10 percent of the applicants are advised they lack this 'potential' and are rejected.

The instructors guide the students from cheerful little cubicles equipped with machines into which they dictate the 'two-page letter of criticism and advice' promised in the advertising. They are, Gordon Carroll told me, former free-lance writers and people with editorial background: 'We never hire professional teachers, they're too *dull!* Deadly dull. Ph.D.s are the worst of all!' (Conversely, a trained teacher accustomed to all that the classroom offers might find an unrelieved diet of FWS students' manuscripts somewhat monotonous.) The annual starting salary for instructors is $8,500 for a seven-hour day, something of a comedown from the affluent and glamorous life dangled before their students in the school's advertising.

As I watched the instructors at work, I detected a generous inclination to accentuate the positive in the material submitted. Given an assignment to describe a period in time, a student had chosen 1933. Her first paragraph, about the election of F.D.R. and the economic situation in the country, could have been copied out of any almanac. She had followed this with 'There were breadlines everywhere.' I watched the instructor underline the breadlines in red, and write in the margin: 'Good work, Mrs. Smith! It's a pleasure working with you. You have recaptured the atmosphere of those days.'

Although the key to the school's financial success is its huge dropout rate ('We couldn't make any money if all the students finished,' Famous Writer Phyllis McGinley had told me in her candid fashion), the precise percentage of dropouts is hard to come by. 'I don't know exactly what it is, or where to get the figures,' said Mr. Lawrence. 'The last time we analyzed it, it related to the national figure for high-school and college dropouts, let's say about two-thirds of the enrolments.'

However, according to my arithmetic based on figures furnished by the school, the dropout rate must be closer to 90 percent. Each student is supposed to send in 24 assignments over a three-year period, an average of 8 per year. With 65,000 enrolled, this would amount to more than half a million lessons a year, and the 55 instructors would have to race along correcting these at a clip of one every few minutes. But in fact (the instructors assured me) they spend an hour or more on each lesson, and grade a total of only about 50,000 a year. What happens to the other 470,000 lessons? 'That's baffling,' said Mr. Carroll. 'I guess you can take a horse to the water, but you can't make him drink.'

These balky nags are, however, legally bound by the contract whether or not they ever crack a textbook or send in an assignment. What happens to the defaulter who refuses to pay? Are many taken to court? 'None,' said Mr. Lawrence. 'It's against our policy to sue in court.' Why, if the school considers the contract legally binding? 'Well – there's a question of morality involved. You'd hardly take a person to court for failing to complete a correspondence course.'

Mrs. Virginia Knauer, the President's Assistant for Consumer Affairs, with whom I discussed this later, suspects there is another question involved. 'The Famous Writers would never win in court,' she said indignantly. 'A lawsuit would expose them – somebody should take *them* to court. Their advertising is reprehensible, it's very close to being misleading.' Needless to say, the debtors are not informed of the school's moral scruples against lawsuits. On the contrary, a Finnish immigrant, whose husband complained to Mrs. Knauer that although she speaks little English, she had been coerced into signing for the course by an importunate salesman, was bombarded with dunning letters and telegrams full of implied threats to sue.

A fanciful idea occurred to me: since the school avers that it does not sue delinquents, I could make a fortune by advertising in the literary monthlies: 'For $10 I will tell you how to take the Famous Writers' course for nothing.' To those who sent in their ten dollars, I would return a postcard saying merely, 'Enrol in the course and make no payments.' I tried this out on Mr. Carroll and subsequently on Bennett Cerf. Their reactions were identical 'You'd find yourself behind bars if you did that!' 'Why? Whom would I have defrauded?' A question they were unable to answer, though Bennett Cerf, in mock horror, declared that the inventive mail order industry would certainly find *some* legal means to frustrate my iniquitous plan.

Both Mr. Lawrence and Mr. Carroll were unhappy about the case of the seventy-two year-old widow when I told them about it – it had not previously come to their attention. It was an unfortunate and unusual occurrence, they assured me, one of those slip-ups that may happen from time to time in any large corporation.

Eventually I had the opportunity to observe the presentation in the home of a neighbor who conjured up a salesman for me by sending in the aptitude test. A few days after she had mailed it in, my neighbor got a printed form letter (undated) saying that a field representative of the school would be in the area next week for a very short while and asking her to specify a convenient time when he might telephone for an appointment. There was something a little fuzzy around the edges here – for she had not yet heard from the school about her test – but she let that pass.

The 'field representative' (like the cemetery industry, the Famous Writers avoid the term 'salesman') when he arrived had a ready explanation: the school had telephoned to notify him that my neighbor had passed the test, and to tell him that luckily for her there were 'a few openings still left in this enrolment period' – it might be months before this opportunity came again!

The fantasy he spun for us, which far outstripped anything in the advertising, would have done credit to the school's fiction course.

Pressed for facts and figures, he told us that two or three of the Famous Fifteen are in Westport at all times working with 'a staff of forty or fifty experts in their specialty' evaluating and correcting student manuscripts . . . Your Guiding Faculty member could be Bennett Cerf, could be Rod Serling depending on your subject, will review at least one of your manuscripts, and may suggest a publisher for it . . . There are 300 instructors for 3,000 students ('You mean, one teacher for every ten students?' I asked. 'That's correct, it's a ratio unexcelled by any college in the country,' said the field representative without batting an eye) . . . Hundreds of university professors are currently enrolled . . . 75 percent of the students publish in their first year, and the majority more than pay for the course through their sales . . . There are very few dropouts because only serious, qualified applicants (like my neighbor) are permitted to enrol . . .

During his two-hour discourse, he casually mentioned three books recently published by students he personally enrolled – one is already being made into a movie! 'Do tell us the names, so we can order them?' But he couldn't remember, offhand: 'I get so darn many announcements of books published by our students.'

Oh, clean-cut young man, does your mother know how you earn your living? (And, Famous Fifteen, do yours?)

The course itself is packaged for maximum eye-appeal in four hefty 'two-toned, buckram-bound' volumes with matching loose-leaf binders for the lessons. The textbooks contain all sorts of curious and disconnected matter: examples of advertisements that 'pull'; right and wrong ways of ending business letters; paragraphs from the *Saturday Evening Post*, *This Week, Reader's Digest*; quotations from successful writers like William Shakespeare, Faith Baldwin, Mark Twain, Mark Wiseman, Winston Churchill, Red Smith; an elementary grammar lesson ('*Verbs* are action words. A *noun* is the name of a person, place or thing'); a glossary of commonly misspelled words; a standard list of printer's proof-marking symbols.

There is many a homespun suggestion for the would-be Famous Writer on what to write about, how to start writing: 'Writing ideas – ready-made aids for the writer – are available everywhere. In every waking hour you hear and see and feel . . . ' 'How do you get started on a piece of writing? One successful author writes down the work "The" the moment he gets to the typewriter in the morning. He follows "The" with another word, then another . . . ' (But the text writer, ignoring his own good advice, starts a sentence with 'As,' and trips himself in an imparsable sentence: 'As with so many professional writers, Marjorie Holmes keeps a notebook handy . . . '

Throughout the course the illusion is fostered that the student is, or soon will be, writing for publication: 'Suppose you're sitting in the office of a magazine editor discussing an assignment for next month's issue . . . ' The set of books includes a volume entitled 'How to Turn Your Writing Into Dollars,' which winds up on a triumphal note with a sample publisher's contract and a sample agreement with a Hollywood agent.

In short, there is really nothing useful in these books that could not be found in any number of writing and style manuals, grammar texts, marketing guides, free for the asking in the public library.

Thrown in as part of the $785–$900 course is a 'free' subscription to *Famous Writers* magazine, a quarterly in which stories written by students appear under this hyperbolic caption: 'Writers Worth Watching: In this section, magazine editors and book publishers can appraise the quality of work being done by FWS students.' According to the schools' literature, 'Each issue of the magazine is received and read by some 2,000 editors, publishers and other key figures in the writing world.' However, Messrs. Carroll and Lawrence were unable to enlighten me about these key figures – who they were, how it is known that they read each issue, whether they have ever bought manuscripts from students after appraising the quality of their work.

The student sales department of the magazine is also worth watching. Presumably the school puts its best foot forward here, yet the total of all success stories recorded therein each year is only about thirty-five, heavily weighted in the direction of small denominational magazines, local newspapers, pet-lovers' journals, and the like. Once in a while a student strikes it rich with a sale to *Reader's Digest*, *Redbook*, *McCall's*, generally in 'discovery' departments in these magazines that specifically solicit first-person anecdotes by their readers as distinct from professional writers: Most Unforgettable Character, Turning-Point, Suddenly It Happens to You.

The school gets enormous mileage out of these few student sales. The same old successful students turn up time and again the promotional literature. Thus an ad in the January 4, 1970, issue of *The New York Times* Magazine features seven testimonials: 'I've just received a big, beautiful check from the *Reader's Digest* . . . ' I've just received good news and a check from *Ellery Queen's Mystery Magazine*. . . . ' 'Recently, I've sold three more articles . . . ' How recently? Checking back through old copies of *Famous Writers* magazine, I found the latest of these success stories had appeared in the student sales department of a 1968 issue; the rest had been lifted from issues of 1964 and 1965.

A FWS graduate who had completed the entire course (and has not, to date, sold any of her storied) echoed the views of many: 'It's tremendously overblown, there's a lot of busywork, unnecessary padding to make you think you're getting your money's worth. One peculiar thing is you get a different instructor for each assignment, so there's not much of the 'personal attention' promised in the brochures.' However, she added, 'I have to be fair. It did get me started, and it did make me keep writing.'

I showed some corrected lessons that fell into my hands to an English professor. One assignment: 'To inject new life and color and dimension into a simple declarative sentence.' From the sentence 'The cat washed its paws,' the student had fashioned this: 'With fastidious fussiness, the cat flicked his pink tongue over his paws, laying the fur down neatly and symmetrically.' The instructor had crossed out 'cat' and substituted 'the burly gray tomcat.' With fastidious fussiness, the lanky, tweed-suited English professor clutched at his balding, pink pate and emitted a low, agonized groan of bleak, undisguised despair: 'Exactly the sort of wordy stuff we try to get students to *avoid*.'

The staggering dropout rate cannot, I was soon convinced, be laid entirely at the door of rapacious salesmen who sign up semi-literates and other incompetents. Many of those who told me of their experience with the school are articulate, intelligent people, manifestly capable of disciplined self-study that could help them to improve their prose style. Why should adults of sound mind and resolute purpose first enrol in FWS and then throw away their substantial investment? One letter goes far to explain:

> My husband and I bought the course for two main reasons. The first was that we were in the boondocks of Arkansas and we truly felt that Famous Writers School under the sponsorship of Bennett Cerf etc. was new in concept and would have more to offer than other courses we had seen advertised. The second was the fact that we had a definite project in mind: a fictionalized account of our experiences in the American labor movement.
>
> I guess the worst part of our experience was the realization that the school could not live up to its advertised promise. It is in the area of the assignments and criticism that the course falls down. Because you get a different instructor each time, there is no continuity. This results in the student failing to get any understanding of story and structure from the very beginning.
>
> My husband completed about eight assignments, but felt so intensely frustrated with the course that he could not go on. He couldn't get any satisfaction from the criticism.
>
> While the school is careful to advise that no one can teach writing talent they constantly encourage their students towards a belief in a market that doesn't exist for beginning writers. For us, it was an expensive and disappointing experience.

The phenomenal success of FWS in attracting students (if not in holding them) does point to an undeniable yearning on the part of large numbers of people not only to see their work published, but also for the sort of self-improvement the school purports to offer. As Robert Byrne points out, what can be learned about writing from a writing course can be of great value in many areas of life, 'from love letters to suicide notes.' For shut-ins, people living in remote rural areas, and others unable to get classroom instruction, correspondence courses may provide the only opportunity for supervised study.

Recognizing the need, some fifteen state universities offer correspondence courses that seem to me superior to the Famous Writers course for a fraction of the cost. True, the universities neither package nor push their courses, they provide no handsome buckram-bound two-tone loose-leaf binders, no matching textbooks, no sample Hollywood contract.

Unobtrusively tucked away in the *Lifelong Learning* bulletin of the University of California Extension at Berkeley are two such offerings: Magazine Article Writing, 18 assignments, fee $55; and Short Story Theory and Practice, 15 assignments, fee $35 ($5 more for out-of-state enrollees). There are no academic requirements for these courses, anybody can enrol. Those who, in the instructor's opinion, prove to be unqualified are advised to switch to an elementary course in grammar and composition.

Cecilia Bartholomew, who has taught the short-story course by correspondence for the past twelve years, is herself the author of two novels and numerous short stories. She cringes at the thought of drumming up business for the course: 'I'd be a terrible double-dealer to try to *sell* people on it,' she said. Like the Famous Writers instructors, Mrs. Bartholomew sends her students a lengthy criticism of each assignment, but unlike them she does not cast herself in the role of editor revising storied for publication: 'It's the improvement in their writing technique that's important. The aim of my course is to develop in each student a professional standard of writing. I'll tell him when a piece is good enough to submit to an editor, but I'll never tell it will sell.' Have any of her students sold their pieces? 'Yes, quite a few. Some have published in volumes of juvenile stories, some in *Hitchcock Mysteries*. But we don't stress this at all.'

In contrast, Louise Boggess, who teaches Magazine Article Writing by correspondence in addition to her classes in 'professional writing' at the College of San Mateo, exudes go-ahead salesmanship: she believes that most of her students will eventually find a market for their work. The author of several how-to-do-it books (among them *Writing Articles That Sell*, which she uses as the text for her course), she points her students straight towards the mass writing market. In her streamlined, practical lessons the emphasis is unabashedly on formula writing that will sell. Her very first assignment is how to write a 'hook,' meaning an arresting opening sentence. What does she think of the word 'The' for openers? It doesn't exactly grab her, she admitted.

During the eighteen months she has been teaching the correspondence course, several of her 102 students have already sold pieces to such magazines as *Pageant*, *Parents*, *Ladies Circle*, *Family Weekly*. She has had but six dropouts, an enviable record by FWS standards.

My brief excursion into correspondence-school-land taught me little, after all, that the canny consumer does not already know about the difference between buying and being sold. As Faith Baldwin said, most advertising is somewhat misleading; as Bennett Cert said, the crux of mail order selling is a hard pitch to the gullible. We know that the commission salesman will, if we let him into our homes, dazzle and bemuse us with the beauty, durability, unexcelled value of his product, whatever it is. As for the tens of thousands who sign up with FWS when they could get a better and cheaper correspondence course through the universities (or, if they live in a city, Adult Education Extension courses), we know from reading Vance Packard that people tend to prefer things that come in fancy packages and cost more.

There is probably nothing actually illegal in the FWS operation, although consumer watchdogs have their eye on it.

Robert Hughes, counsel for the Federal Trade Commission's Bureau of Deceptive Practices, told me he has received a number of complaints about the school, mostly relating to the high-pressure and misleading sales pitch. 'The real evil is in the solicitation and enrolment procedures,' he said. 'There's a basic contradiction involved when you have profit-making organizations in the field of education. There's pressure to maximize the number of enrolments to make more profit. Surgery is needed in the enrolment procedure.'

There is also something askew with the cast of characters in the foregoing drama which would no doubt be quickly spotted by FWS instructors in television scriptwriting ('where the greatest market lies for the beginning writer,' as the school tells us).

I can visualize the helpful comment on my paper: 'Good work, Miss Mitford. The Oakland widow's problem was well thought through. But characterization is weak. You could have made your script more believable had you chosen a group of shifty-eyed hucksters out to make a buck, one step ahead of the sheriff, instead of these fifteen eminently successful and solidly respectable writers, who are well liked and admired by the American viewing public. For pointers on how to make your characters come to life in a way we can all identify with, I suggest you study Rod Serling's script *The Twilight Zone*, in the kit you received from us. Your grade is D-. It has been a pleasure working with you. Good luck!'

Object Lesson (box accompanying original story)

'Every writer worth his salt develops, after a time, his own style.'
Faith Baldwin, *Principles of Good Writing,* FWS textbook.

(But Famous Writers Write Alike)

By Faith Baldwin

If you want to write, my colleagues and I would like to test your writing aptitude. We'll help you find out if you can be trained to become a successful writer. We know that many men and women who could become writers – and *should* become writers – never do. Some are uncertain of their talent and have no reliable way of finding out if it's worth developing. Others simply can't get topnotch professional training without leaving their homes or giving up their jobs.

By Bennett Cerf

If you want to write and see your work published, my colleagues and I would like to test your writing aptitude. We'll help you find out whether you can be trained to become a successful writer. We know that many men and women who could become writers – and *should* become writers – never do. Some are uncertain of their talent and have no reliable way of finding out if it's worth developing. Others simply can't get topnotch professional training without leaving their homes or giving up their jobs.

(Reprinted from postcard inserts currently being circulated in millions of paper-back books.)

Malcolm Knox

Journalist and author Malcolm Knox joined the *Sydney Morning Herald* in 1994. He has written two novels, *Summerland* and *A Private Man*, and the non-fiction book *Secrets of the Jury Room*. In 2004, as the *Herald*'s literary editor, his Walkley Award winning front-page story revealed the literary fraud perpetrated by bestselling author Norma Khouri, whose book *Forbidden Love* allegedly depicted her own experience of fleeing Jordan after her friend's death in an honour killing. Knox's story, which won the Walkley for Investigative Journalism, revealed that Khouri was actually Norma Bagain, an American, married with children, who had faked her identity, fooling her publisher, immigration officials and readers.

HER LIFE AS A FAKE: BESTSELLER'S LIES EXPOSED

Malcolm Knox

Sydney Morning Herald, July 24, 2004

Her tragic story stole readers' hearts and triggered an international outcry. She became a best-selling author in the same league as J. K. Rowling and Michael Moore. She petitioned the United Nations personally, was published in 15 countries, and Australians voted her memoir into their favourite 100 books of all time.

But Norma Khouri is a fake, and so is *Forbidden Love*.

With Australian sales approaching 200,000, the book told of her lifelong friendship with a girl named Dalia in Amman, Jordan. In their 20s, Khouri wrote, she and Dalia started a hairdressing salon together. Dalia met and fell in love with Michael, a Christian army officer. When their chaste affair was discovered, Dalia was murdered – stabbed 12 times – by her father. Norma fled Jordan to Athens, where she said she wrote her book in internet cafes, and ultimately to Australia, where her publisher Random House sponsored her for a temporary residence visa.

Khouri, now 34, spent much of 2003 retelling this story, reducing listeners to tears and anger, in interviews, book festivals, bookshops and other events. She toured the world with the story, from appearing on network television in the US to being selected for a citywide book club in Adelaide.

While making her new home at a secret location in Queensland and fearing for her life, Khouri became a standard-bearer for Arab women and triggered a publishing trend of similar books.

Though Khouri says she stands by what she wrote, the truth is very different, and may affect her residency status in Australia.

Khouri's real name is Norma Majid Khouri Michael Al-Bagain Toliopoulos, and she only lived in Jordan until she was three years old. She has a US passport and lived from 1973 until 2000 in Chicago. She is married with two children, 13 and 11. She has four

American siblings and a mother who are desperate to hear news from her. But she has managed to conceal this double life from her publishers, her agent, lawyers in several continents, the Australian Department of Immigration and, until now, the public.

Her mother, Asma, remembers her estranged daughter as a girl who 'kept deep secrets'. Norma's privacy has a reason: not to protect her safety, but to guard her fabrications.

Khouri's hoax will take its place in a long Australian tradition of literary fraud, from Ern Malley to Helen Darville-Demidenko. But no other fraudulent book has had such wide sales or impact, and in Darville's case the deception only involved her persona, not her book. Khouri has misled the world both on the page and in person.

Suspicion first arose in Jordan, where readers posted on websites their belief that so much in the book was inaccurate, its factual basis was in doubt. A Jordanian women's group discovered that Khouri entered and left Jordan briefly in 2000 but may not have been there at the time of the book's events. The *Herald* found public records evidence of Norma and John Toliopoulos living in Chicago, and put this to Khouri in February. She denied she had ever lived in America, or been there before a publicity tour in 2003. She said the records were 'planted' to trick the Jordanian Government into giving her travel documents to escape.

Subsequently, the *Herald* discovered records of Chicago real estate transactions listing Norma and John Toliopoulos as husband and wife. But as comprehensive as these were, as long as they remained solely on paper they did not necessarily contradict Norma's explanation.

Visiting the addresses this month, however, the *Herald* found members of her family, neighbours and acquaintances who remembered Norma from her 27 years in Chicago, from age three to 30. Her 64-year-old mother keeps dozens of photos of the daughter who disappeared in 2000 and has not spoken to her since. Asma's one hope, she told the *Herald*, was for reconciliation.

Asked how she coped with living secretly, Khouri once said: 'It is very stressful and tiring, and I would not recommend it to anyone.'

There was more than a grain of truth in what she said.

Yesterday the *Herald* put the results of its investigation to Khouri, and she continued to deny she had an American family. Despite the photos, interviews with family and acquaintances, public records of vehicle and real estate ownership and a US marriage, she said her mother, Asma, lived in Jordan.

In *Forbidden Love*, Khouri told how she and Dalia were oppressed by patriarchal Jordanian laws, which protected Dalia's father from prosecution for the alleged murder. Since the book's publication she has embellished the story, saying the only family member she speaks to is an aunt in Jordan and that male relatives might kill her if they found her.

She told an interviewer: 'I know that my mother would support what I'm doing.' And her father? 'I hope he will eventually understand. And it would be nice to have him be proud of me some day, instead of ashamed of me.'

Norma's father, Majid Bagain, does live in Jordan, but that is where the coincidence between truth and fantasy ends.

The *Herald*'s 18-month investigation found that Majid Bagain, a machinist, took his wife Asma and their daughter Norma from Jordan to America in 1973. Majid and Asma separated in 1986 and he returned to Jordan. They divorced in 1994. Asma, now 64, a retired nurse who had open-heart surgery two years ago and now suffers from diabetes, has lived in south-west Chicago since the family came from Jordan and shares a townhouse in South Long Street with Norma's youngest brother, Will, who was born in America in 1980.

Norma has three other younger siblings – Diana, Rita and Mike – who live in Illinois and Indiana. Aside from a handful of emails sent to Diana, Norma has not contacted her family since she left Chicago suddenly about four years ago, at the time she began to write *Forbidden Love*.

Until then, Norma lived a comparatively unremarkable suburban Chicago life, finishing her secondary education at a Catholic school before 'studying computers', her mother says, for four years. She worked in a range of low-paying jobs before meeting John Toliopoulos, a Greek-American.

They had a daughter, Zoe, in 1991, and a son, Christopher, in 1993. Norma and John married on November 27, 1993, in Chicago.

Through the 1990s – at the time of Dalia's 'murder' – Norma and John embarked on a series of property transactions, buying and refinancing houses near Asma's in 1995, 1996 and 1998. Publicly available Illinois State records show that the pair undertook these transactions as 'husband and wife'.

Jordanian authorities state that Norma was issued with a US passport, valid for 10 years, in Chicago on March 26, 1996 – the time when, according to *Forbidden Love*, Dalia was murdered and Norma feared persecution for opposing the honour killing.

Will Bagain said that around 1999 Norma and John moved into a house in Major Street, in a working-class suburb in south-west Chicago. John's brother Steve and her brother Will also lived there. The men clashed, and Will was kicked out. Although the circumstances are in dispute, Will was convicted for a firearms possession offence in 1999 and given a probationary sentence, court records show.

Norma's other brother, Mike, had been convicted for drugs-related felonies and given a four-year prison term in 1997. Norma was a plaintiff in a $30,000 claim against the Northwest National Bank in 1995, but aside from that she and John have no court or criminal records.

For a time Norma lived across the road from her mother in Long Street. A neighbour, Billy Phillips, remembers Norma as 'quiet, OK, good to her mother'. But Toliopoulos and his family are not remembered so fondly among the Bagains.

Norma began to drift away from her family after meeting Toliopoulos. 'To tell the truth, I hate that family,' Will Bagain says. 'I didn't like John from the start. Steve was crazy, thought he was God. I can't think of [John] at all, they make me too angry.'

Norma, John and their children continued living in the area, near Midway Airport, until 2000. Norma sold insurance, her brother said, then enrolled in a bartending school. She drove a 1996 Nissan Sentra. Nobody knew her as a writer, although she owned a laptop and wrote on it, mostly poems, secretively. Then she, her husband and their children abruptly disappeared.

'I don't know why she went,' says Will Bagain. 'She'd kind of run away with John when they first met. Then they came back for a while, but then they went again. One day she was there, the next she was gone.'

Will says he misses Norma, whom he gave away at her 1993 wedding to Toliopoulos, and particularly Zoe and Christopher. 'They're my niece and nephew, you know.'

The reasons for Norma's disappearance remain cloudy. 'I have no idea why they left,' says Asma. 'The mother's always the last to know . . . They hurt me big. I miss them so much. But Norma always kept deep secrets. She kept things to herself.'

Diana Bagain did not want to discuss her sister, saying it was 'unusual that someone would call me to ask about Norma'.

Norma's disappearance from Chicago was the start of a new life. She wrote the book and submitted it piecemeal to Christy Fletcher, a highly reputable New York literary agent. Fletcher edited it for fluency, but did not investigate the truth of Norma's story. He subsequently sold it to 16 publishers around the world, and it was comprehensively vetted by lawyers for Viacom in the US and Transworld in Britain.

None of this uncovered Norma's real life. Having sold the lie, she came to Australia, enjoyed a rapturous welcome from readers, and continued to act out the fabrication.

The *Herald* contacted Norma Khouri about these allegations earlier this year. She denied she had ever lived in America. She said: 'Yes, I have paperwork that shows that I was married to [Toliopoulos]. This was to get my Jordanian passport without my father's involvement.'

Friends, she said, including 'Michael', the man who fell in love with 'Dalia', had 'set up an address in America as though I was there. To get out, I had to show I was married to a foreigner in a foreign country . . .

'I have only ever been to America after the book was published, on a publicity tour. I have never had an American passport.'

After finding proof of Norma's US life, the *Herald* contacted her again yesterday. She repeatedly denied she had lived in the US or had children.

She said: 'I stand by what I wrote. I refute the allegations that you are making, and had I been given more ample time I would have supplied proof. I intend to do so in the future.'

In a statement released last night, her publisher said: 'As a matter of principle, Random House Australia supports its authors and the claims they make. In the case of *Forbidden Love* we were mindful that the issue of concealing Ms Khouri's true identity was central to her fleeing Jordan as described in the book.

'In light of the new information brought to our attention by the *Herald*, we are checking these claims with Ms Khouri.'

Her new book is due out in November. It is said to be a sequel to *Forbidden Love*, covering Norma's clandestine flight from Jordan after Dalia's death. That book's future must now be under question. Its title is *A Matter of Honour*.

Interview with Malcolm Knox

Question *At the beginning of your front-page story you note that Norma Khouri's book has touched readers worldwide and been published in fifteen countries, but you go on to state baldly: 'But Norma Khouri is a fake, and so is* Forbidden Love.*' Was that a scary line to write?*

Knox Yes, it was scary because it would have cost us a seven-figure sum if it had been incorrect. Of course when I wrote the story I was 99 per cent sure I was right, but with so much on the line I couldn't help dwelling on the 1 per cent chance that I was wrong. It was scary because this was a very big story, and without an admission from Norma there was always the chance she would throw up a kind of smoke-and-mirrors act to recover the appearance of credibility. But even though that admission didn't come for some time, her publisher quickly found out that she had been lying and took her book out of the shops. I thought that was a very principled action of theirs, when they could have sold a lot more copies by keeping it out there.

Your front-page scoop was picked up around the world. Why was it an important story?

Because she had defrauded the 250,000 people who had bought the book around the world and thousands more who had borrowed it from libraries, friends, etc, and many thousands on top of that who had heard her speak on the radio or in media – all those people who had given her their sympathies. She had defrauded these people of their emotions and time that will never be refunded. I'm surprised anyone could ask why this is an important story, but with books and the arts, it's not always taken for granted that fraud is a serious matter.

There are people who'll say Norma's book had an 'emotional truth', an underlying truth (presumably about the wickedness of Muslim men), and that she had to tell a literal lie to get this truth across. To those people, I'd say two things. One is that the 'truth' she was telling about Muslim men, now that it is unsubstantiated by evidence, is not actually a truth but an appeal to anti-Muslim prejudices. Her book exploited the laziest kind of racism. The second thing I'd say is that if lies don't really matter, then you have to accept that it's all right if your partner is having an affair and lying to you, it's all right if the car dealer lies to you about how old the car in the lot is, it's all right if your parents and your children lie to you, it's all right if your government lies to you. If you don't mind being lied to, I guess Norma Khouri did nothing wrong by you.

What got the story started?

The impetus for the story came from Jordan, where people had their doubts about Norma and asked some questions of their own. This story had two parts:

establishing that Norma wasn't who she said she was, and establishing who she actually was. For the first part, most of the work was done by those people in Jordan who had no recollection or knowledge of Norma and grave doubts about her story. But that only takes you so far. You can't run a story saying, 'Norma Khouri is a fake because nobody in Jordan can remember her'. That's defamatory. There may be legitimate reasons why they can't remember her. What you need is the other half, which is finding out who she really was.

Legendary American investigator I. F. Stone famously remarked that the best stories come from scouring the public record. Were documents vital in this case?

Up to a point. Documents showed that there was a person 'Norma Bagain' who had lived in Chicago and done certain things. Norma had tried to outsmart this by acknowledging that there was a paper trail in America, but she said it had been fabricated to help her get out of Jordan on an American passport. So the key wasn't finding the documents. The key was getting human witnesses to link Norma Bagain, the American, with Norma Khouri, the writer. Those witnesses were members of her family whom I found by (in the end) walking the streets and knocking on doors.

Can you talk about some of the techniques you used in tracking down your leads?

The most important 'technique' is common courtesy: returning someone's phone call or emails when you don't think they have a story you can use. That's how it was for the first twelve months. I was just keeping in touch with some people in Jordan who seemed honest, but too far from proving their suspicions to have something I could write. The next technique, once I got a few names, was to plough through the White Pages making call after call. The most important technique, if it can be called that, was driving around Chicago and knocking at the doors of the houses I'd found connected with Norma in the phone book. It's not rocket science.

What about the ethical dimensions of a story that is essentially an exposé of a particular person?

You do think about the consequences for that person. Norma and her family led a good life in Queensland, and in breaking the story I would be disrupting that life. But I can't say it weighed too heavily on me. She had defrauded a large number of people (and, as the investigation proceeded, she had committed financial fraud on other individuals in the USA). So she deserved to be caught. I did feel sorry for her children, but in the end they got to move back to be with Norma's family in the States, which by all accounts is the best place for them.

At what point did you contact Khouri herself?

I had first contacted Norma about this story in January 2004. She denied ever having lived in the USA. She said she had only visited there once, on a publicity tour in 2003. I next contacted her in July 2004, when I had assembled the conclusive evidence against her. I contacted her less than 48 hours before the story was published, which she said was too short a time to produce enough evidence to clear her name. Her agent and publisher also asked for more time. In order to buy some time, Norma said she could supply me immediately with photographs and records from her life in Jordan. She couldn't. She gave me an off-the-record explanation of how I had made 'an error of mistaken identity'. Once I heard this explanation (which I did keep off the record), I was convinced that she was lying and that she had no way of clearing her name.

Was it difficult to confront her?

I find any confrontation difficult, let alone one where I'm accusing a person of being a liar. In response, Norma was very cool and convincing. She has an almost hypnotic power to persuade. I was very tempted to believe her, particularly as I was also scared of being wrong. But once I put the phone down and looked at the actual evidence again, I saw that she'd just been trying to snow-job me once again.

How did you cope with her implication that your enquiries would put her in danger? That they might sabotage a false trail laid down deliberately to protect her in hiding?

She said the false trail was to help her get out of Jordan, not to protect her in hiding. She never said I would put her in danger by continuing with the story. (She said that afterwards – that the story had put her in danger. There was no evidence that this was the case.) I never took that very seriously. She was always claiming people were out to kill her, but she only claimed it when she needed to duck a question. Her publishers, on the other hand, had taken it seriously. She had told them that they couldn't investigate her past deeply because it might jeopardise lives. They took her word for it.

Were you inclined to give up on the story at any time?

I was only inclined to give up on it when I thought there was nothing to it. For a long time I followed it out of a sense of responsibility to those people in Jordan whose work against honour killings had been undermined by Norma's book. It's true that she had won a lot of sympathy for her portrayal of a real and troubling issue. But so did the guy who did a big door-to-door collection for the Asian tsunami victims and then scarpered with the money. 'Raising awareness' of an issue doesn't excuse theft.

It must have been difficult working from Sydney when parts of the story were in Jordan and the US? Did you ask the paper to let you travel to advance the research?

I did ask to travel to Jordan and the US, but my supervising editor at the time said she couldn't get that much money. I didn't push it, because at that stage I didn't have much more than a hunch and didn't believe I could pin it down. I ended up going to America in my own annual leave, so I was able to work on the story without the pressure of knowing the paper would expect me to come up with a result.

Despite the knockback, you got to the US, and at that point there was some old-fashioned shoe-leather journalism involved. Can you expand on that?

I had a list of seven addresses where Norma Toliopoulos née Bagain had lived in Chicago, according to searches I'd done on the internet. I went to every one, knocked on the door and showed the occupant a photo of Norma. Funnily enough, none of them did [recognise her], directly. But one of them led me to someone who knew someone who knew her.

How long did the story take?

All up, it was 18 months from the first phone call to the day the story broke. It only took that long because I couldn't get to America until I got my 2004 annual leave. With an unlimited budget it could have happened quicker. I only knew I had it in the bag when I spoke to Will Bagain, Norma's brother. He saw my photo and said it was her. He showed me older photos of her, in America, and we knew we were talking about the same person.

With the shareholders' bottom line dictating cutbacks in newsroom resources is there room for optimism about in-depth investigations in Australian journalism?

Shareholders aren't saying 'cut back on investigations'. It's managers who decide what costs they will cut back on. And it's managers who make cost-cutting a priority over creating new value. Yes, in the past, this has meant cutting back on investigations. But it needn't continue this way in the future. I'm optimistic that newspaper management will be able to persuade their boards and shareholders of the value of in-depth journalism.

There are quite a few journalists turned novelists here and internationally. Do you agree with Tom Wolfe that the disciplines of journalistic research and writing are a good preparation for both literary journalism and fiction?

For a certain type of fiction, perhaps. I think Geraldine Brooks is a good example of a journalist who has turned a compassionate and wise worldview, a doggedness in research, and a gift for clear writing – all of which she developed through journalism – into a career as a fine novelist. But fiction-writing is too individual a practice to succumb to sweeping generalisations of this kind. I don't think it applies to me, and I'm not a journalist who turned to novel-writing anyway. Did the discipline and craft in writing fiction help me when I turned to journalism? Yes.

Discussion questions

Is it acceptable for journalists investigating matters of serious concern to go undercover as a last resort to get at the truth? Why is it discouraged by journalists' codes of ethics? What is the downside?

Experienced journalists say that as editors are replaced by managers respect for journalism that aims to do more than generate profit weakens. What sorts of stories might fall into that category and what might a fall-off in coverage mean?

Cutbacks in newsroom resources are being made in line with concerns for the shareholders' bottom line. Is it fair enough for journalism to be seen as a business like any other?

Further reading

James Ettema and Theodore Glasser, *Custodians of Conscience: Investigative journalism and public virtue*, Columbia University Press, 1998.
Chris Masters, *Inside Story*, Angus & Robertson, 1992.
Chris Masters, *Not for Publication*, ABC Books, 2002.
John Pilger (ed.), *Tell Me No Lies: Investigative journalism and its triumphs*, Jonathan Cape, 2004.
David Spark, *Investigative Reporting: A study of techniques*, Focal Press, 1999.
Brian Toohey and William Pinwill, *Oyster*, William Heinemann, 1989.
Marian Wilkinson and Brian Toohey, *The Book of Leaks*, Angus & Robertson, 1987.

Chapter 5

Essays

Turning personal stories into reflective writing

Willa McDonald

The literary critic Peter Craven calls the essay an 'odd mongrel thing'.[1] And he's right. Sometimes it looks like the best journalism; sometimes its style more closely resembles fiction. It can shapeshift from the stilted version required of school students to a flowing meditation on consciousness and a solar eclipse in the manner of Annie Dillard. Its flexibility allows it to be used by writers to comment on their childhoods, their travels, their hobbies and their politics. In this respect, it's curiously democratic. Anyone can use it to express themselves – and on issues that matter – without claiming expertise in any particular field.

Looking back

The essay can trace its lineage back to the efforts of the sixteenth century French lawyer Michel de Montaigne. Although an aristocrat, Montaigne had little respect for the ecclesiastical cogitations or pandering to high rank typical of the writings of his day. 'On the loftiest throne in the world,' he opined, 'we are still sitting on only our own rump.'[2]

While writers throughout history have pondered their concerns through their prose – for example, St Paul in his *Epistles*, Augustine in his *Confessions* and later Bacon in his *Essays* – it was Montaigne whose groundbreaking secular ruminations enabled writers who came after to examine their own experiences without any theological or instructional purpose in mind. When he chose the term *essais* for his work (from *essayer* – to attempt; to test; to weigh up), Montaigne deliberately chose a label that contains within it the idea of a careful consideration of a topic, a balancing of thoughts, feelings and ideas that has come to denote the personal essay genre as we know it today. As the leaping off point for his *essais* (which were first published in 1580), Montaigne chose his own perceptions. And paradoxically, the deeper he dived into his own life, the better he connected with his readers. That connection has endured across time and place – Montaigne still delights readers with his direct and open conversations on the page.

Thinking local, writing global

In line with Montaigne's legacy, the modern essay is most successful at the point where the public and private meet – where it explores meaning for the individual and, in doing so, inevitably speaks to the many. Helen Garner noted in her interview (see Chapter 6):

> My initial urge is to make sense of things, through writing and all its weird skills and manoeuvres, for *myself*. I'm trying first of all to save myself. From the chaos and terror of meaninglessness. The only way I know how to do this is by writing. Every other purpose follows on from that.

The focus on the personal could be dismissed as self-indulgent. Who wants to hear that Uncle Fred came to dinner last night? Or how long it took you to get to work this morning? But in exploring the microcosm of the individual's world, the accomplished essayist – whether she consciously sets out to or not – always makes broader social, political or philosophical comment. If in recounting your tale about the traffic, you're really commenting on the busyness of modern life or the consequences of poor urban design, then we are more likely to want to listen. First-rate essays always have a deeper layer and always, even if very subtly, deal with 'big' ideas. That's what gives them their lasting value.

Using facts

Emerson once called for newer, younger writers to avoid the rhetoric of the day, to 'pierce this rotten diction and fasten words again to visible things'.[3] As Scott Russell Sanders points out, this is what skilful essayists always aspire to do.[4] They don't write fiction. They don't set themselves up as experts. They fasten their words to concrete facts, garnered not only through their own research but also through their own observations and reactions.

In her essay 'War Talk: Summer Games with Nuclear Bombs', Booker Prize winner Arundhati Roy tackles the real possibility of nuclear war between Pakistan and her home country India. Following a favoured theme in her writing – the relationship between power and powerlessness – Roy peppers her polemic with facts:

> A dear friend, who's an activist in the anti-dam movement in the Narmada valley, is on indefinite hunger strike. Today is the fourteenth day of her fast. She and the others fasting with her are weakening quickly. They're protesting because the Madhya Pradesh government is bulldozing schools, clear-felling forests, uprooting hand pumps, forcing people from their villages to make way for the Maan Dam. The people have nowhere to go. And so, the hunger strike.[5]

The result is an essay that's reasoned and convincing – an essay that challenges humbug and political spin.

Finding the right voice

Arundhati Roy's essay works, in large part, because of the sureness of her voice. It's through the voice – the persona – that the writer conveys the theme, establishes the point of view and strikes the best tone for the piece. Roy's essay reads like a persuasive letter from a reliable and honest friend. The tone is judicious, compassionate and inclusive, yet Roy's narrator actually reveals very little of her life beyond that she is a writer, that her friend is on a hunger strike and that her husband is writing a book about trees and fig wasps. But after finishing the essay we are left knowing more essential things than the facts of the narrator's life – we know her concerns and values and that she is willing to fight for what she believes in. She, her family and friends have become people we care about – and as any activist knows, that makes us care about their issues too.

While the persona may reflect the writer's own personality, it's worth remembering that it's nevertheless created – deliberately – by the writer. The edgy Australian writer John Birmingham's persona in 'S11' isn't the same as the one he used in his humorous books *He Died with a Felafel in his Hand* and *The Tasmanian Babes Fiasco*.[6] It's also different from the one he uses in his more serious works of non-fiction such as *Leviathan* or his *Quarterly Essay* on East Timor, 'Appeasing Jakarta'.[7]

Birmingham's point in writing 'S11' wasn't to defend snarling, howling anarchists, streakers against globalisation or Swamis for Peace. He was calling on his personal experience of this protest to defend the power of ideas and our right to express them, to condemn the violence of the state and the corruption of the media.[8] The persona in 'S11' helps him to pull that off. It's angry, indignant and contemptuous and underpins Birmingham's frank and wryly funny take-no-prisoners approach.

Allowing yourself to be vulnerable

Humourist David Sedaris' popularity with readers is a reflection of the pleasure he gives them. He wrote 'Today's Special' not only to poke fun but also *for* fun. Using an old trick of humorous columnists, he has made the persona in 'Today's Special' slightly bumbling and self-deprecating – a common device of essayists who want to avoid the cardinal sin of being boring. After all, who wants to listen to an egomaniac prattling on about his or her own life? Vulnerability is much more appealing to readers, so essayists often exaggerate their faults. As the essayist and commentator Phillip Lopate says: 'The spectacle of baring the naked soul is meant to awaken the sympathy of the reader who is apt to forgive the essayist's self-absorption in return for the warmth of his or her candour.'[9]

James Thurber, Garrison Keillor, Lennie Lower, Kaz Cooke, Wendy Harmer, Richard Glover, and many other writers, use such awkward, gauche narrators with humour and charm, but they also always give them acute observations. The combination attracts regular readers to them as if they're old friends.

Being funny, being serious

The most successful humorists use their ability to raise a laugh to leaven a message. While Sedaris' story is very funny, it's also essentially serious in theme. Says writing instructor William Zinsser:

> Humour is not a separate organism that can survive on its own frail metabolism. It's a special angle of vision granted to certain writers who already write good English. They aren't writing about life that's essentially ludicrous; they are writing about life that's essentially serious . . .[10]

While writing teachers can tell us about the use of humour, Sedaris shows us how it's done. In this brief story he's taken the position of an outsider looking in; he uses overstatement to heighten a 'truth'; he doesn't strain for laughs by trying to be funny in every line, but let's the reader breathe between jokes; he uses surprise and leaves the reader with a warm feeling about the incongruity of life and human behaviour, including the reader's own. While we can't help laughing in recognition at the antics of the narrator, we're also gently prodded to think about ourselves and the sillier side of our consumerist desires.

And that is the nub of the personal essay. Regardless of its final structure – whether it's long or short, funny or serious, descriptive or full of dialogue – its purpose is to stir a common understanding, or at least invite deliberation on a common question. It reaches out in conversation across generations and cultures to touch others with its particular take on the world.

John Birmingham

John Birmingham, once mostly known for his humorous writing – *He Died with a Felafel in his Hand, The Tasmanian Babes Fiasco* – is now equally well recognised for his political commentary and his science fiction thrillers. He began his writing career in student magazines and the street press before moving on to mainstream publications including the *Age*, the *Sydney Morning Herald* and the *Australian* newspapers. He has been a contributing editor at a number of magazines such as *Rolling Stone, Penthouse* and *Inside Sport*. Birmingham has won many writing and journalism awards, including the National Non-Fiction Award for his book *Leviathan*.

S11

John Birmingham

The Best Australian Essays, 2000

His lips were, dare I say it, unAustralian. They were lavishly, almost lasciviously pink, and seemed unnaturally full, as though injected with collagen in the minutes before going to air. His hair was blonde, and maybe thinning a little, but not ruinously so. Just enough, perhaps, to lend a little gravitas to an otherwise childish face. His eyes shone, but with a synthetic flicker. They were like lovingly polished marbles which threw off the blaze of the studio's high powered lighting. He seemed to pause before speaking, just long enough for a smirk – I was sure it was a smirk – to form on those curiously feminised lips.

'So much for nonviolence,' he read.

I actually gasped. I had been prepared for something special, this being Packer's network after all. But the arrogance, the contempt and the reflexive, unthinking stupidity compressed into that fleshy pink smirk and those four brief words were still literally breathtaking. The news reader was two or three pars into his lead story, the first morning of the S11 protest in Melbourne, before I recovered sufficiently to follow what he was saying.

Violence had flared, angry scenes had broken out, clashes had erupted between demonstrators and police. A sixteen-year-old code cutter could have hacked up a simple piece of software to generate the story from a database of network-approved phraseology. It might have been a little more challenging to load the computer-generated script with the appropriate subtext, a narrative of brave, beleaguered officers standing fast against a violent threat to civilised society. But it wasn't that subtle a subtext, so I'm guessing it could be done. And the news reader, with his eyes of glass and the heart of a tape recorder? Could he also be replaced by a cgi construct? A third or fourth generation Max Headroom to give protohuman expression to his ultimate owner's will to power. It would certainly be more efficient, more economically rational, and less harmful to the immortal souls of those currently forced by their lucrative contracts to utter such malicious bullshit as, 'So much for nonviolence.'

I doubt these thoughts bothered my pink-lipped friend though. He sailed on with a sort of spiteful cheeriness, throwing to vision of a flying wedge of police officers ploughing into a seething, screaming mass of protesters. The cops were attempting a rescue of WA premier Richard Court who had unwisely decided to emulate Bob Askin by 'driving over the bastards'. Unfortunately the bastards had surrounded his vehicle, cutting it off and subjecting the occupants to a sustained barrage of abuse and anti-mandatory-sentencing graffiti. One Aboriginal activist mounted the bonnet and danced a jig while informing Court he was under citizen's arrest for state crimes against indigenous people. The premier, he announced, now knew how the country's first inhabitants felt, being held to ransom for 200 years.

It was a wild scene, as baton charges always are, but it was unrepresentative. Most of the first day actually passed off without significant conflict, as the police struggled to counteract the fluid tactics of the blockaders. Mobile phones and message runners gathered reinforcements to any point where it seemed the blockade might fail. Horses were ineffectually deployed against picket lines, which had been trained to close up against them, leaving no gaps for the mounted police to break through. No central authority existed to organise the dozens of disparate groups which composed S11 and that lack of a command structure seemed to unhinge the police response. A number of megaphone-wielding enthusiasts from the International Socialists, the Democratic Socialist Party and its youth wing Resistance did try with varying success to marshal numbers into a couple of flash points, but many of the anarchically inclined protesters reacted as badly to their demands as they did to the cops'.

Despite the emphasis on conflict which dominated the mainstream news coverage, the reports of hundreds of eyewitnesses which quickly flooded onto the internet spoke of hours of inactivity, punctuated by short bursts of intense turbulence at isolated locations where forum delegates attempted to run the barrier. These moments provided the sound and fury on which television reporters insist if they are to have a story worthy of air time. They constituted only a fraction of the day's content however, with thousands of people protesting peacefully while trying to stay dry in the morning's downpour. Streakers against globalisation jogged past a swami-for-justice sitting on a bed of nails. Christians prayed, and true believers from One Nation railed against worldwide conspiracy as dreadlocked forest dwellers broke out the drums, rolled some joints and got jiggy with it.

The baton charge to rescue Court, in which one man lost seven teeth, provided much of the broadcast media action. The balance was down to one freelance guardian of the forum delegates' right to assembly – who sailed into a knot of picketers, windmilling his fists until taken to the ground with a bloody nose – and a group of three men tagged as neo-Nazis by some witnesses, and casino security by others. They attacked a thin line of protesters after a brief conversation with nearby police. One was alleged to have used a set of keys held inside his fist as a weapon.

The media, which had been indecently tumescent at the prospect of a week of Seattle-style street warfare just before the Olympics in Sydney, seemed unable to deconstruct their own imagery. Having composed a narrative in which foreign activists joined forces with domestic nutters to sabotage Australia's fifteen minutes of fame, many journalists and almost all commentators were incapable of understanding a simple premise. The vast majority of protesters were, in fact, nonviolent. Many had been trained in nonviolent dissent. Just as many had extensive experience of nonviolent protest. For all of their fearsome imagery, for all of the savage, howling mayhem of protest, the violence, when it came, was initiated by the agents of authority, not by the dissenting citizenry. Citizens do not launch baton charges or mounted attacks. They are the targets of baton charges and mounted attacks.

Allegations of protester villainy did surface, with the *Age* retailing instances of 'fish hooks being dangled from bridges to try to disable police; nuts and bolts being thrown at police; and ball bearings being thrown under police horses' hooves'. The Nine network also carried a story of unidentified anarchists invading an ambulance and assaulting the crew. At no time however, were any of these allegations proved. Indeed, no evidence in support of them was even advanced. No urine-soaked police uniforms were produced. No assaulted ambulance drivers were interviewed. No dangling fish hooks were ever photographed despite the presence of hundreds of still and video cameras. A horse which was supposed to have been stabbed turned out to have a grazed nose, according to police media (most likely sustained in a charge against a picketline full of vegetarian animal rights activists).

This crucial disconnection between the world of real things and the world of fantastic narrative was to prove disastrous as the week progressed. With somewhere between one and two-thirds of conference delegates barred from the casino on the opening day, the rhetoric of press and electronic coverage shifted from a sort of pre-emptive *schadenfreude* to spluttering, belligerent outrage. Tabloid attack dogs and Victorian premier Bracks alike called on the police to bring down the hammer. The protesters were 'unAustralian' (even 'unVictorian') and therefore seemingly unentitled to the due regard of those authorised to use deadly force on behalf of the society they had so publicly betrayed and embarrassed. Bracks was reported to have said that the protesters deserved everything they got. Although he did not elaborate on whether these deserving victims of muscular law enforcement also included those hundreds of school students, previously characterised as innocent victims of a Resistance recruiting campaign, who were also in attendance. Apparently, in crossing over the Rubicon of civil disobedience, they too became unAustralians and thus unworthy of any previous concern for their wellbeing.

I suppose I should guard against a hint of outrage entering my tone. Weary resignation would be more appropriate. For what happened at S11 is an old, old story and I have both heard and written it many times before; in Queensland through the 1980s, at Aidex in Canberra at the turn of the decade, at any number of places in the last ten years – Coffs Harbour, Sydney, Parliament House, the waterfront. I have seen enough political violence to know that far from being unAustralian, it is in fact completely banal. And that rather than being the result of wild, antisocial renegades, it is almost inevitably an outcome of tactical decisions taken by the police commander on the scene, occasionally at the behest of political interests further up the food chain. I also know, down in my meat, that when the beast is unleashed the most dangerous place to be is not on a police line, but in front of one.

My first encounter with a police riot took place in 1989, at the University of Queensland. I was covering a series of demonstrations on that campus for *Rolling Stone* magazine and was lucky enough to be present when about thirty or forty cops stormed a sit-in. The students knew the raid was coming and had voted to carry on the occupation, but only with volunteers. Most wisely abandoned the building. About a dozen remained. Following the advice of the late Tasmanian war correspondent Neil Davis, that it is always safer to go in with the first wave, I charged in with the cops rather than waiting with the occupiers for them to arrive. I wasn't all that surprised at the chaos within. The vicious fights between weedy, underfed college students and Bjelke-Petersen's praetorian guard were predictably one-sided. But I was totally blown out by the sight of one young, probationary constable who was so far gone in the moment, that when he could find nobody to punch, he launched himself at a wall-mounted telephone and ripped it right off its moorings before throwing it to the ground. Perhaps it was an unAustralian telephone.

After that I made the study of police officers during violent demonstrations something of an avocation. I travelled to the National Exhibition Centre in Canberra for the infamous Aidex Arms Fair riots, which I still regard as the most frightening police rampage I have ever personally witnessed. For three days I slept under a bush in a ditch by the side of the road while a medieval caravan of greenies, ferals, vegans and communists fed themselves into a threshing machine. I saw one cop shoot his entire wad, his eyes rolled back to whites, thin lips drawn back from his teeth in a canine grimace as he flayed into a knot of hippies with a riot baton. The nightstick was a blur, like a particularly impressive special effect, which conjured up flying clumps of scalp and gouts of blood wherever he cared to lay it. I saw another cop smashing the head of a female reporter from a community radio station into the side of a police wagon as yet another diverted metres out of his way to crack the kneecap of a woman who had broken through the line and was threatening to carry the demonstration a couple of metres closer to the arms manufacturers ensconced within the Exhibition Centre.

This too was another nonviolent demonstration. Like S11, Aidex was a largely uncoordinated effort by dozens of different groups, most of them green rather than red. Decisions were mediated through a sort of mass fishbowling conference held at the start of each day, with the angry left of the ISO and DSP – or the Socialist Workers Party as I think they still were then – unable to swing the numbers behind a more confrontational approach. Nonviolence was a sort of mantra the majority of protesters invoked to protect themselves from some imagined karmic backlash. Its efficacy against a real world backlash was questionable at best. One of the saddest things I ever saw was a couple of hundred of these poor dumb bastards joining hands and dancing onto the road in front of the Centre, like children playing ring-a ring-a-rosie. A baton charge broke them up in less than ten seconds, hundreds of blows falling on the exposed forearms of the enchanted circle people while the hard core Left, who had opted out of that particular doomed action, watched on with spastic rage.

I have never known the media, which is always prompt with reports of injury to individual police officers and fictional ambulance drivers, to fully detail the casualties on the receiving end of the baton attack. To wander through the camp outside Aidex each day was to bear witness to hundreds of broken ribs, fingers, wrists and jaws amongst an abundance of livid bruises, weeping wounds and black eyes. At S11, volunteer medical staff toted up a similar butcher's bill. One first aid co-ordinator posted to the indymedia website that on the first day at Crown they treated about 130 protester injuries, sending eleven to hospital by ambulance. On the second day, they tallied another 200, with thirty-one hospitalised, before he stopped counting. Most required stitches to the scalp and face, many from baton strikes to the fingers, kidney, liver and breasts (in the case of women). After being interviewed by a Melbourne newspaper the aid worker was upset to find his figures rounded down to about 'twenty hurt' on both days.

Fortunately the atomisation of reportage by the internet has meant that we are no longer hostage to the likes of Kerry Packer's pink-lipped vassal for accounts of such civil atrocities. Cheap digital recording equipment transformed hundreds of witnesses at Crown into reporters. Even those without access to camcorders could and did post extended personal narratives which invariably contradicted the mainstream media's initial reporting. (After a number of journalists were assaulted by the Victorian police their enthusiasm for Steve Bracks' enforcers was noticeably diminished. By late in the week some had even shifted their rhetorical ground enough to openly speculate on topics such as 'police brutality'. It's amazing how much the change from observer to participant can alter one's perspective on these matters.)

Dozens of hotlinked websites now carry thousands of pages of first person narrative and video footage from S11. It would be a great pity if this archive were to be lost to future researchers as I believe it is an infinitely more accurate depiction of what happened there.

A.C., writing on the Melbourne indymedia site, captured some of the frustrating but reasonably peaceful tactics of the police. (The following extracts are reproduced verbatim):

> . . . the day quietens down, but there is a sense of danger that is more palpable than Monday. A sound system is set up at King's Way on the overpass, which is teaming with people. This afternoon at King's Way, police engage in an exercise of psychological warfare designed to confuse, and tire the remaining crowd. Squads of police change formation, march from one entrance to another, put goggles on, remove goggles, display canisters of capsicum spray, put them away . . . the dog squad is brought out and lined up inside the compound. Unfortunately for the cops one of the dogs bites his trainer. Riot police march through a foot overpass back and forth from building to building. It works. The crowd expends its energy running from one entrance to another, is revved up by marshals, engages on one boring chant after the next – in other words reacts exactly as to be expected. It's easy to say this in hindsight, of course. At the time, how do you tell the difference between a formation of riot police designed to psyche you out, and a formation of riot police about to charge?

A young woman named Maya, in an article entitled 'How I was clubbed like some baby seal (or, thank god for the black bloc)', described her panic, and what she thought of as her own cowardice when she realised she was the weak link in a picket-line which would soon be targeted. (The 'black bloc' refers to groups of masked anarchists):

. . . then people were hugging me and telling me I wasn't weak, I was strong and asking if I wanted to go further back or leave altogether. Nothing could have made me leave after that, but a little while later they attacked us and I couldn't hold the line. The truth is, even though I'm not very strong, I wasn't really holding on that tightly. I think I was panicking already. I was panicking. I started panicking the second they moved the Nimbin hippie bus.

. . . One of the cops hit me in the throat with his baton. I went strait down and thought I would be trampled by the police that were running past our former front line. The cop dragged me up by the neck (throat), which at least stopped me being trampled. I was screaming 'I can't breathe, I can't breathe, you're killing me, you're killing me.' Of course I can't identify him. A lot of the riot cops' masks were completely fogged up from their breath.

. . . After about 30 seconds or less, this cop picked me up and threw me backwards. I don't remember all of this. I know I ended up on the ground with a group of other (mostly) women from the bloackade, and a group of at least four or five just went for us. If you could manage to get away, they would drag you back in.

During this, one of the uniformed cops bit me. I have tooth marks in my arm. I don't know if this happened to anyone else. The truth is, I'll never be able to get my head around any of this. At the time he was still yelling 'Get back! Get back!' while he was holding on to me to prevent me getting away.

After the cop bit me I was really, really panicking. Either him or another cop picked me up and threw me at the police line. I wasn't really thinking straight at this point, but we could see that if you got too close to the line, they would just beat you and throw you back in. I was terrified of the cops, I was terrified of the horses, I felt like I was about to die. There was no way I could have gotten out of all that by myself.

Someone grabbed me. I don't know who. I think, (I think) he was with the black bloc. I'm pretty sure I saw a mask or balaclava. Maybe I just think that because I couldn't see his face very well.

But this black bloc guy grabbed me and dragged me through the line and no one touched us. I don't even remember how, but he got me out of the fighting. Maybe he saved me from a broken limb. Maybe he saved my life.

Then he left me with someone else and went back into the fighting.

Thankyou thankyou thankyou thankyou. I hope I'm not overdoing it. I hope this is an appropriate forum to thank you a billion times and still feel it's not enough. I don't think anything is enough . . .

By the third day of the protest, some mainstream journalists, who realised they may have backed a loser on the opening day, began to log on to the independent sites to access this motherlode of alternative data. It is possible that the net's erosion of the old media cartel, organised around the twin poles of the Murdoch and Packer empires, influenced the eventual response of both the cartel and the State. Just as some of the media at last changed tack in the face of a terrible and sustained assault on a small group of dissenting citizens, so too was the political superstructure forced to adjust to a new reality. Steve Bracks began the week by claiming that the protesters deserved everything they got and finished it by inviting the heroes of the emergency services to a State-funded barbecue. But he was soon forced to withdraw the invitation after sections of his own party sided with the churches in condemning the actions of the police. Even the forum delegates began to get the message. Those who managed to attend the first day's much depleted sessions had to accept that theirs may not be the only story worth hearing.

It may be argued then that the violence at Crown had a positive, heuristic effect. Had the protests taken the form preferred by critics like Bracks, Court, and Bob Carr – that is, had they been nothing more than a meaningless piece of irrelevant street theatre which had no discernible effect on the lives of the conference goers – they would have been contemptuously ignored. That is the subtext whenever a politician supports the 'right to protest' as long as it doesn't interfere with the legitimate concerns of others – I think 'people going about their business' is the preferred phrase. To label anyone who demurs from that line as unAustralian is an attempt to define them out of civil society. In the past this proved easier because of a commonality of interest between the owners of the means of communication and the State which protected their interests. (And because those threatening that arrangement were often so easily demonised anyway.) It may prove less so in future with the web providing the demons with their own means of mass communication.

The use of the term 'unAustralian' seemed to cause nearly as much anger online as the tactics of the police. More than one internet correspondent drew out the hypocrisy of political leaders trying to shame the demonstrators for violence which was actually the chosen strategy of the State itself. Australian history is debauched with violence; the institutionalised savagery of the convict era; the massacres of both black and white on the frontier in the nineteenth century; the slaughter at the Eureka Stockade; the anti-Chinese pogroms on the gold fields; the street wars of the Depression between fascist and communist private armies; the civil rights demonstrations in Queensland; the vicious attack by New South Wales police on Sydney's first gay Mardi Gras. These were all defining moments in Australian history, occasions when the nation's cultural narrative stopped and turned and lurched off in a new direction, driven by violent impetus towards light or dark, but always onwards, never back.

Interview with John Birmingham

Question *'S11' is a piece of factual writing, without any pretence at the 'objectivity' traditionally foisted on journalism as a requirement. How important is it to your purpose as a writer that you make your own thoughts and feelings clear?*

Birmingham I never wanted to be a reporter, as such. Although I began my writing career in non-fiction, I purposely steered away from the conventional career path of degree, cadetship, roundsman and so on. I decided to work in fringe publications to begin with, because they afforded me almost complete freedom to frame my stories. One of the major freedoms was that of opinion. I believe that straight, factual, non-biased reporting is very important (but quite rare), but for my own purposes, as an 'activist writer', the autonomy to make judgements quite openly was crucial. As long as I stated my biases up front, the readers were then free to make their own judgements on the content of the story.

The observational details included in 'S11' are tellingly rendered. How important are they to the success of this piece and to non-fiction narrative in general?

Fact selection is of prime importance because every event is infinitely describable. The very act of choosing what to write about within an event imposes an observer effect and can make a mockery of claims to objectivity. In technical terms, inappropriate fact selection will leave you with a boring or misdirected piece which serves your readers poorly. But every selection brings with it the weight of the reporter's own agendas, prejudices, and so on. In that sense, a thorough grounding in traditional techniques of reportage is vital, no matter what your intent as a writer.

As part of its subject matter 'S11' deals with 'the crucial disconnection between the world of real things and the world of fantastic narrative' (as perpetrated by mainstream media coverage). Yet all writers shape the experience they're writing about, make decisions about what to include, whom to interview, what to edit. Were you conscious of that balancing act in writing 'S11'?

I'm conscious of it every time I write. All writers and readers should be. I became aware of the disconnect in my early days of covering demonstrations and riots. The mainstream media had a standard set of procedures for covering such events which did very little to actually explain them. 'S11' is my explanation of that process, based on years of participant/observation.

There is a sense of real anger that comes across in this piece, a sense that you believe important things have gone wrong. To what extent did that drive the piece?

Anger drives all my best writing. As a young writer it had to because I wasn't making much money on the work. In fact, I'd lose money every time I wrote a long piece for a magazine such as *Rolling Stone* because they didn't pay expenses. I considered the loss an investment on my part.

In the context of the fact versus fiction debate, is there a line beyond which creative non-fiction writers cannot go?

Yes. You cannot make stuff up. It is wrong. It is bad. You should be driven from the profession for doing so.

How important is it to remember to be a storyteller?

If you want people to read your stories, it is of paramount importance. Most people are time poor, and are daily bombarded with any number of distractions which can drag them away from a long magazine piece. The harder you make it on your readers, the less of them you will have and the more pointless will be your exertions.

How crucial is the structure to the effectiveness of a story?

Once a piece gets to a certain length (about 1200 words or more) you will be dealing with a complex series of images, ideas, arguments, and so on. If you have not planned out the structure of the piece you will be unable to keep all of those balls in the air and will find yourself lost in your own copy. It may be possible to save the situation with a rewrite or five. But planning the structure before you begin will save you time and make for a much stronger piece.

Is this form of first-person essay/reportage a peculiarly democratic form – in that it offers a way of breaking silence over something in which the writer may have no expertise except as regards their personal experience?

I think that may be right, although we will have to watch how blogging develops over the next few years to make a definitive answer. With the ability to publish online it certainly challenges the hegemony of the mainstream media.

What do you think about profile writing?

I try to avoid profile writing wherever possible, but occasionally an interesting subject or a looming mortgage payment will send me back to the salt mines. The voice of the author is a vexed question in profile writing, because for once it really isn't all about you anymore. That's partly why I avoid them. But they are also conflicted because you tend to be dealing with subjects who are either completely naïve about the publicity machine into which they have fallen, or those who are entirely cynical and manipulative. When the subject such as a politican, celebrity, or business leader is surrounded by the machinery of image creation you find yourself in battle with that machinery as well. It's best left to the experts like Bill Zehme.

Are there writers you particularly admire, or who have greatly influenced you and the course you have taken as a writer?

I was drawn into feature writing by the works of Hunter S. Thompson and Michael Herr. I was kept there by E. Jean Carroll, Pete Hamill and Chip Brown. They're all fine writers who chose to work with non-fiction.

If you could give one piece of advice to up-and-coming writers, what would it be?

Four hours a day reading. Four hours a day writing. Each split up into two hour blocks with a stretch and a cup of tea between.

Arundhati Roy

Booker Prize winner Arundhati Roy began her working life as an architect, before turning to acting and scriptwriting. Since winning the Booker for her first novel *The God of Small Things* she has been writing finely wrought polemical essays, agitating for peace and social justice. In 2004, she accepted the Sydney Peace Prize as a writer rather than an activist, but in 2006 she turned down the literary Sahitya Akademi Award in protest against the Indian Government toeing the US line by 'violently and ruthlessly pursuing policies of brutalisation of industrial workers, increasing militarisation and economic neo-liberalisation'.

WAR TALK: SUMMER GAMES WITH NUCLEAR BOMBS

Arundhati Roy

Frontline, 2002

When India and Pakistan conducted their nuclear tests in 1998, even those of us who condemned them balked at the hypocrisy of Western nuclear powers. Implicit in their denunciation of the tests was the notion that Blacks cannot be trusted with the Bomb. Now we are presented with the spectacle of our governments competing to confirm that belief.

As diplomats' families and tourists disappear from the subcontinent, Western journalists arrive in Delhi in droves. Many call me. 'Why haven't you left the city?' they ask. 'Isn't nuclear war a real possibility? Isn't Delhi a prime target?'

If nuclear weapons exist, then nuclear war is a real possibility. And Delhi is a prime target. It is.

But where shall we go? Is it possible to go out and buy another life because this one's not panning out?

If I go away, and everything and everyone – every friend, every tree, every home, every dog, squirrel, and bird that I have known and loved – is incinerated, how shall I live on? Whom shall I love? And who will love me back? Which society will welcome me and allow me to be the hooligan that I am here, at home?

So we're all staying. We huddle together. We realize how much we love each other. And we think, what a shame it would be to die now. Life's normal only because the macabre has become normal. While we wait for rain, for football, for justice, the old generals and eager boy-anchors on TV talk of first-strike and second-strike capabilities as though they're discussing a family board game.

My friends and I discuss *Prophecy,* the documentary about the bombing of Hiroshima and Nagasaki.[1] The fireball. The dead bodies choking the river. The living stripped of skin and hair. The singed, bald children, still alive, their clothes burned into their bodies. The thick, black, toxic water. The scorched, burning air. The cancers, implanted genetically, a malignant letter to the unborn. We remember especially the man who just melted into the steps of a building. We imagine ourselves like that. As stains on staircases. I imagine future generations of hushed schoolchildren pointing at my stain . . . That was a writer. Not she or he. *That.*

I'm sorry if my thoughts are stray and disconnected, not always worthy. Often ridiculous.

I think of a little mixed-breed dog I know. Each of his toes is a different color. Will he become a radioactive stain on a staircase too? My husband's writing a book on trees. He has a section on how figs are pollinated. Each fig only by its own specialized fig wasp. There are nearly a thousand different species of fig wasps, each a precise, exquisite synchrony, the product of millions of years of evolution.

All the fig wasps will be nuked. Zzzz. Ash. And my husband. And his book.

A dear friend, who's an activist in the anti-dam movement in the Narmada valley, is on indefinite hunger strike. Today is the fourteenth day of her fast. She and the others fasting with her are weakening quickly. They're protesting because the Madhya Pradesh government is bulldozing schools, clear-felling forests, uprooting hand pumps, forcing people from their villages to make way for the Maan Dam. The people have nowhere to go. And so, the hunger strike.[2]

What an act of faith and hope! How brave it is to believe that in today's world, reasoned, non-violent protest will register, will matter. But will it? To governments that are comfortable with the notion of a wasted world, what's a wasted valley?

The threshold of horror has been ratcheted up so high that nothing short of genocide or the prospect of nuclear war merits mention. Peaceful resistance is treated with contempt. Terrorism's the real thing. The underlying principle of the War Against Terror, the very notion that war is an acceptable solution to terrorism, has ensured that terrorists in the subcontinent now have the power to trigger a nuclear war.

Displacement, dispossession, starvation, poverty, disease – these are now just the funnies, the comic-strip items. Our Home Minister says that Nobel laureate Amartya Sen has it all wrong – the key to India's development is not education and health but defense (and don't forget the kickbacks, O Best Beloved).[3]

Perhaps what he really meant was that war is the key to distracting the world's attention from fascism and genocide. To avoid dealing with any single issue of real governance that urgently needs to be addressed.

For the governments of India and Pakistan, Kashmir is not a *problem,* it's their perennial and spectacularly successful *solution.* Kashmir is the rabbit they pull out of their hats every time they need a rabbit. Unfortunately, it's a radioactive rabbit now, and it's careening out of control.

No doubt there is Pakistan-sponsored cross-border terrorism in Kashmir. But there are other kinds of terror in the valley. There's the inchoate nexus between jihadist militants, ex-militants, foreign mercenaries, local mercenaries, underworld Mafiosi, security forces, arms dealers, and criminalized politicians and officials on both sides of the border. There's also rigged elections, daily humiliation, 'disappearances,' and staged 'encounters.'[4]

And now the cry has gone up in the heartland: India is a Hindu country. Muslims can be murdered under the benign gaze of the state. Mass murderers will not be brought to justice. Indeed, they will stand for elections. Is India to be a Hindu nation in the heartland and a secular one around the edges?

Meanwhile the International Coalition Against Terror makes war and preaches restraint. While India and Pakistan bay for each other's blood, the coalition is quietly laying gas pipelines, selling us weapons, and pushing through their business deals. (Buy now, pay later.) Britain, for example, is busy arming both sides.[5] Tony Blair's 'peace' mission a few months ago was actually a business trip to discuss a one-billion pound deal (and don't forget the kickbacks, O Best Beloved) to sell sixty-six Hawk fighter-bombers to India.[6] Roughly, for the price of a *single* Hawk bomber, the government could provide one and a half million people with clean drinking water for life.[7]

'Why isn't there a peace movement?' Western journalists ask me ingenuously. How can there be a peace movement when, for most people in India, peace means a daily battle: for food, for water, for shelter, for dignity? War, on the other hand, is something professional soldiers fight far away on the border. And nuclear war – well, that's completely outside the realm of most people's comprehension. No one knows what a nuclear bomb is. No one cares to explain. As the Home Minister said, education is not a pressing priority.

The last question every visiting journalist always asks me is: Are you writing another book? That question mocks me. Another book? Right *now*? This talk of nuclear war displays such contempt for music, art, literature, and everything else that defines civilization. So what kind of book should I write?

It's not just the one million soldiers on the border who are living on hair-trigger alert. It's all of us. That's what nuclear bombs do. Whether they're used or not, they violate everything that is humane. They alter the meaning of life itself.

Why do we tolerate them? Why do we tolerate the men who use nuclear weapons to blackmail the entire human race?

1. *Prophecy*. 16mm. Nagasaki, Japan: Nagasaki Publishing Committee, 1982.
2. See Aruna Roy and Nikhil Dey, 'Words and Deeds,' *India Together*, June 2002, and 'Stand-Off at Maan River: Dispossession Continues to Stalk the Narmada Valley,' *India Together*, May 2002. Available on-line at http://www.indiatogether.org/campaigns/narmada/. See also 'Maan Dam,' Friends of River Narmada, available on-line at http://www.narmada.org/nvdp.dams/ maan/.
3. 'Nobel laureate Amartya Sen may think that health and education are the reasons why India has lagged behind in development in the past 50 years, but I think it is because of defence,' said Home Minister L.K. Advani. See 'Quote of the Week, Other Voices,' *India Today*, June 17, 2002, p.13.
4. See Human Rights Watch, 'Behind the Kashmir Conflict: Abuses by Indian Security Forces and Militant Groups Continue,' 1999. Available on-line at http://www.hrw.org/reports/1999/kashmir/summary.htm.
5. See John Pilger, 'Pakistan and India on Brink,' *The Mirror* (London), May 27, 2002, p.4. Neil Mackay, 'Cash from Chaos: How Britain Arms Both Sides,' *The Sunday Herald* (Scotland), June 2, 2002, p.12.

6. See Richard Norton-Taylor, 'U.K. Is Selling Arms to India,' *The Guardian* (London), June 20, 2002, p.1. Tom Baldwin, Philip Webster, and Michael Evans, 'Arms Export Row Damages Peace Mission,' *The Times* (London), May 28, 2002. Agence France-Presse, 'Blair Peace Shuttle Moves from India to Pakistan,' January 7, 2002.
7. Pilger, 'Pakistan and India on Brink,' p.4.

David Sedaris

Sedaris' comic writing career began with his reading of his 'Santaland Diaries' – stories about his real-life experiences as a Macy's elf – on National Public Radio's *Morning Edition*. His subsequent books include *Barrel Fever, Holidays on Ice, Dress Your Family in Corduroy and Denim* and *Children Playing before a Statue of Hercules: An anthology of outstanding stories*, as well as the collections of personal essays, *Naked* and *Me Talk Pretty One Day*. In 2001, he won the Thurber Prize for American Humor and was named by *Time* magazine as 'Humorist of the Year'. His essays appear regularly in the *New Yorker* and *Esquire*.

TODAY'S SPECIAL

David Sedaris

Esquire, c. 1999

It is his birthday, and Hugh and I are seated in a New York restaurant, awaiting the arrival of our fifteen-word entrées. He looks very nice, dressed in the suit and sweater that have always belonged to him. As for me, I own only my shoes, pants, shirt and tie. My jacket belongs to the restaurant and was offered as a loan by the maître d', who apparently thought I would feel more comfortable dressed to lead a highschool marching band.

I'm worrying the thick gold braids decorating my sleeves when the waiter presents us with what he calls 'a little something to amuse the palette.' Roughly the size and color of a Band-Aid, the amusement floats on a shallow, muddy puddle of sauce and is topped with a sprig of greenery.

'And this would be . . . what, exactly?' Hugh asks.

'This,' the waiter announces, 'is our raw Atlantic swordfish served in a dark chocolate gravy and garnished with fresh mint.'

'Not again,' I say. 'Can't you guys come up with something a little less conventional?'

'Love your jacket,' the waiter whispers.

As a rule, I'm no great fan of eating out in New York restaurants. It's hard to love a place that's outlawed smoking but finds it perfectly acceptable to serve raw fish in a bath of chocolate. There are no normal restaurants left, at least in our neighborhood. The diners have all been taken over by precious little bistros boasting a menu of indigenous American cuisine. They call these meals 'traditional,' yet they're rarely the American dishes I remember. The club sandwich has been pushed aside in favor of the herb-encrusted medallions of baby artichoke hearts, which never leave me thinking, Oh, right, those! I wonder if they're as good as the ones my mom used to make.

Part of the problem is that we live in the wrong part of town. SoHo is not a macaroni salad kind of place. This is where the world's brightest young talents come to braise caramelized racks of corn-fed songbirds or offer up their famous knuckle of flash-seared crappie served with a collar of chided ginger and cornered by a tribe of kiln-roasted Chilean toadstools, teased with a warm spray of clarified musk oil. Even when they promise something simple, they've got to tart it up – the meatloaf has been poached in sea water, or there are figs in the tuna salad. If cooking is an art, I think we're in our Dada phase.

I've never thought of myself as a particularly finicky eater, but it's hard to be a good sport when each dish seems to include no fewer than a dozen ingredients, one of which I'm bound to dislike. I'd order the steak with a medley of suffocated peaches, but I'm put off by the aspirin sauce. The sea scallops look good until I'm told they're served in a broth of malt liquor and mummified litchi nuts. What I really want is a cigarette, and I'm always searching the menu in the hope that some courageous young chef has finally recognized tobacco as a vegetable. Bake it, steam it, grill it, or stuff it into littleneck clams, I just need something familiar that I can hold on to.

When the waiter brings our entrées, I have no idea which plate might be mine. In yesterday's restaurants it was possible both to visualize and to recognize your meal. There were always subtle differences, but for the most part, a lamb chop tended to maintain its basic shape. That is to say that it looked choplike. It had a handle made of bone and a teardrop of meat hugged by a thin rind of fat. Apparently, though, that was too predictable. Order the modern lamb chop, and it's likely to look no different than your companion's order of shackled pompano. The current food is always arranged into a senseless, vertical tower. No longer content to recline, it now reaches for the sky, much like the high-rise buildings lining our city streets. It's as if the plates were valuable parcels of land and the chef had purchased one small lot and unlimited air rights. Hugh's saffron linguini resembles a miniature turban, topped with architectural spires of shrimp. It stands there in the center while the rest of the vast, empty plate looks as though it's been leased out as a possible parking lot. I had ordered the steak, which, bowing to the same minimalist fashion, is served without the bone, the thin slices of beef stacked to resemble a funeral pyre. The potatoes I'd been expecting have apparently either been clarified to an essence or were used to stoke the grill.

'Maybe,' Hugh says, 'they're inside your tower of meat.'

This is what we have been reduced to. Hugh blows the yucca pollen off his blackened shrimp while I push back the sleeves of my borrowed sport coat and search the meat tower for my promised potatoes.

'There they are, right there.' Hugh uses his fork to point out what could easily be mistaken for five cavity-riddled molars. The dark spots must be my vegetable.

Because I am both a glutton and a masochist, my standard complaint, 'That was so bad,' is always followed by 'And there was so little of it!'

Our plates are cleared, and we are presented with dessert menus. I learn that spiced ham is no longer considered just a luncheon meat and that even back issues of *Smithsonian* can be turned into sorbets.

'I just couldn't,' I say to the waiter when he recommends the white chocolate and wild loganberry couscous.

'If we're counting calories, I could have the chef serve it without the crème fraîche.'

'No,' I say. 'Really, I just couldn't.'

We ask for the check, explaining that we have a movie to catch. It's only a ten-minute walk to the theater, but I'm antsy because I'd like to get something to eat before the show. They'll have loads of food at the concession stand, but I don't believe in mixing meat with my movies. Luckily there's a hot dog cart not too far out of our way.

Friends always say, 'How can you eat those? I read in the paper that they're made from hog's lips.'

'And . . . ?'

'And hearts and eyelids.'

That, to my mind, is only three ingredients and constitutes a refreshing change of pace. I order mine with nothing but mustard, and am thrilled to watch the vendor present my hot dog in a horizontal position. So simple and timeless that I can recognize it, immediately, as food.

Discussion questions

Is the persona assumed in an essay really just the personality of the writer? Or is it a complete invention?

Is there such a thing as the 'common human condition' into which the essayist taps? Or is that an outdated view? Why?

Further reading

The Best American Essays (series), Houghton Mifflin Company, Boston.

The Best Australian Essays (series), Black Inc., Melbourne.

Alexander J. Butrym (ed.), *Essays on the Essay: Redefining the genre,* University of Georgia Press, 1989.

Phillip Lopate, *The Art of the Personal Essay: An anthology from the classical era to the present,* Anchor/Doubleday, 1994.

Brian MacArthur, *The Penguin Book of Twentieth-Century Protest,* Penguin, 1998.

Michel de Montaigne, *Essays*, 1580–1592, Charles Cotton (trans.), available online at *Project Gutenberg,* <http://www.gutenberg.org/etext/3600>.

Chapter 6
Memoir

Examining our own lives

Willa McDonald

We love to read life stories. We read them to escape. We read them to better understand ourselves and the world we live in. We read them to find out how other people manage life, filled as it always is with hardships, challenges and joys. Described as an interrogation of consciousness rather than of fact, memoir is the form of the personal essay that most directly tries to explore and convey a history of the writer's own life and experiences – a job usually done in a more disguised form by fiction.

Consequently, memoir is a particularly grey area in the 'fact or fiction' debate. In part, this is because it deals with that slippery critter 'memory', but also because its construction and concerns come closest on the non-fiction continuum to the 'literary' rather than the journalistic. Philosophers will tell you that language can only signal reality. Policemen and historians will tell you that the memories of eyewitnesses are notoriously unreliable. A person caught in the chaos of a burning building may not correctly remember the number of fire engines that attended. A 25-year-old doesn't remember events in exactly the same way as she experienced them as an 8-year-old. Writers, with all good intentions, may not be able to help but change the memories in recalling them and arranging them into a narrative, even if only in subtle ways.

Honouring the true

Clearly, all stories, non-fiction or otherwise, are constructed. Memoir is no exception. As Helen Garner, the author of 'The Violet Jacket', says in her interview:

> Only a terribly naïve reader believes that a story already exists in nature – that the writer just picks it up, brushes the dirt off it, and puts it in a book. A story is what you get when you mould the mess of everything into a shape . . .

But memoir is not fiction, and the challenges of writing memoir are no excuse to make it so. The basic rule is not to deceive the reader. Memoir is based on real occurrences, real situations. The facts, as best they can be known, must be honoured even though, in this form of the personal essay, they take a backseat. The world of journalism and non-fiction writing is full of cautionary tales about people who have used their writing to lie. Literary and journalistic frauds – Stephen Glass, Jayson Blair, Eric Slater, Barbara Stewart, Leon Carmen, James Frey and the one recorded in this collection, Norma Khouri – litter the past decade, many of the perpetrators having lost their jobs or their publishing contracts because of their fabrications.

Yet, not all embellishment amounts to lying. Pico Iyer reminds us that:

> Bruce Chatwin's books seem to dance around the distinction between fact and fancy. V. S. Naipaul's recent book *A Way in the World* was published as a non fictional 'series' in England and as a 'novel' in the United States. And when some of the stories in Paul Theroux's half-invented memoir, *My Other Life*, were published in *The New Yorker*, they were slyly categorized as 'Fact and Fiction'.[1]

That these writers have successfully moved between invention and fact, and in an exciting way, is largely because the reader understands what the writer intended. Through the choice of subject matter and the way the texts have been constructed, the writing comes closer on our continuum to imaginative, personally interrogative literature, fictional literature. But it's a thin grey line – and writers do well to remember it must be negotiated with skill, clarity and fairness.

Creating a clear contract with the reader

What counts, for readers and critics alike, is the contract that's forged between the writer and the reader and the extent to which that's been honoured. The more the text claims to be reportage, the stronger the expectation on the part of the reader that the story will be both true *and* accurate. Garner famously became the subject of controversy with her book *The First Stone: Some questions about sex and power*,[2] a riveting and beguiling investigation of a sexual harassment incident.

The storm that followed the book's publication was in part caused by the political stance Garner took, but also for reasons of journalistic ethics – in particular that, at the behest of her publishers, she changed one person, Dr Jenna Mead, into six or seven characters to avoid a possible defamation suit. Some readers argued (including Mead in her book *bodyjamming,* written in response to the debate) that the changes wrongly created the impression of a 'feminist conspiracy' and made the text untrustworthy.[3] It raised ire because it claimed in its introduction to be reportage. Says Garner now: 'I did a dumb thing in *The First Stone* . . . It was a loss of nerve, and it distorted the particular story, which I crossly regret, but I don't think it disturbed the thrust of the book's argument.'[4]

The book's polished, observational style and the strength of Garner's personal reflections – factors more commonly found in good fiction – have helped win *The First Stone* a stable of staunch defenders who argue that it stands for a 'truth' that the distortion of some of the facts can't shake – an argument that, as we see in the Malcolm Knox interview, resurfaces frequently in discussions of how memory should be written and read.

Fundamental to how forgiving readers will be is the contract with the reader, the amount of fabrication and the intentions of the author. Two cases illustrate the point. In 1999 it was revealed by the anthropologist David Stoll[5] that the Nobel Peace Prize winning author of the 1982 autobiography *I, Rigoberta Menchú* had changed some of the facts concerning the murders of her family at the hands of Guatemalan security forces.[6] Yet the prize committee allowed her to keep the award because the murders, and the general suffering described, did take place, although not always in the ways depicted. Menchú, it was said, had found a narrative means to tell the story of her people. The changes were minor and didn't contradict the larger 'truth' of her tale.[7]

In contrast is the case of James Frey, the author of the bestselling memoir *A Million Little Pieces*, who was revealed as a fraud in 2006 by *The Smoking Gun*. The book, which had zoomed to the top of the bestseller lists once it was chosen for Oprah's Book Club, was shown to be almost entirely made-up. Frey, however, continues to rationalise his memoir on the grounds that it reflects the 'emotional truth' of his life as an alcohol and drug addict. Many don't agree. In a landmark legal settlement, Frey and his publishers have promised to reimburse any readers who sign a statutory declaration that they believed they were buying a memoir rather than a novel. The distinction between the two clearly exists at law.

Taking honesty as far as it can go

While not all writers would follow the Oprah Winfrey school of baring what might be better left in one's closet, there is a trend in personal essays, particularly memoir, to reveal and explore those parts of the writer's life that society has said must be kept hidden. And it's a trend that has given us strong, moving writing that has expanded the parameters of public discussion.

In 'Tuesday's Child', journalist Kathy Evans describes a landscape of grief and confusion, but ultimately love and joy, that's rarely the subject of discussion in public circles – the birth of a child with Down syndrome. This piece is an example of the way in which memoir has been liberating. This is especially so for women and minorities who might not otherwise have been heard in the mainstream media, or if they were, then in ways that may have been distorted because of the manner in which society allowed certain topics to be discussed or certain language to be used.

Many previously taboo topics – topics that underpin people's lives such as menstruation, intercourse, childbirth – are now written about, and in personal terms not just clinical terms, because changing mores have allowed women to openly describe themselves and their circumstances.[8] Self-revelation can break silence and assert authority.[9] As the writer Audre Lorde said when discussing the usefulness of memoir to black women: 'If we do not define ourselves for ourselves, we will be defined by others – for their use and to our detriment.'[10]

Taking the reader with you

It is always important, even in memoir, that the writer doesn't get in the way of the story. One of the reasons the pieces in this section are convincing is because readers are taken along on the journeys of the writers. As we've seen, the surest way to do this is to *'show, not tell'*. If you re-create the scene, the readers begin to feel emotions because of their *own* memories of similar situations. This doesn't happen if you simply tell the reader what occurred – 'telling' puts the writer in front of the story. It may engage the readers' minds, but not their hearts.

In 'Tuesday's Child', Evans retraces her pregnancy and the birth of her daughter, Caoimhe. By describing, in tangible details, the chronological facts of her experiences, as well as recounting one by one all her questions about the future of her daughter – questions laden with fear, hope, love and sadness – she takes the reader on the narrative path with her, provoking companion emotions in the reader who cannot help but be moved by the force of the story. Evans doesn't labour these emotions. She doesn't wallow in self-pity or pity for her child. She doesn't tell the reader what to feel. Instead, she writes simply about her circumstances, letting readers feel their own way along this journey.

Garner, in 'The Violet Jacket', takes her readers on the same sort of emotional journey. By re-creating the scene in the bushgear shop – through the discriminating use of description and dialogue – she calls up the characters of the shoppers and the young man serving them. By showing us what happened to the friendly boy, line by line, she conveys her feelings about the brief exchange:

> Our eyes met. The sparkle had gone out of his open, cheerful face; it was closed and sombre now. He was carrying in silence the load of the horrible story. I signed quickly, thanked him, took my parcel, said goodbye, and hurried out on to the street.

Garner stirs in the reader corresponding feelings to her own – and in doing so she gives us a world of information about women and the way they chat; about relationships across gender divisions and across generations; about the sympathy and respect she has for the people she encounters; and she subtly sets up her point that men, in general, are to be honoured, not dismissed because of the barbarous actions of the few.

Similarly, Mark Mordue's story 'Pissing in the Wind' would not be as successful if he hadn't re-created for us what it was like for an adolescent to live in a 1970s Northern Territory town:

> My best friend when I was 14 was his younger brother Steven. Steven Stevens. You'd think they coulda come up with something more. He always seemed to be in the shadow of his brother, who hadn't been arrested then, and I didn't understand then what I do today: that there was an anger starting to sprout up inside of him. I can't even remember Steven's face now. Just the sinews on his arms turning tighter. And how there was something prematurely manly about him, as if the boy in him didn't last long.

While the voice of Mordue's teenage self resonates through the essay – reminiscent of Holden Caulfield in *The Catcher in the Rye* – the real narrator is the adult Mordue, the 38-year-old writer living in New York who is remembering his young and naïve self. By telling his coming-of-age tale, Mordue takes us back not only to his boyhood but to our own youth, our own naïveté and confusions, our own need to make hard decisions and learn from our own choices – but also our pleasure in being young and energetic and alive.

Kathy Evans

The story 'Tuesday's Child' won a Walkley Award for Kathy Evans in 2004. Evans had already been a finalist for the award in 2001. Born in North Wales in 1966, she trained as a journalist on her local evening paper, later becoming a feature writer for national papers, based firstly in London and then in Dublin. In 1996 she moved to Melbourne and became a senior feature writer with the *Sunday Age*. She is currently living in Co. Down, Northern Ireland, with her partner and three children, where she is writing her first book based on her experiences of having a child with Down syndrome.

TUESDAY'S CHILD

Kathy Evans

Sunday Age, September 28, 2003

Let me start by saying that Conor and I are good parents. Everyone says so. When our third daughter was born with Down Syndrome, the same sentiment echoed through the congratulation cards; it couldn't have happened to a nicer family.

We appreciated the comments and the spirit in which they were made. They were attempts to be consoling by people who were lost for words, not knowing whether to offer congratulations, or commiserations. Still, sifting through the cards in the aftermath of our crisis, Conor remarked dryly: 'Next time I'm coming back as a Complete Bastard.'

Not that either of us believes in an afterlife. That's our problem, Conor and I, we're devout atheists. At this moment of reckoning in our life, when people turn to their faith for support, we couldn't even draw comfort that Caoimhe was the baby that God had sent us or that this was our Fate; there was no spiritual buffer. No, we had been starkly confronted by a random act of the universe, Caoimhe McCooey was the one in seven hundredth baby born with Down Syndrome, and suddenly our lives had changed forever.

It was, we reflected later, as if we had gone on a road trip, lost the map and ended up in a town inhabited by aliens. Overnight we had entered the strange new world of disability where up until now, my only acquaintance with such places had been occasionally sneaking into a wheel chair allocated parking spot.

We had spent months agonising over whether to have a third child. We already had two headstrong, capricious yet delightful daughters, and wondered what a third child could bring. But the primal urge to reproduce eventually drowned out the small, but insistent voice of reason at the back of my mind which banged on about lack of money and time, and last October I became pregnant. Right from the start there was something wrong. First, a low, nagging pain, and then a blood test which revealed the levels of human Chorionic Gonadotrophin, the hormone needed to sustain this pinprick of life, were

rising at a snail's pace. An ultrasound at six weeks showed our baby, a tiny star in a vast black universe winking down at us from the monitor. Next to her, a puddle of grey spilled across the screen like the Milky Way. I was bleeding internally and was, as the medical jargon puts it, about to 'spontaneously abort'.

I was devastated. Even at this early stage she was still my baby. I went home, wrote her a letter and waited for the inevitable. It never happened. Instead, a vague sickness crept over me, which grew stronger and stronger as the days passed. An eight-week scan showed a healthy embryo with a strong heartbeat and a 90 per cent plus chance of survival.

We decided not to have the 11-week tests for Down Syndrome. At that point, we were just thankful she'd survived. Termination, with its jumbled spaghetti of ethics and emotions, was not something we could contemplate. And of course, we believed it would never happen to us. For a start, I was only 35, at the crest of fertility's slippery slope. I ate well, didn't drink, didn't smoke, and was physically healthy. How naive I was! Now I know that 80 per cent of babies with Down's are born to women under 35, who, perhaps like me, believe the odds are strongly in their favour.

We did have the 18-week scan. The doctor who performed it raved about the new technology which showed our baby pirouetting in the womb in glorious colour 3D. Conor thought she looked perfect, but when a close-up of her face loomed large on the screen, I couldn't help but exclaim, 'Blimey she looks like Spud from *Bob the Builder*.'

The name stuck. From then on, my bump was known as Spud. We bought clothes for Spud, made plans for Spud. In my fantasies I saw her with red hair cascading down her back, long, delicate fingers running up and down the piano with an effortless grace that I had never acquired in all my years of practice. My daughters painted endless pictures of Spud. Spud on a horse. Spud going shopping. Spud in her pram. And as the due date got nearer and nearer, they'd ask, 'Will Spud come out today?'

Spud needed a proper name. Her Irish father was determined it would be Gaelic and we decided to call her Caoimhe (pronounced Keeva) which means grace.

On Tuesday, June 17, at five-o clock in the afternoon, in the middle of a clothes shop in North Brighton, I went into labour, six days overdue. Not the gradual escalation of pain, but sharp peaks erratically spaced. I went home and played the piano, crashing out disharmonious chords which crescendoed with each contraction. At 10 pm, we headed for the hospital. In that drunken euphoric state of active labour, I remember chanting: 'Tuesday's child is full of grace'. At 11.45 pm, my friend Annabel who was acting as birth attendant said: 'If you want this child to be born on a Tuesday, you'd better hurry up.' Caoimhe emerged eight minutes later.

She was beautiful. At seven pounds three ounces, she was smaller than my second child, bigger than my first. There was nothing to suggest anything was wrong. She wriggled and grimaced with all the vigour of a typical newborn who had been rudely evicted. And when she opened her huge eyes I could see they were slate blue, with the promise of hazel, like her sisters.

I held her to my breast but for some reason, she couldn't suck. The next morning I was still struggling to get her to feed. A midwife, whose face remains seared on my brain, casually asked me if I'd had had any screening tests in pregnancy. Puzzled, I asked her why she wanted to know, and she told me it was believed my baby had Down Syndrome.

Heavy words, so lightly thrown. It couldn't possibly be true. I snatched up Caoimhe and looked at her. How could I have not seen it? Her beautiful eyes were indeed slanted, her tiny ears folded down at the tops. From that point on, it was as if Spud had evaporated and a changeling placed in the crib. Whenever I looked at this strange new baby, I could no longer see her beauty, just her defects.

No one at the hospital really seemed to know what to do from that point. It was left up to me to break the news to Conor. He'd taken our two daughters out to celebrate with chocolate cake and baby chinos, and came home to find my broken message on the answering machine. Naturally he was devastated. In some ways it was harder for him. While I could allow myself the luxury of tears cocooned from the humdrum of everyday reality, he struggled to be stoic for the sake of our two daughters.

The rest of the week passed in a blur. The public hospital was a busy, bustling place but I felt suspended in time. Staff came and went, watering the roses, collecting food trays, slipping in and out like shadows. My feelings of grief and sadness, and overwhelming sense of isolation felt so out of place on a maternity ward where happiness hangs like thick smog. On the second night, the mother in the next bed held a party to celebrate the birth of her first child. As the champagne corks popped, and the cameras flashed, I stifled sobs into my pillow for the baby I hadn't had.

Conor and I were left alone to deal with the nuclear fall out of our dreams. On reflection, I find it ironic that couples agonising over whether to terminate a foetus with Down Syndrome are offered counselling by trained professionals, whereas we hardly got as much as a cup of tea. There was a general awkwardness among the staff when it came to talking about her diagnosis; or else it was ignored completely. Maybe I came across as a person who was coping, whereas inwardly, I was flooded with the strangest sensations. Grief, anger, disappointment, fear and an overwhelming love for this tiny creature who was still my child, and who was struggling with the very basic survival skill of sucking. Every minute was spent trying to get her to feed, but her low muscle tone made it achingly difficult. I felt so helpless after each attempt left us both angry and confused.

Sitting with her on my lap, stroking the muscles of her cheeks and throat in an attempt to stimulate a reflex, there were fleeting moments when I hated her for being different. I felt impatient with her for not being able to do something so basic, and terrified that this was a pattern that was going to be recreated all her life.

How old would she be before she was toilet trained? Would she be able to read and write? Hold a conversation? I wanted to know everything about Down Syndrome, but I was too terrified to find out. The nurses gave us a badly printed handout from the internet, but the words ran off the page, and didn't make sense anyhow.

I managed to absorb the fact that Caoimhe had standard Trisomy 21, which meant that in every cell of her body lurked an extra chromosome ready to cause potential damage. I could still manage a twisted smile to think of all the years I've militantly refused to buy genetically modified food, yet I'd given birth to a genetically modified child.

As the days passed, I continued to struggle with the breastfeeding, with little support. I remember feeling incensed when one of the midwives called her lazy. I knew nothing about Caoimhe's condition, but I could see her gamely trying to latch on and I could feel her frustration when each attempt failed.

There were blissful moments too. When the ward was quiet, Conor and our two girls had gone home, and I could look down at her and she was just my beautiful baby with perfect skin and big dark eyes. It was like the two of us were encased in a safe warm bubble, but then thoughts of the future would barge into my mind like a gatecrasher at a party and the moment would be lost.

I couldn't equate this perfect child with my image of a person with Down Syndrome. I feel embarrassed now, twelve weeks down the track, with my ignorance. But I have had very little contact with anyone with the condition, and my images were outdated. Growing up in a small village in the north of England, there had been a home for the mentally handicapped on the periphery and I'd seen them there. Badly dressed, overweight men and women with pudding bowl haircuts, who talked funny. People to be feared and avoided.

Nobody wants that for their child. I felt like the 13th fairy from Sleeping Beauty had come along and cast a wicked spell. For Down Syndrome strikes at the heart of society's two most valued attributes; looks and intelligence. Needless to say, I was ashamed of such thoughts. I'd worked hard to bury my prejudices and develop some sort of godless spirituality. Neither *Hi-5* nor Barbies are encouraged in our house because I do not want my girls to grow up obsessed by their appearance. But look at me now! Crying because my youngest daughter may end up with a bull neck.

Four days passed in the hospital, with me struggling to contain my intense and ambivalent feelings, not to mention the incessant thoughts which ricocheted around my brain like boiling bubbles in a closed pan. On the fifth day she came home and we attempted to reconstruct family life from the wreckage of our crashed hopes. I remain eternally grateful to friends who rallied round with their quiches, cooked dinners, and bottles of wine, who'd take our children on outings to give us space to grieve, without expecting anything in return. Conor and I are both private people who up till now have been crap at asking anyone for help, even each other. We felt gauche and awkward in the face of such kindness; our vulnerability made us cringe.

Slowly we began taking bigger forays into the world of Down Syndrome, only to beat a hasty retreat when we inevitably bit off more than we could chew. We'd go to the local library and arm ourselves with books we were too afraid to read. The higher incidence of disease and illness to which Caoimhe was prone, read like a shopping catalogue. Heart problems, respiratory infection, leukemia, epilepsy, blah blah. Like children watching a horror movie we'd peep through latticed fingers at the black and white photos contained within the pages and then cover our eyes. I could only go so far before casting the book aside in favour of a Jilly Cooper blockbuster I'd also picked up to cushion the shock. How lovely it was at the end of the day to run away to Larkshire, where all the people were sleek and gorgeous and the only thing they cared about was humping each other.

The problem was that the literature we found was woefully outdated. Reading the bibliographies at the back of one book, with titles such as *Bernard: bringing up our mongol son* and *Johnny's so bright, what a shame he's retarded*, left us bleating with laughter whereas just a few months ago, we'd have been too politically correct to see the humour. Conor reckoned it was like Irish jokes, only the Irish are allowed to tell them. Similarly it was OK for us to laugh because we were now part of this world. Black humour, but then there is no place where laughter is more needed than in the dark.

We lost count of the number of people who kept telling us that babies with Down's are 'happy and loveable', which was like being offered a consolation prize on school sports day. It annoyed me because I felt it denied Caoimhe the chance to be seen as an individual with her own personality. I didn't want her to belong to a homogeneous group of happy halfwits.

She is a jolly baby, but so were her sisters. In fact, if it wasn't for the obvious physical differences, there isn't much to set her apart. So far, she has reached all the expected milestones and slowly we are daring to dream.

When she started babbling – early too – I proudly joked about her being the first person with Down's to graduate from Monash. In Ireland a teenage girl with Trisomy 21 was in the newspaper last week after scoring three As in her Inter-cert (Year 10) exams. Perhaps we are only on the cusp of realising what these people can do given the chance.

Still, the worry remains. There are so many questions we long to ask but are too afraid of the answers. The nights are the worst, when life's existential questions rain down like a meteorite shower. Who will look after her when Conor and I die? The natural order of life sees your child gradually unravel from your apron strings till they are mature independent adults. People sigh about their children growing up too fast, but I panicked at the thought of Caoimhe being with us for good. I know there is sheltered housing for people with disabilities which gives them semi-independence, but I imagine I'd never stop worrying if she was OK.

Would I come to terms with the disappointment? Ours is a society that is used to getting what it wants and while we can tolerate and accept people like Caoimhe, nobody actually wants a child with a disability. Pre-natal screening and terminations exist to relieve us of the fear of difference and the pain, heartache and responsibility, which go with it. Here, in the midst of a reproductive heatwave, the fertility gods can design babies right down to their eye colour. Sperm sold on the internet boasts of its owner's high IQ. Perhaps mine are the misshapen memories of youth, but as a child I saw more people with Down Syndrome than I do today. I worry that by the time Caoimhe emerges into adulthood children like her will be gone forever.

Paradoxically, the future is brighter today for people with Down Syndrome than it's ever been. The average life expectancy is 55 plus, and there is a whole smorgasbord of experts out there who can help my child live as normally as possible. At 10 weeks into life she is already hooked up with a physiotherapist and speech pathologist. Chances are she'll attend the same state school as her sisters. I can't help wonder what it would be like for her, though, to be the only child in the class with Down Syndrome. I worry she'll be the butt of playground teasing. Sometimes in my mind's eye I see her as a teenager, boarding a bus and everyone staring at her. I see her trying to buy an ice cream and being laughed at as she struggles to count her money. I see her wanting to look like the pop diva of the day, and crying because she never will. But these are piffling concerns compared with others I have. They are too scary to voice.

Meanwhile, I throw myself into early intervention programs. With my other two daughters, I took all their milestones for granted. They were both early movers and shakers without much input from me. I thumbed my nose at the so-called educational toys and left them to play with their imagination. Now I'm filling the house with brightly coloured squishy rattles that ping and buzz and mobiles that play canned lullabies. I read somewhere that listening to Baroque music can improve the number of brain synapses, and Bach's rhythmic, methodic counterpoints fill the space between conversations in every room. Bach at breakfast, Bach at bathtime, Bach at bedtime. Baching mad.

Sometimes I wonder if the therapy is about helping her, or me, by making her more acceptable to a critical society and giving me something to focus on. I had no say in constructing a child with her condition, but I can play a part in how she develops. Yet in doing so, I sometimes wonder uneasily if I'm creating a child who is too sophisticated for institutions, but still too vulnerable for the real world.

I hope in time as her personality continues to emerge, I will get better at separating the child from the condition. My two daughters can help me with this. When the time was right, I told them as matter-of-factly as I could, that Caoimhe had a condition called Down Syndrome and would learn everything that they learnt, but in a different way. The next week my eldest child stood up in front of her class and told everyone about her little sister whom she accepts unconditionally.

Will my sadness ever leave? Probably not, I decided. It will continue to be trammelled by a whole host of other feelings most of all joy. Time, that great Band-Aid, will see emotions shake and settle like the flakes in a child's snow dome.

I guess that's why I am writing this. To make sense of the senseless, to create some order from the chaos in my head, so perhaps I can sleep at night. The days are too busy to pay attention to the incessant thoughts, which form a continual backdrop of interference. So far, Caoimhe's life's been a conveyor belt of tests and appointments which provide reassurance, but leave little time for me to get on with the job of mothering. It takes a plethora of professionals to raise a child with a disability and I can't help but feel at times that my nose has been put out of joint, my role diluted.

Still, we've come a long way in a short time. A lot of my initial fears remain unfounded, as is so often the case. People ask if I wished I'd have discovered her condition in pregnancy but the answer remains an emphatic no.

Fear permeates our perceptions, it is easy to be afraid of the unknown, to create monsters where there are none to be found. From the very beginning, holding her has been my strength. I can bury my nose in her neck and she will grab my finger. In these moments, nothing else matters.

I've ceased to anticipate what people might think. I used to dread people's reactions, especially the elderly. I envisaged a weathered face peering in the pram, buckling with shock, and a voice exclaiming, 'Oh! a mongol!' But when Conor wheeled her down to the local milk bar the old lady who runs it merely smiled and said: 'What beautiful eyes.'

There are people who don't know what to say, who stumble over comments about her lack of hair, her tiny size. But there are plenty that admire her beauty, who can see beyond the physical traits that go with Down's, to find Conor's cheeks, my mouth, an expression of her sister's.

I look at my baby, with her beautiful almond eyes, and her slow smile, which starts at the top and spreads downwards so that her whole face beams. All my fears are momentarily quashed, my prejudices melt away. She raises her hands and waves her fingers with all the grace of a Balinese dancer. They are beautiful fingers, long and tapered. Just right for playing the piano. We are back in our bubble, Caoimhe and I, and life is good. The feelings that wrap around my bones are blissful; they warm the very core of my existence. Beautiful girl, we are so lucky to have you. I don't know where she fits in society, but a family is a world in microcosm. And I do know that right here, right now, she fits perfectly within my arms.

Helen Garner

Helen Garner has been described as Australia's foremost non-fiction writer, although she has worked extensively as a novelist, journalist, reviewer and screenwriter. After a string of publicly acclaimed novels, including *Monkey Grip*, *Honour and Other People's Children*, *The Children's Bach* and *Cosmo Cosmolino*, she published her first book of non-fiction, the controversial *The First Stone,* in 1995. Other works of non-fiction have followed – the collections *True Stories* (1996) and *Feel of Steel*, as well as *Joe Cinque's Consolation*. In 1993, she won a Walkley Award for her feature for *Time* magazine about the death of 2-year-old Daniel Valerio.

THE VIOLET JACKET

Helen Garner

Age, 1993

In Hobart, on my way to a more remote spot for some walking, I went to a bushgear shop to buy myself a waterproof jacket. A young man in his early twenties served me, friendly and knowledgeable. He showed me a jacket of a pretty violet colour. 'It's specially designed for women,' he said. 'The sleeves are not too long, but they come right down over your wrists, to keep you warm. And the whole thing isn't too . . . voluminous.'

I put it on.

'See how it's made?' he said. 'They've sewn it so that even when your rucksack strap comes across here, in front on your shoulder, you can still get things out of your top pockets.'

'How clever – isn't it clever!' I was zipping and unzipping and ripping the strips of velcro. I got it all done up and swanned about in it, in front of the long mirror. The young man laughed. Together we admired the ingenuity of the jacket, its simple practicality, the outcome of somebody's careful thought. The price tag made me wince, but I said, 'I'll take it.'

As I slipped it off, I noticed among the wall display of heavy hiking boots a strange shoe, which was dangling toe down, hooked to a peg by a little loop of leather stitched to its heel. Its upper was of stiff cloth firmly laced, and its sole was made of black rubber, moulded so closely to the curves of a human instep that it looked as light and tight as a ballet slipper, but tougher: springy, graceful and peculiar. 'What sort of shoe is that?'

'It's for rock-climbing.'

'You'd think it was made for a dancer,' I said. 'It's strong, but it's almost dainty.'

'Beautiful, isn't it,' he said, taking it down and passing it to me. 'You have to buy them tight. Your foot has to be right up against the end, so that when you get the top of the shoe over a hold, your toes are over it as well. You have to be able to get a *grip*.' He made clawing movements with his bent fingers, laughing, and glanced back over his shoulder as if into a yawning chasm. My hair stood on end. I put the shoe back on its hook and followed him to the counter.

'Are you going walking?' he said.

'Yes – do you think the weather will be good?'

He flashed me a joyful look. 'Last weekend I was down at Freycinet,' he said, 'and I could see snow on the Hazards! Maybe you'll be lucky!'

At the cash register a woman customer was telling the other shop assistant, also a woman, that she had just that morning got out of doing jury duty.

'Didn't you want to do it?' I asked.

'I would have – but I was challenged.'

'Why?'

She shrugged. The woman assistant and I ran our eyes up and down her. She was in her forties, with a lot of flustered wiry blonde hair and a big smiling mouth full of uneven teeth. She wore a rain jacket, a money belt, heavy boots.

'Maybe you looked a bit . . . alternative?' I suggested.

'Or were they getting rid of the women?' said the assistant. 'Was it a rape case, maybe?' she shuddered. 'I'd hate to have to do a rape case. I'd be so outraged – I don't think I'd be able to be objective. Or imagine if you were on the jury of that bloke who killed his wife and cut up her body into pieces.' She lowered her voice. 'He put bits of her down the drain. Some of her he put into a blender.'

We three women looked at each other without speaking, our eyebrows raised and our lips stretched back off our clenched teeth, through which we sharply sucked in air.

'A friend of mine,' continued the woman shop assistant, who was wearing spectacles with unusual, sophisticated frames, 'knows someone who knew the social worker that the wife went to. Apparently the social worker warned her. The wife came to her and said, "I'm leaving him." And the social worker said, "Well, get help – because you could be in real danger." But the wife said, "Don't worry. I can handle it." '

'She *told* people he was violent,' cut in the rejected juror passionately, 'she *told* people, but no one would do anything about it.'

During this exchange, the young man was right in the middle of us, shoulder to shoulder with his colleague, working modestly and efficiently, keeping his eyes down and filling out the credit card docket, folding my new coat and sliding it neatly into a big paper bag with string handles. He waited till there was a pause, then handed me the pen, to sign.

Our eyes met. The sparkle had gone out of his open, cheerful face; it was closed and sombre now. He was carrying in silence the load of the horrible story. I signed quickly, thanked him, took my parcel, said goodbye, and hurried out on to the street.

There are two men in this story. Two. Out of all the many sorts of men that exist in the world. And so I'm determined that I will acknowledge and value and remember the young man who laughed with me and showed me the clever jacket and the beautiful shoe, for at least as long as I'll remember the other one, the murderer and dismemberer.

Interview with Helen Garner

Question *Did you set out to write 'The Violet Jacket' with a particular intent?*

Garner 'The Violet Jacket' encounter happened in 1993, at a time when I was already engaged in two other pieces of writing, one big and one small. At home in Melbourne, I was researching the book that would eventually become *The First Stone*. I didn't have a publisher's advance for the book yet, so I had to keep on making my usual between-books living from feature journalism: a travel magazine had sent me to Tasmania to write a piece about a new eco-tourist resort. I was already up to my neck in work – certainly not on the look-out for more.

After I'd bought this pretty Gore-Tex jacket in Hobart, I drove down to the eco-tourist resort. I was supposed to slog over a small mountain and round a couple of bays, eat the resort food, sleep two nights in a handsome little timber cabin, and write a couple of thousand words about the whole experience. But as soon as I put down my bag in the cabin, I was attacked by an irresistible urge to write about the conversation I'd had in the outdoor gear shop where I'd bought the jacket.

In other words, I didn't *choose* the story. It got hold of my lapels and shook me till I paid it full attention.

It's a long time ago. I don't recall what I thought the story was going to be about, when I set up my typewriter to have a bash at it. This is something that has happened to me over and over again, but that I still can't get my head around: you can sit down with one sort of story in mind, and when you get up, hours later, you find it's come out completely different. Of course it's ultimately your job to shape the story, but you also – at least at the start – have to let it guide you. You have to 'let the unconscious take precedence', as Jung says somewhere.

Anyway, I do recall how it felt to be sitting there in that cabin, crouching over the typewriter while I was supposed to be writing something else. It was a painful and obsessive feeling.

For a year I'd been trying to get a handle on the *First Stone* story. I was struggling to make sense of a certain kind of contemporary campus feminism, which I hated and was afraid of. It had an unforgiving, punitive tone to it, and it gloried in women's victimhood. The story of a bloke who'd murdered and dismembered his wife would have fitted neatly into the way such feminists seemed to see the world – and naturally I'd felt a spontaneous female comradeliness with the other two women at the shop counter – it was such a brutal and disgusting crime.

But what hurt me, in the shop that day, was the way the light went out of the face of the friendly young guy who was selling me the jacket. As soon as we women began to talk about the murder, he gave up his claim to a share in the conversation. He deferred to us. The look on his face showed that he was just as appalled by the crime as we were, but his opinion was not invited. All his wit and openness couldn't prevail. Because he was a man, he was closed out of the encounter. And I hated being a part of that.

OK. I can spell out the meaning of it now, thirteen years later, but that day, when I had the urge to write it down, I was still under the spell of the actual people I'd met in the shop, what they looked like, their hair, their teeth, their boots, their glasses; what they'd said, and what expressions passed over their faces while they were saying it. I was still enchanted by 'The Violet Jacket' and the rock-climbing shoe. Material things that engage my senses are what make me want to write. I never start with an idea. I always start with things, including people. Ideas ooze up between the cracks.

You are known for the economy of your style, the exactness of your writing – how important is that to you?

I don't want sub-editors to be hacking my stuff, so before I file it I cut it back as hard as I can. For a year I wrote a weekly column with a limit of 770 words. That was fabulous discipline. It's amazing how much of what you write is throat-clearing. You can almost always throw out the whole first page. Have no mercy. You have to learn to cut till it bleeds.

You use dialogue to great effect in 'The Violet Jacket' – firstly in creating the character of the young man, and secondly in the discussion of male violence amongst the women. Obviously, dialogue is central to much journalism. How useful is it to you as a non-fiction writer?

I adore dialogue. The way people speak makes me dizzy with joy – all those curls and leaps and sudden silences. But there's a great art in quoting. My hero, the American writer Janet Malcolm, is brilliant on this in *The Journalist and the Murderer:* 'Only the most uncharitable (or inept) journalist will hold a subject to his literal utterances and fail to perform the sort of editing and rewriting that, in life, our ear automatically and instantaneously performs.' The art of it is in choice, but also a kind of inspired and totally legitimate mimicry. And there are times when you have to paraphrase, or the reader will die of boredom. I learnt this the hard way when I was writing *Joe Cinque's Consolation* – I had to précis a barrister's whole submission in a murder trial, but still make it sound like talking. Hardest work I've ever done. But it gave me a terrific sense of being in command.

How crucial to the writing are the details and descriptions you have included?

I'm always trying to arrange material objects and events and dialogue on the page in such a way that *they* do the heavy lifting, so I won't have to interpret or pontificate. This is a fictional technique, I suppose. I want to haul readers right into the text. Push them right up against the people and the situation – make them feel and smell things, so they have to react.

There is a musical quality in your writing that seems to suggest you deliberately write for the ear. Is that so?

There's a lot you can achieve emotionally, if the sentence sounds right. I read everything out loud so it'll make sense aurally, and be pleasing or purposely jarring. I don't like sounds or words to repeat themselves except for a reason. I want to be in control of the music of it. If I spot a repetition that I missed in editing, I kick myself. I don't like the last two lines of 'The Violet Jacket', for example. The ending feels clumsy, and truncated. I wish I'd rounded it off with a couple more words, something graceful, to make it sing.

An underlying theme of some of your non-fiction work is the idea that men also occasionally need protecting – that not all men are bad and that they too can be victimised by women – e.g. The First Stone, The Consolation of Joe Cinque. *Is 'The Violet Jacket' an early glimpse of an enduring concern of yours?*

Like most women, I complain a lot about the awful things men do, and I was hopeless at being married, but on the whole – specially now I'm in my 60s and living happily without one – I like men. I greatly enjoy their company, and would like to get on with them. I have quite a few men friends of my daughter's generation, and I observe their struggles with a sympathy that wasn't available to me when I was still out there in the world of sex and marriage and romantic love. I can see their delicacy, and their decency, and their particular way of suffering. I find it moving.

You are recognised as the foremost non-fiction writer in Australia and at the same time your much admired feature writing has won you the national Walkley Award for Journalism. What do you think of the much discussed divide between the two in terms of literature? Are they really so different?

In my experience the differences are largely ones of scale. Also, I'm aware that my feature stories are going to be read much more skimmingly than my non-fiction books. I couldn't count the number of times people have said to me, 'I really loved your story last week, the one about – uhm – what was it about, again?' At least with a book you know a reader's probably going to remember a bit more about it – that you haven't poured all that energy into tomorrow's fish and chip wrappers.

One thing you don't do that journalists are so often urged to do is to pretend to be objective or to hide behind a litany of facts. You always take a position and your presence is always strong in your work. Could you write any other way?

Maybe I *could*, but the question is, would I want to? Janet Malcolm says, and I think she's right, 'The "I" in journalism is almost pure invention'. It's a persona, a mask – a device you can use, partly to get yourself past certain ethical roadblocks (you can say 'I wanted to find out X, but I wasn't able to, so I'm telling you why I couldn't, and what I think that failure means, and where it leaves me vis à vis the story') and partly to hold up for scrutiny your own personal response to the story, so that readers can compare it with theirs – fruitfully, you hope.

Much important journalism has been done by people who have also taken strong positions (Knightley on thalidomide, Pilger on Cambodia, Fisk on the Middle East). Yet traditional journalism is less overtly personal. Do you see a difference between what you are trying to achieve and what those sorts of journalists are doing?

Yes, a huge difference. They are political writers who have urgent international arguments to run, backed by massive and risk-taking external research. I'm much more of a fiction writer who has moved sideways into non-fiction. I'm interested in smaller, closer, more personal stories, and if they involve a crime and thus fan out in the end into something with broader relevance, it's not because I planned it that way. I don't start with a political or world-changing aim, and I never will. I just respond to the very small, intimate worm of curiosity.

A feature of your work is that you interrogate your own thoughts and feelings as much as the situation and people you are writing about. How important is that to your purpose as a writer?

People don't want to hear this, I suppose, but my initial urge is to make sense of things, through writing and all its weird skills and manoeuvres, for *myself*. I'm trying first of all to save myself. From the chaos and terror of meaninglessness. The only way I know how to do this is by writing. Every other purpose follows on from that. And I bet this is true of the Fisks and Pilgers of this world, too, except that they'd probably never admit it.

What about the need to be a storyteller in the context of concerns raised in the fact vs fiction debate in recent years? For example, there is an emotional honesty in 'The Violet Jacket'. Would it matter if you tweaked an anecdote in some way if those changes helped to move the story along but that emotional honesty was still there?

All writers tweak things all the time. Only a terribly naïve reader believes that a story already exists in nature – that the writer just picks it up, brushes the dirt off it, and puts it in a book. A story is what you get when you mould the mess of everything into a shape. Huge amounts of labour are required to make a story. There are lines that you know it would be distorting and immoral to cross. There is a contract, in non-fiction: you're saying, *Trust me, this really happened*. It must be maddening to hear writers keep saying this, but the rules can't be carved in stone. The line has to be drawn free-hand every time, and the writer is accountable, even if only to her own conscience.

Have your opinions on that changed since the controversy that surrounded the publication of The First Stone*?*

I did a dumb thing in *The First Stone*. One person involved in the story worked very hard behind the scenes to stop me from writing it, and made a lot of threatening noises. What I wrote about her was supported by plenty of reliable evidence, but because the publisher feared that she might sue me, I called her by a different name every time she appeared in the text. It was a loss of nerve, and it distorted the particular story, which I crossly regret, but I don't think it disturbed the thrust of the book's argument. When the book was published she took pride in identifying herself publicly, so it all back-fired!

You seem to have been writing more non-fiction than fiction in recent years. Is there a reason for that?

I didn't want to be in rivalry with a novelist I was married to. So I shifted off the common turf. It was unconscious at the time, of course – but blindingly obvious when I look back. The marriage ended anyway; so now I would like to jump back across the border to fiction, but I'm worried that I've forgotten how to do it. Non-fiction suits me, though. I love poking my nose into other people's business. Fiction is awfully lonely. You have to pull it out of your guts, like a spider. With non-fiction you can spend hours, weeks, months in rooms with total strangers, watching them work. What a privilege!

If you could give one piece of advice to up-and-coming writers, what would it be?

Read. Read, read, read. Practise every day. And don't use too many adverbs.

Mark Mordue

Mark Mordue is a writer and journalist whose work has appeared in many leading Australian news and literary publications, as well as in a range of international magazines – *The Nation*, *Salon*, *Madison* and *Speak* in the USA, *Melody Maker* and *Sight + Sound* in the UK, *Purple* in France and the *Kyoto Journal* in Japan. He was the founding editor of *Australian Style* (1992–97) and in 1992 was awarded a Human Rights Media Award for his journalism. In 2001 he was the Asialink writer-in-residence at Beijing University. Mordue's first book, a collection of travel stories, is called *Dastgah: Diary of a headtrip*.

PISSING IN THE WIND

Mark Mordue

Purple, 1999

You know whenever I put Neil Young on the stereo, I find myself fifteen years old, learning to drive on the long free roads of Australia's Northern Territory, a bauxite redness in the land and the pale, ghost greys and lean tawns of the gum trees jittering past like wilting bones. The air seems to burn in the bush, to crackle in the sun, hot breath in an old man's ribcage. Nothing is moving, but the whole place seethes. This big, vast silence, crackling, while 'Ambulance Blues' pumps on the cassette player and my mother has to keep seizing the wheel and pulling it towards her as I keep getting hypnotised by oncoming cars, drifting toward them as I watch them approach. Took me a while to get the hang of watching where I was going. Watch the fucking road, for god's sake, watch the road. Jesus.

I'm 38 years old now, listening to Neil Young in New York City, snowflakes out my window, getting carried home to Australia and the dry heat of growing up in an isolated mining town. To those times. It's his voice. The weight of his guitar. Both embedded in me.

My mother had picked up on Neil Young from a couple of Canadian hippies who lived across the road in Nhulunbuy. They were mostly famous for smoking pot, walking around their house nude, and their two young sons, who had nearly waist-length blond hair and seemed to run feral, although Carol their mum – who the kids called by her first name – used to teach them herself and they usually got good grades that no one felt they deserved. The boys were twins. One would grow up to be an artist in Sydney, the other stayed in town as a miner.

It could be a brutal town for choices. I used to watch the next-door neighbour's husband falling asleep standing up at the 6 am bus stop opposite our home. His wife was fucking another guy, and he was trying to literally work it out, doing 'doublers', long 24 hour shifts in solid blocks of two by twelve hours. As if he could pummel himself back into shape. Eventually he couldn't take it anymore, and he left town in a 4-wheel drive. There were no roads in or out of Nhulunbuy, so this was a dangerous business at the best of times. About a week later they found his truck bogged in a dry river-bed, with him crouching dead beside it. My father was called in to identify his friend and neighbour, but he came home weeping, not able to recognize his dark-haired workmate at all: his whole body had been cooked black by the sun, his hair had turned white as a ghost. The sun had made him into something else.

Down the road from us were the Stevenses. Nothing but trouble. The older brother Tim was a skinny guy with black hair, a bad tattoo of a heart on his arm and a leather jacket in tropical weather. Just fucking dumb, acting cool without even knowing what cool was. By the time he was seventeen he would already be in some kinda jail for a few break-and-enters in a town so small everybody knew who was having affairs with whom, and when you went out to buy groceries, and probably what you bought as well.

My best friend when I was 14 was his younger brother Steven. Steven Stevens. You'd think they coulda come up with something more. He always seemed to be in the shadow of his brother, who hadn't been arrested then, and I didn't understand then what I do today: that there was an anger starting to sprout up inside of him. I can't even remember Steven's face now. Just the sinews on his arms turning tighter. And how there was something prematurely manly about him, as if the boy in him didn't last long. But when I felt I knew him there was a looseness to what we did. We could just wander all day. Things weren't hard. Whether we took an axe to the tops of termite mounds just to see how long they would take to grow back, or simply walked down to the local garbage dump to scrounge in the smoke, we were animated slowly, hovering in our scenery, not quite shaped in what we did, what we were.

I was also slowly drawn to his sister Jenny, who was just a year older than me and Steven. The way she could glance at you. The cup of her neck.

One time I went to Steven's place to see if he was there. I knocked, called out and walked in. It seemed like no one was home, even though the door was open. The dry season heat streamed in like a balloon sagging over the entrance and into the air-conditioned room. I was glad to get inside, to pull myself beyond its weight and into the centre of the room. It was midday. Most sensible people were staying still, staying under cover. I stood there nervously in the lounge room, and called out again.

I heard a voice call me back deeper into the house. It was Jenny. So I walked down the white hall, past paintings of horses drinking and purple-blue impressions of Spanish señoritas. When I came to Jenny's room, she was still getting dressed. It's the first time I can recall having an erotic moment, her back, its nakedness, the false way she pretended to cover up, but unhurried, brazen, inviting me into her room without saying a word – if I wanted to make my own decision, I could.

I backed away, frightened, wishing I could somehow step forward. Not even understanding what I was feeling. She just called out then that Steven wasn't home. 'Okay, see ya later. Tell him I came over,' I said in a flat, hollow way, making how I spoke rougher, as if to protect myself from her. To sound further away, less interested, drier than I really was.

Later that same season Steven and I would go spearfishing in a local mangrove. We had our own spears of bamboo with three metal prongs made out of clothes-hanger wire, and we chased fish through the open, undulating shadows and shallows that faced onto the sea. The water was so peaceful you could still see footprints in the sandy beds where Aboriginal people had been there hunting earlier and smarter that morning. I didn't know what sunstroke was, and after a few hours I began to feel faint. Eventually I went to sit under a saltbush. But it made no difference to the nausea spinning over me. Steven didn't give a fuck and went back to hunt in the mangroves. Eventually I realised something was seriously wrong and I started to walk home, staggered really, losing my head to the sky.

It was a half-hour walk through the bush to town. The noisiest silence you could ever struggle through. A goanna came running, like a fuse along the dry ground, *so fast*, rattling twigs and leaves. I had startled it, and it me. Its whipping run caused me to go off-balance and almost vomit with a rush of fear. It slithered up a tree and some bark peeled slowly to the ground from where it had furiously scratched its way up the trunk. Birds screamed, something whistled a way off in the distance, I heard my own footsteps as if they were coming from someone near me.

Finally I passed through the local 'golf course', really just cleared ground then on the outskirts of town. The greens weren't anything more than flattened sand and clay beds. Pathetic shit. It mocked itself and the fantasies of leisure that the town was trying to have.

I had that head-tipping momentum, where you start to fall forward rather than walk. It may have been 30 or 40 minutes since I had left the mangroves, but it felt like hours.

Later my mother would tell me I had walked straight through the fertilizer sprays. I was so out of it I didn't even know. Walking through all these trucks set up to spout out some noxious shit to make this new world grow. Just desperate to make it home.

It was a brand new mining town and the whole place was still being set up. Still being civilized, from cyclone-proof homes to the golf course. The sprays were part of the making of the town, the invention of lawns. Quite a process. It had taken weeks. First people were encouraged to dig up and soften their yards with hoes. Then trucks had come round with decent quality dirt to make a topsoil. They'd dumped it in giant mounds out the front of each person's home. Then it was a case of spade or wheelbarrow, just spreading the dirt, beautiful and sweet, shit brown, rich, all over your yard. People had then been encouraged to go out into the bush and look for grass roots and runners to help with the next phase. So we went out and pulled them up like green rope, then replanted them, yellowing already. Giant trucks then came around and sprayed the lawns on, with what were like fire hoses spouting out this blue-green algae, a high-powered mix of seeds, mulch and fertilizer. Then it was a case of water the hell of it in this dry season. And water it some more. A whole suburban landscape drenched in psychedelic blue.

I came stumbling through a fortnight later, having spread some of the original dirt myself, the blue magic already comfortably, normally green, blades sprouting in fresh earth. A new round of trucks was respraying with a softer, clearer essence. And I just staggered through the fertile mist.

My mother started yelling at me about what the hell I was doing you bloody idiot, swearing at me in a kind, worried way. I just tried to act like I was alright. Not wanting her to know what I had been up to. They hadn't wanted me going to the mangroves, didn't even know I'd gone – now I remember the day, it was probably lucky we didn't get taken by the crocodiles that hunted there. Innocence is bliss sometimes.

Whatever my story, it became pretty apparent to my mum that I was in a fucked-up state. She was relieved to realize it was sunstroke rather than the sprayed poison I'd been blasted with. Figuring I was dehydrated, she made me drink water, lots of water, then she offered me a cold, sweet, strawberry lemonade that I promptly vomited back out.

Don't remember much else. Apparently I lost almost 24 hours in a delirium. Thinking of fish in pools darting away from me, cars coming towards me, bush ghosts, lizards, blue grass, blue skies, sweat, and me running, staggering, not even knowing my own name, not even lying down on a bed, just spinning through space.

When I came out of that world, I felt so weak it was unbelievable. Sticky and drained. My mother had water for me, bread, some chicken soup with not too much chicken. I could barely make it through this geriatric's meal. Where had I been? It was frightening to land back in my own body and realize I could go so far away from it.

I didn't see Steven after that. And I was kinda pissed off with him for leaving me to make my own way home when I was so sick. For deserting me so he could keep spearfishing.

Then all of a sudden the holidays were over and I went away again down south to school. Didn't see him for a whole year. When I came back it had all changed. By now Steven's brother was in jail, no longer the rebel, just a dickhead loser. Steven's sister Jenny looked sexier than ever, but she was known as 'the town bike', easy to ride. No decent guy should go near her. And Steven was headed down the same road as his brother, dropped outta school, no job, getting pissed, doing casual vandalism on phone booths and street lights, and small-time theft that everybody knew he'd done, or said he'd done, though somehow he hadn't been caught yet.

I'd already been told to stay away from him and his family as soon as I arrived. His sister smiled at me down at the shopping centre and I had to just smile back and ignore her then with a nod of the head and I'm on my way. She knew straight away what I was doing and I burned with shame. She was wearing tight jeans and a soft, old checked green shirt. She didn't look like a slut to me.

Steven called round a few times but I didn't call back. He finally caught me at home reading one day – there wasn't much else for me to do that holiday – and we sat on the morning verandah in the rising heat and talked. But it was all stiff. I couldn't invite him inside, though my mother did relent and bring us out some soft drinks. Then Steven tried to intimidate me into being his friend, to threaten me somehow. He had become much harder and I was repulsed by this toughness and frightened too. I did not know how to remake our old familiarity. Or even if it had existed.

He'd get busted trying to break into my parents' car a week later. My father just kicked his arse. Told him to fuck off and never show his face anywhere near him again. And that was the absolute end of Steven Stevens for me and my family. I don't know where he or Jenny ended up, what happened to them – eventually they just all moved out of town. I heard stories about jail and babies, but nothing certain. I was away studying and when I came back they were just gone. That was what a mining town was like. New people were living in their house. It was like they didn't exist anymore, except in old talk – and because of it being a mining town, with lots of people coming and going, not many people could talk the old talk anyway.

Funny to think how it all began with whispers that I could sorta hear. Then it became a fact without hardly anything being said. They were just an untouchable family. Then they didn't exist any more.

I felt like a guilty witness to something. And I found it hard to go from being best friends with someone one year to not speaking to them at all the next. It just wasn't my way. But it was imposed upon me – by my family, by circumstances, by Steven too and the way he behaved. Like he challenged our friendship out of existence.

I was pretty bored whenever I came home after that. So bored I used to kill time riding around town on the free bus, just sitting up the back, looking at the streets, watching the few passengers get on and off. This wasn't an uncommon way for Nhulunbuy youths to entertain themselves. Round and round a two-suburb circuit.

Alternatively, I'd cruise the sports shop, mostly running my hands over fish-hooks, diving masks, snorkels and shark chains, feeling the thickness of lines and weights, all the murder of the water. Or I'd go down to the chemist, which had a records section where I pondered *Kiss Alive* for a whole three months like it was an indecipherable mystery before I finally bought it. Read *Catch-22* in like three days. Then ploughed through a bunch of *Archie* comics, plus my dad's collection of crap westerns, a lesbian vampire novel and heaps of science fiction. A highlight was seeing Bruce Lee in *Enter The Dragon* at the local pictures when he had to fight in a hall of mirrors. I gave the trees, the telegraph poles and my sisters hell on the way home after that.

In the end though, I was experiencing most things on my own, trying to deal with how my world had shifted. Trying to fill up the space. Or live with it in my head.

My mother had changed a lot in this time too. I arrived back from studying to find her doing the vacuuming to 'Get It On'. She switched me on to T-Rex's *Electric Warrior* completely and at least a little Neil Diamond, though I could never hack my father bellowing 'Song Sung Blue'. I started to explore music then, to find out about stuff that wasn't in the Top 40. To listen to things I didn't even understand. That was when my mother started to teach me to drive on red dirt roads just off the highway to get me away from those oncoming cars. We'd listen to Neil Young's *On The Beach*, our mutual favourite, and sing 'they're all just pissing in the wind' and laugh and drive down to the sea, where a blue-pocked moon could sometimes be seen on pale afternoons, half-formed, hanging like an ear in the sky.

Discussion questions

Can facts ever be changed? In what circumstances?

How far should writers go in revealing the 'truths' of their lives? Are there limits to what is acceptable confession?

Further reading

There are too many enjoyable, enlightening memoirs that have been published to single out one or two for special mention, but the following books may prove useful to the aspiring memoirist.

Carmel Bird, *Writing the Story of Your Life*, Fourth Estate, 2007.

Natalie Goldberg, *Writing Down the Bones: Freeing the writer within*, Shambala, 1986.

Vivian Gornick, *The Situation and the Story: The art of personal narrative*, Farrar, Straus and Giroux, 2001.

Jill Ker Conway, *When Memory Speaks*, Vintage/Random House, 1998.

William Zinsser, *Inventing the Truth: The art and craft of memoir*, Houghton/Mifflin Company, 1998.

Chapter 7

Writing about Place

Placing readers in the world

Willa McDonald

Writing about place matters. It matters in features. It matters in memoir. It matters in virtually every story because we human beings don't live divorced from our surroundings. We are fundamentally connected through our senses to the environment in which we live. Too little sunlight causes sadness; thunderstorms trigger skittishness; we respond physically and emotionally to our world as if we're part of nature, not separate from it. That's why writing about place is one of the best tools we have for bringing a subject out of the abstract and anchoring it firmly in the concrete of a reader's mind. As Sydney-based writer Ashley Hay advises, this needn't take much space in an article. All that's really necessary are:

> two or three critical pieces of information – tactile, sensual, physical pieces of information – that throw your reader out of the familiar comfort of wherever they are (a bus, a train, a bed, a bath, a chair) and make the place you want them to be familiar and immediate . . . If you give your reader a little bit of place – a little bit of extra *where* to go with their *who, what, when* and *why* – I think they might carry your story with them longer. You'll give them setting.[1]

Hay should know. Her essay 'Ultramarine', commissioned for Mark Tredinnick's *A Place on Earth: An anthology of nature writing from Australia and North*

America,[2] conveys such an infectious fondness for Australia – particularly the Sydney coastline, laced as it is by the blue Pacific – that parts of it were used in a publicity campaign by the United Kingdom branch of Tourism Australia. Hay's advice on 'place' can be applied to any essay, but 'Ultramarine' goes further. Its colourful images and anecdotes effectively conjure up so many aspects of Australia, but especially the landscape, that it is also at home in that fast-growing category – 'Nature Writing'.

Bearing witness to the landscape

Emily Dickinson once observed that places speak and the poet learns to listen.[3] Writing that 'listens' to the land holds a special place in the world of essays, increasingly in Australia, but particularly in North America which has a fine tradition of landscape writing dating back to Emerson, Thoreau and the Transcendentalist movement – that group of writers and thinkers who revered and looked to nature for guidance and inspiration. That this type of writing has been emerging in such secular, urbanised societies, built largely on immigration, is perhaps not surprising. As Pico Iyer tells us, the twenty-first century is the era of the 'global soul'[4] – a time when many people belong both everywhere and nowhere. While for some this may be liberating, for others it's dislocating. Witnessing the places that are important to us – 'new' places as well as old, rural as well as urban – helps to affirm our sense of belonging to them, physically, aesthetically, spiritually. It helps to affirm our sense of home.

Being real

Standout nature writing – like any effective writing – aims to connect us deeply to our world and our own humanity. There's a wildness in the best of it – an acknowledgement that under the aspirations and achievements of civilisation, life is fundamentally about survival. Too much nature writing is reverential; too much is oppressively pretty and fails to have an edge.[5] 'What about wall rubble and discarded plastic toys and a broken tile in the weeds?' asks the filmmaker, writer and Zen Roshi Susan Murphy in her essay 'Zen and the City':

> Every fragment of our regular world of human trouble and riches waits as patiently as mountains and waters. To fail to attend truly to them is to lay waste [to] the place right where we are, where we live our lives. It is to agree to live with habitual distance or indifference, which breaks the spell of life . . .[6]

Observing with a purpose

Nature writing shouldn't be a safe escape – for the writer or the reader. When Thoreau wrote *Walden*, one of this genre's founding texts, he claimed he went to the woods because he wished to live deliberately, to front only the essential facts of life.[7] He used his two years and two months at Walden Pond, where he built himself a house on land owned by Emerson, to experiment in living well. Because of his opposition to slavery and the Mexican–American War, he also refused to pay his taxes. One of the essays that emerged from that experience – 'On the Duty of Civil Disobedience' – influenced and inspired many later activists, including Tolstoy, Gandhi and Martin Luther King Jnr. As David Gessner points out, the best nature writing, if not all writing, has a quest in mind – a searching for an answer to that raw question that has plagued humanity since ancient times: How can I live a good life?[8]

Making the structure work for the content

No one's ever accused Pulitzer Prize winner Annie Dillard's writing of being too nice. 'Total Eclipse' takes the horror writer's approach to nature – it doesn't sanitise the experience of the eclipse, but draws the reader ever deeper into a terrifying moment of awe in the face of omnipotent nature. One of the reasons why this essay works so well is because of the clever and complex structure Dillard has chosen. For an essay to be successful, it must flow according to its own internal logic, and that in turn depends on how well the structure shapes the writer's ideas and intentions into a coherent whole. The structure should assist, not interfere, with what the writer is trying to communicate to readers.

According to Dillard, finding the right structure in this instance was a challenge. Confronted by a 'most interesting technical problem' – how to give narrative form to less than a minute of experience, she settled on a structure that was influenced by Faulkner's approach in *As I Lay Dying*.[9] She took that single brief moment of the eclipse and returned to it again and again in the writing, unravelling and re-ravelling it, to construct an essay that recreates the unfolding layers of her responses to that fearful moment of human insignificance on the Washington mountainside:

> The sky snapped over the sun like a lens cover. The hatch in the brain slammed. Abruptly it was dark night, on the land and in the sky . . . There was no sound. The eyes dried, the arteries drained, the lungs hushed. There was no world. We were the world's dead people rotating and orbiting around and around, embedded in the planet's crust, while the earth rolled down.

'Total Eclipse' shows how well a 'nature' essay can work, particularly when the writer keeps a tight grip on the structure while stretching her own perceptions to the limit. The result – as unsettling as it's compelling – is a contemplation of consciousness itself.

Connecting in new ways

Writers like Dillard and Hay evoke nature – evoke the landscape – through their writing. Not stereotypical representations of landscape, but the land and nature they experience directly, to which they're deeply attached. Their non-fiction narratives are about not only witnessing, observing, interpreting, but also imagining and creating. Hay, for example, gives us this description from 'Ultramarine':

> My blue line runs this hundred or so miles. It flows and shifts, turning in less than 12 hours, striping the edge of the country, the space out to the horizon, and runs against sand and rocks. This grounding colour of blue that I stand and watch and fall into; crave if I'm not here; guzzle when I come home.
>
> It's this colour – not wide brown or sunburnt red or that monotonous khaki that used to be pinned on the eucalypts: it's this colour that holds my place in shape.

Writers of non-fiction, like the writers of history, convey a personal perspective bound to observable fact. It's in the tension between perspective and fact that new ways of connecting are created – and in this genre that means new ways of connecting with the land, new ways of belonging to place. Connections our war-torn, environmentally degraded world desperately needs.

Ashley Hay

Ashley Hay has written two books of narrative non-fiction, *The Secret: The strange marriage of Annabella Milbanke and Lord Byron* (2000), and *Gum: The story of eucalypts and their champions* (2002). The author of many short stories and essays – including *Herbarium* (2004), a collaboration with the Australian photographer Robyn Stacey – she has worked as a journalist for publications such as the *Independent Monthly* and the *Bulletin*. She is currently literary editor of the *Bulletin*, and is working on her first novel and on another collaboration with Stacey, inspired by the collections of the Macleay Museum at the University of Sydney.

ULTRAMARINE

Ashley Hay

A Place on Earth, 2003

This island, this shape: it's like an oblong squeezed hard in the middle and left – orange and gold, with sandstone made from chocolate and rose, and green edges – to make up its own plants, its own animals, its own people. A lap of deep blue all around it, an arc of high blue stretching over it, and the sharp line where they meet.

This place has different shapes, different colours that mark it as special, depending on who's telling its story. It's gum-tree shaped, ashy-green. It's desert-open, rich reds. It's inner-city, flat grey pavement. It's opportunity, gold piled up. It's dispossession, black and white. It's stripes on a football scarf, whatever colours. It's summer sun, the feeling of sand.

In my story, it's a blue line that runs a hundred miles or so, along the coast where the first white people came to stay: from the beaches north of Wollongong, where Cook tried to make his landing, over Bell's Point, through the Royal National Park, past Cape Banks and Point Solander that hug around Botany Bay, up to Coogee and the path that runs along the cliffs to Bondi. And on to South Head, where Arthur Phillip posted men to scan the horizon for sails – as if their gaze might make ships come faster from the rest of the world. Now, there's a lighthouse, its hopeful yellow flare pushing east into the ocean, pushing west into that deep bubble of ultramarine called Sydney Harbour.

My blue line runs this hundred or so miles. It flows and shifts, turning in less than 12 hours, striping the edge of the country, the space out to the horizon, and runs against sand and rocks. This grounding colour of blue that I stand and watch and fall into; crave if I'm not here; guzzle when I come home.

It's this colour – not wide brown or sunburnt red or that monotonous khaki that used to be pinned on the eucalypts: it's this colour that holds my place in shape.

My mother gave me this story.

A man arrives in Australia from Holland, a couple of years ago, with tubes of artists' paint in his bag, and a roll of brushes. He enrols himself in an artclass, sits down in front of his first Australian landscape, and smears stripes of colour across his palette. He looks around at the other people in the class, at the rainbows of pigment on their boards. There's something different, he thinks, but he can't put his finger on what it is. He begins to paint.

At the end of the morning he steps back from the canvas. The scene in front of him runs replicated around a circle of stretched frames. Still something. He squints at his picture. He squints at the sky. The teacher comes over to him. She rests her finger on his cold, unmixed Antwerp blue. We're a much more cobalt country, she says. Or ultramarine.

This place has blue in its soul.

Arthur Phillip brags of his harbour. The finest in the world, he says, and he skites about the extraordinary number of ships that could be comfortably moored in its waters. So deep. So blue. They have sent him to set up a life on the other side of the world. The antipodean side. The inverted side. They have sent him there to try to survive on the edge of the harbour's richness.

He does feel, he writes a little plaintively, the want of several people who may have helped him make sense of this new place. He can't help but comment on the fact that he is without anyone with a notion of coal and mining, making him completely ignorant of half the resources he may be walking around on, and more and more dependent on the ungiving wood his men fell from the gum-trees. And there, too, he can't help but remark that it might have been useful if he'd been given a botanist – even a gardener. The place Cook landed, he says, was definitely teeming with the stuff it had been named for. [1] But here he is, 12,000 miles away from Kew Gardens, with only the garden-bed horticultural knowledge of a couple of surgeons and officers available, and a bunch of natives – who had lived on the plants forever and could have told him the use of everything growing on the harbour's edge – with whom he can't communicate.

This gulfing space between black and white, crouched together around the harbour's blue.

The harbour itself is all about blue. Specifically, it's about ultramarine. More specifically, it's Winsor and Newton ultramarine: 'Winsor and Newton Deep Ultramarine oil colour,' Brett Whiteley salivates on the harbour's edge almost 200 years after Phillip, 'has an obsessive ecstasy-like effect upon my nervous system quite unlike any other colour.'[2] The colour of the harbour: rich, inky, sensuous.

Naturally-occurring ultramarine has always been precious – so precious that halos used to be painted this colour to demonstrate the generosity of the Church, and contracts between patrons and their Renaissance artists specified how much extra funding would be laid on to buy in the all-important blue. The first ultramarine known to come to the new settlement of Sydney – pure, precious – is sent in 1812 to John William Lewin by his friend and former student Alexander Huey. [3]

And then, in 1828 – when Sydney has stepped from simply surviving to feeling itself established, settled, contemplative – someone on the other side of the world works out how to fake that blue: you no longer need to grind vast quantities of lapis lazuli into pigment. You can take clumps of china clay, quartz or sand (for silica), sulfur, charcoal or coal (to burn for carbon) and any spare anhydrous sodium sulfate and/or carbonate you have lying around. You grind them, take them up to red hot and keep them there – in an airless atmosphere – for a few hours to create a mess. Grind the mess, wash it, dry it, and reheat it to 500° C to bring out the blue colour. [4]

And then you may consider the precise painting of Sydney's harbour and the inky line of its coast's horizon – at a starting price (in the 1830s) of 400 francs per pound as opposed to the 2500–3000 francs you'd pay for a pound of the real stuff. England's Winsor and Newton has it parceled up in anticipation of Brett Whiteley's ecstasy by 1832 – although they're still selling oil colours in pigs' bladders, a decade or so away from the invention of metallic tubes. [5]

Think about ecstasy. Think about the way the light plays on the navy of the water on a clear day, about leaning towards it, mouth open to it slightly, head tilted slightly to open your throat as you try to inhale it. This place that pulls you up every time you see it, laid out under full sun.

Sit here on this eastern edge of Australia's land, facing directly out to the horizon, anywhere along that hundred-odd miles. Let the sides of your gaze register the warm golds and oranges, roses and chocolates of the cliffs. Let the top of your gaze register how high and blue and clear the sky is, its apogee so far against the blackness of space that you can't quite focus on it. Pour the rest of yourself towards that point where the solid ultramarine of the ocean meets the diffuse cobalt of the sky.

This thing is constant: this horizon is hypnotic. An eye gazing at an infinite point tells its brain to release lithium, and a brain releasing lithium feels happier. Does this make a line of seascape fascinating? Is it what makes me sit looking over the water, watching its water rise and fall, swell and turn? Is this what Goethe means when he says that blue is a strange paradox of a colour that pulls away from you, receding, yet draws you after it, compelled?

The horizon is hypnotic: the horizon is fixed. Someone arriving on this point of the Australian coast in 1788, someone possessing it and surviving in it, and changing and losing and trampling all the things that are already there – someone then would have seen the same point that you see now. Someone would have seen that same point two days, two years, two millennia before those ships arrived.

It is a constant.

Under this blue, the blue that arches over Arthur Phillip's fine, deep water and Brett Whiteley's ecstasy, there used to be a language that called the sky *burra*. [6] It's one of the first words someone writes down. *Burra*: sky. *Minak* for darkness. *Mulumulu* for stars that fall in a cluster. And *birrung* for stars that stay where they are.

A man who builds rockets for NASA gave me the only story he knows about Australia.

When the Americans build the first spaceships that they trust to fly men, they send an astronaut up to orbit the Earth and come back down again. Yuri Gagarin has done this already, and has come back to say that the planet is really the most extraordinarily lush blue. The Americans want their own vision splendid. And because they are American and are used to performing things for the world, they make this man's flight an international event – where the Russians have crash-landed Gagarin in a field somewhere hoping no one will notice until they can make him look like a hero. So the Americans say, can you please ask the people of your cities to turn all their lights on as our spaceship goes over, to hang out a bit of a welcome for our guy?

The world obliges.

And he passes over the huge bulk of his own continent, on over the vast black-blue of the Pacific Ocean, over the top of Brisbane, on over central Australia. 'Can you thank the people of Brisbane for all that light?' he radios down to the ground. 'And then the next city in to the west from that, in the middle of Australia – the really huge one: whatever they did,' says the American astronaut, 'was just so pretty. I'm flying over with this deep blue around me and they're pushing up so much light that it's like I'm surrounded by fireflies or crackers or something.'

This is the only story the man who works for NASA knows about Australia. He wants to know what the big, big city – west of Brisbane, in the middle of the country – is called, the one that put on such a show for that rocketman. He's always thought he'd like to go there, he tells me.

I say to him: but there is no big city in the middle of Australia, west of Brisbane. There's country, space, some towns, and a huge thickness of histories and stories. No big city.

Under this blue, on the edges of Sydney Harbour, there was a language that was gentle enough to have a word for this: I will warm my hands in front of the fire, and then I will squeeze your fingers with mine, and you will feel the warmth. *Buduwa*.[7] Linguists say that blue is one of the last colours to be given a word in most languages: it occurs less frequently in the natural world – there's the sea, there's the sky, but if you have words for them you don't really need a blue-word to describe anything else. Better, maybe, to have a word for sharing warmth.

I try to make sense of my blue, to make sense of why I carry it. In the middle of words about colour from the other side of the world, I find this; a Frenchman suggesting that blue, situated between black and white, indicates an equilibrium.[8] After all, people from Aristotle to Leonardo da Vinci have believed that blue is really a lovely composite of black and white.

It means something, I think, carrying this strip of coast and the water that runs out from it as far as I can see, that runs in towards its centre, up the harbour. Watching it change through light twice every day. Watching the impossibility of water hitting land, of sky falling sharply into ocean. Watching these things coexist, the clear blue lines of one brushing against the other.

Blue, between black and white.

1. Gov. Arthur Phillip in Britten, A. (ed.), *Historical Records of New South Wales*, vol. i, pt. Sydney: Lansdowne Slattery & Co., 1978, pp. 122, 128. Tench, Watkin, *1788*. Melbourne: Text, 2004, p. 72.
2. McGrath, Sandra, *Brett Whiteley*. Sydney: Bay Books, 1992, p. 214.
3. Burgess, Erica, and Paula Dredge, 'Supplying Artists' Materials to Australia 1788–1850', in Ashok Roy and Perry Smith (eds), *Painting Techniques: History, Materials and Studio Practice*. London: The International Institute for Conservation of Historic and Artistic Works, 1998, p. 199.

4. Roy, Ashok (ed.), *Artists' Pigments*. Washington: OUP/National Gallery of Art, 1993, p. 56.
5. Harley, R. L., *A Brief History of Winsor and Newton*. Wealdstone: Winsor and Newton, 1982, pp. 3–4.
6. Troy, Jakelin, *The Sydney Language*. Canberra: Panther, 1994, p. 50.
7. Troy, p. 70.
8. Bachelard, in Cirlot, J. E., *Dictionary of Symbols*. London: Routledge, 1993, p. 54.

Interview with Ashley Hay

Question *'Ultramarine' appears to be about the colour blue, but it goes much deeper than that and explores ideas of belonging and reconciliation in Australia. Did you mean the essay to end up saying all that it did?*

Hay I was looking for a way to make the blue mean more, and I was looking for a way to talk about the things that people in Australia might have in common – a love of some part of this place, a view of the same horizon now as they might have had, staring out to sea, hundreds or even thousands of years ago. Finding the information about an old idea – that ran from Aristotle to Leonardo at least – that blue might be a combination of black and white seemed almost too good to be true.

I wanted the essay to make a greater point than just how beautiful this part of the world was, and how much I loved it – but I wasn't sure until I was almost at the end of the drafting process how to do that. And I'm not sure I felt the weight of the ending until much later when I read the essay again after it had gone through the editing process.

It comes across as a personal and passionate piece. How did you come to write it?

I think I've been collecting the anecdotes that turned up in 'Ultramarine' for most of my life – it's one of the reasons I think I'd never be able to write another piece like this. My mother's story about the man in her art class who had the wrong colour blue on his palette: that's probably fifteen years old. Brett Whiteley's line about the ecstasy of Winsor and Newton Deep Ultramarine: I probably read that when he died in 1992. John Lewin asking for the first ultramarine pigment to be sent to Sydney in 1812: Humphrey McQueen sent me looking for that five or six years ago. The man from NASA: he was in a church in Venice a decade ago now.

I wrote an essay about the history of blue for my Honours year in 1995, and I think I'd always wanted to write something somehow more poetic about it. [Then I was] commissioned by Mark Tredinnick to contribute a piece to his anthology, *A Place on Earth*[10] – it was a lovely wide brief to write a lyrical essay about a particular place and our connections with it. The combination of Mark's enthusiasm for a piece about a place that meant something, and all those bits and pieces of information, turned into this.

There is a strong sense of place in this piece – a love of place. How do you create that for the reader?

Because the whole point of this essay was about place it's probably much more explicit than in other things I've written. But if there is a trick to catching place it might be to do with finding two or three critical pieces of information – tactile, sensual, physical pieces of information – that throw your reader out of the familiar comfort of wherever they are (a bus, a train, a bed, a bath, a chair) and make the place you want them to be familiar and immediate.

You have to find the way to make the place feel real, whether you're talking about the piece of coast you looked at half an hour ago – and that they might know themselves – or about a time and place that doesn't exist anymore. If you give your reader a little bit of place – a little bit of extra *where* to go with their *who, what, when* and *why* – I think they might carry your story with them longer. You'll give them setting.

When I was trying to write about Byron in London, in 1812,[11] I got my head around its place through things like the fact that there was so much deep mud on the side of the roads that women wore shoes almost like stilts to walk along them. That it was the time of the first gaslights pushing warm yellow light into the city's previously impenetrable nights. And that grand houses had inside lavatories that had to be emptied manually, leaving nasty smells to waft through even the most opulent and aristocratic residence until that emptying took place.

If you could get someone to imagine the stick of the mud, the shock of being able to see in the night for the first time, and the stench of waterclosets without sewage systems, then you might be able to give them a headstart towards breaching the space between that particular then, and now.

How important is it to write for the senses?

I have a strong visual sense – I blame my mum, who's an artist, and my dad, who's an engineer; they both have very visceral imaginations – and I think I always tried to take literally that injunction to show rather than tell. There's a sense of music and rhythm tied up in it too.

I know when I was looking for the seven people around which to build *Gum*,[12] I was conscious that each needed to have at least one very illustrative anecdote about their interaction with eucalypts: I ended up with Major Mitchell in the chronology because of that one very 'picturable' story about him riding back up New South Wales, being literally stopped in his tracks by a gorgeous gum tree, and having to stop so he could sketch it. I think you can say a lot with a story that's quite sensual – the explorer riding home after months of bushwhacking, arrested so shudderingly by a thing of beauty that he has to stop and draw it.

And you need a good lead and a good ending in any piece of writing – something to draw readers in, something to finish them off. That would be as true of fiction, of narrative non-fiction, of a piece of journalism, as it is for an essay.

How important is honesty to the craft of essay writing/non-fiction writing? How far can you go in moving from fact to tell a deeper truth?

Honesty is extremely important in this kind of writing – but of course you tweak some of the anecdotes, just by virtue of the fact that we all change things and misremember things and rewrite them as we carry them in our memories – usually subconsciously. So there has to be a certain amount of latitude, and I think tweaking is a very different thing to changing facts.

In a piece I wrote about the sixtieth anniversary of Hiroshima, I talked about a garden in Cornwall and the gardener being concerned about a heron getting her fish. I had myself seen the heron at the end of that conversation whereas I think it actually turned up the next day – maybe a day later, or maybe it had flown over before we had the conversation. I can't remember now, but I thought that was OK. Then I decided maybe it would be better not to have the heron turn up at all. I guess you make decisions based on structure and poetry, and these might shuffle things a bit. That's very different to saying, 'this happened', 'this person did this', 'this person said this', when that's an invention – a fiction, a lie. Although, of course, perhaps this distinction is disingenuous.

How did you settle on the structure?

In this case, the structure was a very instinctive thing. Because this sprang out of such a disparate collection of stuff, I think it probably ebbed and flowed through its separate moments: here's a nice place for the man who builds spaceships; here's a nice place for my mother; here's a nice place for the first ultramarine pigment requested by a painter in Sydney.

I don't know where the instinct for that structure comes from. I guess you feel the pace and the turns of any narrative as you write it, and it's always interesting finding where peaks and troughs fall throughout words.

Is the narrator of this piece you?

I think that of all the pieces I've written this is perhaps the one in which the narrator is most obviously me. That said, you always craft a persona in writing, don't you? This is a fluffier me – the real me would never lean forward across a table and say, 'Think about ecstasy. Think about the way the light plays on the navy of the water on a clear day, about leaning towards it, mouth open to it slightly, head slightly tilted to open your throat as you try to inhale it.'

When the extract from the essay went up on tube stations and in carriages in London, I realised that I might have created an 'I' that I *would* like to be – I got lots of messages from people saying that they'd seen it, and how it made them homesick, or made them want to come to Sydney and see the blue for themselves. And I thought how good it could be to be that passionate about place and story all the time – I suppose to be that open-hearted about it. It opens up the conversations you can have as a person as much as the conversations you have with readers as a writer.

How important is it that the narrator be trustworthy and reliable?

I think it's very important – and I think there should be a great sense of that among people who read personal pieces, whether they're reading essays or memoirs or reportage. I trust that John Hersey is telling me the truth about what he saw in Hiroshima in 1945. I trust that Robert Fisk is telling me the truth about Baghdad's libraries burning in 2003. These are much more extreme versions of things than a pretty essay about a piece of coast tied up with a gentle wish for rapprochement, but I think you do have to be able to trust that non-fiction is exactly that.

I don't know why you trust a writer, though. I suppose partly you trust them if they make you feel you're actually seeing something yourself, or if they give you something that allows you to empathise as much as you can with a situation of which you've had no direct experience. I think also perhaps you trust writers who don't present themselves as having all the answers, who say, 'I'm going to tell you as much as I know about this, and I'm going to let you see the things that still puzzle me as well – the bits I can't answer. And maybe when you read as much as I've managed to get down, you'll see a bit of the answer that I can't yet.'

Is essay writing a way of breaking silence and claiming authority over something, even though the writer has no expertise?

It was only when I was re-reading 'Ultramarine' that I started to see the sneaky things that happened between its words – the things that end up in a piece of writing that you don't pick as you write it, only as you read it; it was like the way people see things in the words you write that you don't see yourself. I saw an emotion that was in it, a rawness, an openness that I'd never be able to sit down and write deliberately.

And what's also true is that by writing about these strange blue fragments I could write with some kind of authority. I'm not sure who else would be carrying such a weird bundle of fragments about with them, or would try to lace them together into something that meant something.

This was one of the things that writing 'Ultramarine' helped me to put my finger on. It wasn't just about finding language to try to evoke a place which, for me, was my most significant geography – a changeable combination of blues above and below the horizon that have an imaginative, physical and aesthetic impact on me. It was about finding that all the threads of being and blueness could wind into an obscure piece of colour theory that might say something hopeful and positive about a topic as vast and important as reconciliation.

There is something democratic about essays – I try to excuse myself by saying I want to tell stories for readers in general and that my own haphazard (rather than specific or expert) background lets me do that. I'm not sure that essays give you that claim to authority that you suggest: they just open up a forum for you to meditate on and worry at something.

Your writing crosses journalism, creative non-fiction, essays and now fiction. Are there things you can say in an essay that you can't say in any other form?

An essay is like one of those Russian dolls that opens to reveal another and another and another; it's a way of trying to say large things through small things – it lets you think about huge questions in very intimate and domestic contexts. I suppose that's how most of us try to make sense of the magnitude of the world and its concerns against our own square metres of space and life.

I think David Malouf has said something about a writer's body of work changing with the addition of every new piece, and essays give you yet another lens through which you can consider the stories or the themes or the characters or the bits and pieces of information that you're carrying around with you.

There's a richness and potential in essay writing that makes its structures and forms and rhythms lovely and helpful things to keep in mind no matter what you're working on – maybe that's to do with its democracy.

I don't know that I have an identifiable underlying purpose to the things I write – I suppose all you'd like is for what you write to find some readers, to open a window for those people, or give them something that makes them think or smile. I'm not sure you can ask for any more than that.

Annie Dillard

Annie Dillard is renowned for her narrative essays that use poetic language and theological musings to explore the natural world. In 1975 she won the Pulitzer Prize (for non-fiction) for her book *Pilgrim at Tinker Creek,* a meditation based on a journal she kept while living at Tinker Creek following a life-threatening bout of pneumonia. Dillard's many books have included *Tickets for a Prayer Wheel, Holy the Firm, Living by Fiction, Teaching a Stone to Talk, Encounters with Chinese Writers, An American Childhood, The Writing Life, For the Time Being* and her novel *The Living*. Her essays continue to most inspire up-and-coming writers.

TOTAL ECLIPSE

Annie Dillard
1982

I

It had been like dying, that sliding down the mountain pass.

It had been like the death of someone, irrational, that sliding down the mountain pass and into the region of dread. It was like slipping into fever, or falling down that hole in sleep from which you wake yourself whimpering. We had crossed the mountains that day, and now we were in a strange place – a hotel in central Washington, in a town near Yakima. The eclipse we had traveled here to see would occur early the next morning.

I lay in bed. My husband, Gary, was reading beside me. I lay in bed and looked at the painting on the hotel-room wall. It was a print of a detailed and lifelike painting of a smiling clown's head, made out of vegetables. It was a painting of the sort that you do not intend to look at and that, alas, you never forget. Some tasteless fate presses it upon you; it becomes part of the complex interior junk you carry with you wherever you go. Two years have passed since the total eclipse of which I write. During those years I have forgotten, I assume, a great many things I wanted to remember – but I have not forgotten that clown painting or its lunatic setting in the old hotel.

The clown was bald. Actually, he wore a clown's tight rubber wig, painted white; this stretched over the top of his skull, which was a cabbage. His hair was bunches of baby carrots. Inset in his white clown makeup, and in his cabbage skull, were his small and laughing human eyes. The clown's glance was like the glance of Rembrandt in some of the self-portraits: lively, knowing, deep, and loving. The crinkled shadows around his eyes were string beans. His eyebrows were parsley. Each of his ears was a broad bean. His thin, joyful lips were red chili peppers; between his lips were wet rows of human teeth and a suggestion of a real tongue. The clown print was framed in gilt and glassed.

To put ourselves in the path of the total eclipse, that day we had driven five hours inland from the Washington coast, where we lived. When we tried to cross the Cascades range, an avalanche had blocked the pass.

A slope's worth of snow blocked the road; traffic backed up. Had the avalanche buried any cars that morning? We could not learn. This highway was the only winter road over the mountains. We waited as highway crews bulldozed a passage through the avalanche. With two-by-fours and walls of plyboard, they erected a one-way, roofed tunnel through the avalanche. We drove through the avalanche tunnel, crossed the pass, and descended several thousand feet into central Washington and the broad Yakima valley, about which we knew only that it was orchard country. As we lost altitude, the snows disappeared; our ears popped; the trees changed, and in the trees were strange birds. I watched the landscape innocently, like a fool, like a diver in the rapture of the deep who plays on the bottom while his air runs out.

The hotel lobby was a dark, derelict room, narrow as a corridor, and seemingly without air. We waited on a couch while the manager vanished upstairs to do something unknown to our room. Beside us, on an overstuffed chair, absolutely motionless, was a platinum-blonde woman in her forties, wearing a black silk dress and a strand of pearls. Her long legs were crossed; she supported her head on her fist. At the dim far end of the room, their backs toward us, sat six bald old men in their shirtsleeves, around a loud television. Two of them seemed asleep. They were drunks. 'Number six!' cried the man on television, 'Number six!'

On the broad lobby desk was a ten-gallon aquarium, lighted and bubbling, that contained one large fish; the fish tilted up and down in its water. Against the long opposite wall sang a live canary in its cage. Beneath the cage, among spilled millet seeds on the carpet, were a decorated child's sand bucket and matching sand shovel.

Now the alarm was set for six. I lay awake remembering an article I had read downstairs in the lobby, in an engineering magazine. The article was about gold mining.

In South Africa, in India, and in South Dakota, the gold mines extend so deeply into the earth's crust that they are hot. The rock walls burn the miners' hands. The companies have to air-condition the mines; if the air conditioners break, the miners die. The elevators in the mine shafts run very slowly, down, and up, so the miner's ears will not pop in their skulls. When the miners return to the surface, their faces are deathly pale.

Early the next morning we checked out. It was February 26, 1979, a Monday morning. We would drive out of town, find a hilltop, watch the eclipse, and then drive back over the mountains and home to the coast. How familiar things are here; how adept we are; how smoothly and professionally we check out! I had forgotten the clown's smiling head and hotel lobby as if they had never existed. Gary put the car in gear and off we went, as off we have gone to a hundred other adventures.

It was before dawn when we found a highway out of town and drove into the unfamiliar countryside. By the growing light we could see a band of cirrostratus clouds in the sky.

Later the rising sun would clear these clouds before the eclipse began. We drove at random until we came to a range of unfenced hills. We pulled off the highway, bundled up, and climbed one of these hills.

II

The hill was five hundred feet high. Long winter-killed grass covered it, as high as our knees. We climbed and rested, sweating in the cold; we passed clumps of bundled people on the hillside who were setting up telescopes and fiddling with cameras. The top of the hill stuck up in the middle of the sky. We tightened our scarves and looked around.

East of us rose another hill like ours. Between the hills, far below, was the highway that threaded south into the valley. This was the Yakima valley; I had never seen it before. It is justly famous for its beauty, like every planted valley. It extended south into the horizon, a distant dream of a valley, a Shangri-la. All its hundreds of low, golden slopes bore orchards. Among the orchards were towns, and roads, and plowed and fallow fields. Through the valley wandered a thin, shining river; from the river extended fine, frozen irrigation ditches. Distance blurred and blued the sight, so that the whole valley looked like a thickness or sediment at the bottom of the sky. Directly behind us was more sky, and empty lowlands blued by distance, and Mount Adams. Mount Adams was an enormous, snow-covered volcanic cone rising flat, like so much scenery.

Now the sun was up. We could not see it; but the sky behind the band of clouds was yellow, and, far down the valley, some hillside orchards had lighted up. More people were parking near the highway and climbing the hills. It was the West. All of us rugged individualists were wearing knit caps and blue nylon parkas. People were climbing the nearby hills and setting up shop in clumps among the dead grasses. It looked as though we had all gathered on hilltops to pray for the world on its last day. It looked as though we had all crawled out of spaceships and were preparing to assault the valley below. It looked as though we were scattered on hilltops at dawn to sacrifice virgins, make rain, set stone stelae in a ring. There was no place out of the wind. The straw grasses banged our legs.

Up in the sky where we stood, the air was lusterless yellow. To the west the sky was blue. Now the sun cleared the clouds. We cast rough shadows on the blowing grass; freezing, we waved our arms. Near the sun, the sky was bright and colorless. There was nothing to see.

It began with no ado. It was odd that such a well-advertised public event should have no starting gun, no overture, no introductory speaker. I should have known right then that I was out of my depth. Without pause or preamble, silent as orbits, a piece of the sun went away. We looked at it through welder's goggles. A piece of the sun was missing; in its place we saw empty sky.

I had seen a partial eclipse in 1970. A partial eclipse is very interesting. It bears almost no relation to a total eclipse. Seeing a partial eclipse bears the same relation to seeing a total eclipse as kissing a man does to marrying him, or as flying in an airplane does to falling out of an airplane. Although the one experience precedes the other, it in no way prepares you for it. During a partial eclipse the sky does not darken – not even when 94 percent of the sun is hidden. Nor does the sun, seen colorless through protective devices, seem terribly strange. We have all seen a sliver of light in the sky; we have all seen the crescent moon by day. However, during a partial eclipse the air does indeed get cold, precisely as if someone were standing between you and the fire. And blackbirds do fly back to their roosts. I had seen a partial eclipse before, and here was another.

What you see in an eclipse is entirely different from what you know. It is especially different for those of us whose grasp of astronomy is so frail that, given a flashlight, a grapefruit, two oranges, and fifteen years, we still could not figure out which way to set the clocks for daylight saving time. Usually it is a bit of a trick to keep your knowledge from blinding you. But during an eclipse it is easy. What you see is much more convincing than any wild-eyed theory you may know.

You may read that the moon has something to do with eclipses. I have never seen the moon yet. You do not see the moon. So near the sun, it is as completely invisible as the stars are by day. What you see before your eyes is the sun going through phases. It gets narrower and narrower, as the waning moon does, and, like the ordinary moon, it travels alone in the simple sky. The sky is of course background. It does not appear to eat the sun; it is far behind the sun. The sun simply shaves away; gradually, you see less sun and more sky.

The sky's blue was deepening, but there was no darkness. The sun was a wide crescent, like a segment of tangerine. The wind freshened and blew steadily over the hill. The eastern hill across the highway grew dusky and sharp. The towns and orchards in the valley to the south were dissolving into the blue light. Only the thin river held a trickle of sun.

Now the sky to the west deepened to indigo, a colour never seen. A dark sky usually loses colour. This was a saturated, deep indigo, up in the air. Stuck up into that unworldly sky was the cone of Mount Adams, and the alpenglow was upon it. The alpenglow is that red light of sunset which holds out on snowy mountaintops long after the valleys and tablelands are dimmed. 'Look at Mount Adams,' I said, and that was the last sane moment I remember.

I turned back to the sun. It was going. The sun was going, and the world was wrong. The grasses were wrong; they were platinum. Their every detail of stem, head, and blade shone lightless and artificially distinct as an art photographer's platinum print. This colour has never been seen on earth. The hues were metallic; their finish was matte. The hillside was a nineteenth-century tinted photograph from which the tints had faded. All the people you see in the photograph, distinct and detailed as their faces look, are now dead. The sky was navy blue. My hands were silver. All the distant hills' grasses were finespun metal that the wind laid down. I was watching a faded colour print of a movie filmed in the Middle Ages; I was standing in it, by some mistake. I was standing in a movie of hillside grasses filmed in the Middle Ages. I missed my own century, the people I knew, and the real light of day.

I looked at Gary. He was in the film. Everything was lost. He was a platinum print, a dead artist's version of life. I saw on his skull the darkness of night mixed with the colors of day. My mind was going out; my eyes were receding the way galaxies recede to the rim of space. Gary was light-years away, gesturing inside a circle of darkness, down the wrong end of a telescope. He smiled as if he saw me; the stringy crinkles around his eyes moved. The sight of him, familiar and wrong, was something I was remembering from centuries hence, from the other side of death: yes, *that* is the way he used to look, when we were living. When it was our generation's turn to be alive. I could not hear him; the wind was too loud. Behind him the sun was going. We had all started down a chute of time. At first it was pleasant; now there was no stopping it. Gary was chuting away across space, moving and talking and catching my eye, chuting down the long corridor of separation. The skin on his face moved like thin bronze plating that would peel.

The grass at our feet was wild barley. It was the wild einkorn wheat that grew on the hilly flanks of the Zagros Mountains, above the Euphrates valley, above the valley of the river we called *River*. We harvested the grass with stone sickles, I remember. We found the grasses on the hillsides; we built our shelter beside them and cut them down. That is how he used to look then, that one, moving and living and catching my eye, with the sky so dark behind him, and the wind blowing. God save our life.

From all the hills came screams. A piece of sky beside the crescent sun was detaching. It was a loosened circle of evening sky, suddenly lighted from the back. It was an abrupt black body out of nowhere; it was a flat disk; it was almost over the sun. That is when there were screams. At once this disk of sky slid over the sun like a lid. The sky snapped over the sun like a lens cover. The hatch in the brain slammed. Abruptly it was dark night, on the land and in the sky. In the night sky was a tiny ring of light. The hole where the sun belongs is very small. A thin ring of light marked its place. There was no sound. The eyes dried, the arteries drained, the lungs hushed. There was no world. We were the world's dead people rotating and orbiting around and around, embedded in the planet's crust, while the earth rolled down. Our minds were light-years distant, forgetful of almost everything. Only an extraordinary act of will could recall to us our former, living selves and our contexts in matter and time. We had, it seems, loved the planet and loved our lives, but could no longer remember the way of them. We got the light wrong. In the sky was something that should not be there. In the black sky was a ring of light. It was a thin ring, an old, thin silver wedding band, an old, worn ring. It was an old wedding band in the sky, or a morsel of bone. There were stars. It was all over.

III

It is now that the temptation is strongest to leave these regions. We have seen enough; let's go. Why burn our hands any more than we have to? But two years have passed; the price of gold has risen. I return to the same buried alluvial beds and pick through the strata again.

I saw, early in the morning, the sun diminish against a backdrop of sky. I saw a circular piece of that sky appear, suddenly detached, blackened, and backlighted; from nowhere it came and overlapped the sun. It did not look like the moon. It was enormous and black. If I had not read that it was the moon, I could have seen the sight a hundred times and never thought of the moon once. (If, however, I had not read that it was the moon – if, like most of the world's people throughout time, I had simply glanced up and seen this thing – then I doubtless would not have speculated much, but would have, like Emperor Louis of Bavaria in 840, simply died of fright on the spot.) It did not look like a dragon, although it looked more like a dragon than the moon. It looked like a lens cover, or the lid of a pot. It materialised out of thin air – black, and flat, and sliding, outlined in flame.

Seeing this black body was like seeing a mushroom cloud. The heart screeched. The meaning of the sight overwhelmed its fascination. It obliterated meaning itself. If you were to glance out one day and see a row of mushroom clouds rising on the horizon, you would know at once that what you were seeing, remarkable as it was, was intrinsically not worth remarking. No use running to tell anyone. Significant as it was, it did not matter a whit. For what is significance? It is significance for people. No people, no significance. This is all I have to tell you.

In the deeps are the violence and terror of which psychology has warned us. But if you ride these monsters deeper down, if you drop with them farther over the world's rim, you find what our sciences cannot locate or name, the substrate, the ocean or matrix or ether that buoys the rest, that gives goodness its power for good, and evil its power for evil, the unified field: our complex and inexplicable caring for each other, and for our life together here. This is given. It is not learned.

The world that lay under darkness and stillness following the closing of the lid was not the world we know. The event was over. Its devastation lay round about us. The clamoring mind and heart stilled, almost indifferent, certainly disembodied, frail, and exhausted. The hills were hushed, obliterated. Up in the sky, like a crater from some distant cataclysm, was a hollow ring.

You have seen photographs of the sun taken during a total eclipse. The corona fills the print. All of those photographs were taken through telescopes. The lenses of telescopes and cameras can no more cover the breadth and scale of the visual array than language can cover the breadth and simultaneity of internal experience. Lenses enlarge the sight, omit its context, and make of it a pretty and sensible picture, like something on a Christmas card. I assure you, if you send any shepherds a Christmas card on which is printed a three-by-three photograph of the angel of the Lord, the glory of the Lord, and a multitude of the heavenly host, they will not be sore afraid. More fearsome things can come in envelopes. More moving photographs than those of the sun's corona can appear in magazines. But I pray you will never see anything more awful in the sky.

You see the wide world swaddled in darkness; you see a vast breadth of hilly land, and an enormous, distant, blackened valley; you see towns' lights, a river's path, and blurred portions of your hat and scarf; you see your husband's face looking like an early black-and-white film; and you see a sprawl of black sky and blue sky together, with unfamiliar stars in it, some barely visible bands of cloud, and over there, a small white ring. The ring is as small as one goose in a flock of migrating geese – if you happen to notice a flock of migrating geese. It is one 360th part of the visible sky. The sun we see is less than half the diameter of a dime held at arm's length.

The Ring Nebula, in the constellation Lyra, looks, through binoculars, like a smoke ring. It is a star in the process of exploding. Light from its explosion first reached the earth in 1054; it was a supernova then, and so bright it shone in the day time. Now it is not so bright, but it is still exploding. It expands at the rate of seventy million miles a day. It is interesting to look through binoculars at something expanding seventy million miles a day. It does not budge. Its apparent size does not increase. Photographs of the Ring Nebula taken fifteen years ago seem identical to photographs of it taken yesterday. Some lichens are similar. Botanists have measured some ordinary lichens twice, at fifty-year intervals, without detecting any growth at all. And yet their cells divide; they live.

The small ring of light was like these things – like a ridiculous lichen up in the sky, like a perfectly still explosion 5000 light-years away: it was interesting, and lovely, and in witless motion, and it had nothing to do with anything.

It had nothing to do with anything. The sun was too small, and too cold, and too far away, to keep the world alive. The white ring was not enough. It was feeble and worthless. It was as useless as a memory; it was as off kilter and hollow and wretched as a memory.

When you try your hardest to recall someone's face, or the look of a place, you see in your mind's eye some vague and terrible sight such as this. It is dark; it is insubstantial; it is all wrong.

The white ring and the saturated darkness made the earth and the sky look as they must look in the memories of the careless dead. What I saw, what I seemed to be standing in, was all the wrecked light that the memories of the dead could shed upon the living world. We had all died in our boots on the hilltops of Yakima and were alone in eternity. Empty space stoppered our eyes and mouths; we cared for nothing. We remembered our living days wrong. With great effort we had remembered some sort of circular light in the sky – but only the outline. Oh, and then the orchard trees withered, the ground froze, the glaciers slid down the valleys and overlapped the towns. If there had ever been people on earth, nobody knew it. The dead had forgotten those they had loved. The dead were parted one from the other and could no longer remember the faces and lands they had loved in the light. They seemed to stand on darkened hilltops, looking down.

IV

We teach our children one thing only, as we were taught: to wake up. We teach our children to look alive there, to join by words and activities the life of human culture on the planet's crust. As adults we are almost all adept at waking up. We have so mastered the transition, we have forgotten we ever learned it. Yet it is a transition we make a hundred times a day, as, like so many will-less dolphins, we plunge and surface, lapse and emerge. We live half our waking lives and all of our sleeping lives in some private, useless, and insensible waters we never mention or recall. Useless, I say. Valueless, I might add – until someone hauls the wealth up to the surface and into the wideawake city, in a form that people can use.

I do not know how we got to the restaurant. Like Roethke, 'I take my waking slow.' Gradually I seemed more or less alive, and already forgetful. It was now almost nine in the morning. It was the day of a solar eclipse in central Washington, and a fine adventure for everyone. The sky was clear; there was a fresh breeze out of the north.

The restaurant was a roadside place with tables and booths. The other eclipse-watchers were there. From our booth we could see their cars' California license plates, their University of Washington parking stickers. Inside the restaurant we were all eating eggs or waffles; people were fairly shouting and exchanging enthusiasms, like fans after a World Series game. Did you see . . . ? Did you see . . . ? Then somebody said something that knocked me for a loop.

A college student, a boy in a blue parka who carried a Hasselblad, said to us, 'Did you see that little white ring? It looked like a Life Saver. It looked like a Life Saver up in the sky.'

And so it did. The boy spoke well. He was a walking alarm clock. I myself had at that time no access to such a term. He could write a sentence, and I could not. I grabbed that Life Saver and rode it to the surface. And I had to laugh. I had been dumbstruck on the Euphrates River, I had been dead and gone and grieving, all over the sight of something that, if you could claw your way up to that level, you would grant looked very much like a Life Saver. It was good to be back among people so clever; it was good to have all the world's words at the mind's disposal, so the mind could begin its task. All those things for which we have no words are lost. The mind – the culture – has two little tools, grammar and lexicon: a decorated sand bucket and a matching shovel. With these we bluster about the continents and do all the world's work. With these we try to save our very lives.

There are a few more things to tell from this level, the level of the restaurant. One is the old joke about breakfast. 'It can never be satisfied, the mind, never.' Wallace Stevens wrote that, and in the long run he was right. The mind wants to live forever, or to learn a very good reason why not. The mind wants the world to return its love, or its awareness; the mind wants to know all the world, and all eternity, and God. The mind's sidekick, however, will settle for two eggs over easy.

The dear, stupid body is as easily satisfied as a spaniel. And, incredibly, the simple spaniel can lure the brawling mind to its dish. It is everlastingly funny that the proud, metaphysically ambitious, clamoring mind will hush if you give it an egg.

Further: while the mind reels in deep space, while the mind grieves or fears or exults, the workaday senses, in ignorance or idiocy, like so many computer terminals printing out market prices while the world blows up, still transcribe their little data and transmit them to the warehouse in the skull. Later, under the tranquilizing influence of fried eggs, the mind can sort through these data. The restaurant was a halfway house, a decompression chamber. There I remembered a few things more.

The deepest, and most terrifying, was this: I have said that I heard screams. (I have since read that screaming, with hysteria, is a common reaction even to expected total eclipses.) People on all the hillsides, including, I think, myself, screamed when the black body of the moon detached from the sky and rolled over the sun. But something else was happening at that same instant, and it was this, I believe, that made us scream.

The second before the sun went out, we saw a wall of dark shadow come speeding at us. We no sooner saw it than it was upon us, like thunder. It roared up the valley. It slammed our hill and knocked us out. It was the monstrous swift shadow cone of the moon. I have since read that this wave of shadow moves 1,800 miles an hour. Language can give no sense of this sort of speed – 1,800 miles an hour. It was 195 miles wide. No end was in sight – you saw only the edge. It rolled at you across the land at 1,800 miles an hour, hauling darkness like plague behind it. Seeing it, and knowing it was coming straight for you, was like feeling a slug of anesthetic shoot up your arm. If you think very fast, you may have time to think: Soon it will hit my brain. You can feel the deadness race up your arm; you can feel the appalling, inhuman speed of your own blood. We saw the wall of shadow coming, and screamed before it hit.

This was the universe about which we have read so much and never before felt: the universe as a clockwork of loose spheres flung at stupefying, unauthorized speeds. How could anything moving so fast not crash, not veer from its orbit amok like a car out of control on a turn?

Less than two minutes later, when the sun emerged, the trailing edge of the shadow cone sped away. It coursed down our hill and raced eastward over the plain, faster than the eye could believe; it swept over the plain and dropped over the planet's rim in a twinkling. It had clobbered us, and now it roared away. We blinked in the light. It was as though an enormous, loping god in the sky had reached down and slapped the earth's face.

Something else, something more ordinary, came back to me along about the third cup of coffee. During the moments of totality, it was so dark that drivers on the highway below turned on their cars' headlights. We could see the highway's route as a strand of lights. It was bumper-to-bumper down there. It was eight-fifteen in the morning. Monday morning, and people were driving into Yakima to work. That it was as dark as night, and eerie as hell, an hour after dawn apparently meant that in order to *see* to drive to work, people had to use their headlights. Four or five cars pulled off the road. The rest, in a line at least five miles long, drove to town. The highway ran between hills; the people could not have seen any of the eclipsed sun at all. Yakima will have another total eclipse in 2019. Perhaps, in 2019, businesses will give their employees an hour off.

From the restaurant we drove back to the coast. The highway crossing the Cascades range was open. We drove over the mountain like old pros. We joined our places on the planet's thin crust; it held. For the time being, we were home free.

Early that morning at six, when we had checked out, the six bald men were sitting on folding chairs in the dim hotel lobby. The television was on. Most of them were awake.

You might drown in your own spittle, God knows, at any time; you might wake up dead in a small hotel, a cabbage head watching TV while snow piles up in the passes, watching TV while the chili peppers smile and the moon passes over the sun and nothing changes and nothing is learned because you have lost your bucket and shovel and no longer care. What if you regain the surface and open your sack and find, instead of treasure, a beast, which jumps at you? Or you may not come back at all. The winches may jam, the scaffolding buckle, the air-conditioning collapse. You may glance up one day and see by your headlamp the canary keeled over in its cage. You may reach into a cranny for pearls and touch a moray eel. You yank on your rope; it is too late.

Apparently people share a sense of these hazards, for when the total eclipse ended, an odd thing happened.

When the sun appeared as a blinding bead on the ring's side, the eclipse was over. The black lens cover appeared again, backlighted, and slid away. At once the yellow light made the sky blue again; the black lid dissolved and vanished. The real world began there. I remember now: we all hurried away. We were born and bored at a stroke. We rushed down the hill. We found our car; we saw the other people streaming down the hillsides; we joined the highway traffic and drove away.

We never looked back. It was a general vamoose, and an odd one, for when we left the hill, the sun was still partially eclipsed – a sight rare enough, and one that, in itself, we would probably have driven five hours to see. But enough is enough. One turns at last even from glory itself with a sigh of relief. From the depths of mystery, and even from the heights of splendor, we bounce back and hurry for the latitudes of home.

Discussion questions

Do you need to know a place well to write about it? If you've never been to the Arctic Circle, can you still re-create it in a non-fiction story for your readers? If so, why? How?

Chronological structures are typically used by writers who want to re-create their journeys. Would a chronological structure have worked for Dillard's account of her trip to Washington to watch the eclipse? If she had used such a structure, what would her story have looked like? What information might it have contained? Would it have conveyed the same underpinning theme?

Further reading

There are many writers, writing across very many genres, whose books emphasise place, both urban and rural. And there are many whose work is about nature – ranging from Aldo Leopold and his scientific approach to the poetry of Gary Snyder, the memoirs of Terry Tempest Williams and the delightful but varying stories produced by travel writers such as those mentioned in the next chapter. But here are a few collections to get the budding nature/place essayist started.

Daniel Halpern and Dan Frank (eds), *The Picador Nature Reader*, Eco Press, 1996.

Henry David Thoreau, *Walden; or, Life in the Woods*, 1854. (Complete online versions of Thoreau's works are available, including his essays 'Walking', 1862, and 'On the Duty of Civil Disobedience', 1849, through, for example, *The Thoreau Reader: The works of Henry David Thoreau, 1817–1862* (A Project in Cooperation with the Thoreau Society, © 1999–2006 Richard Lenat, all rights reserved), at <http://thoreau.eserver.org/default.html>.

Mark Tredinnick, *A Place on Earth: An anthology of nature writing from Australia and North America,* University of Nebraska Press, Lincoln & London/University of New South Wales Press, 2003.

Chapter 8
Travel Writing

Taking to the road to learn about ourselves

Willa McDonald

There's a wanderlust in all of us – a yearning to escape to exotic climes and new locales, to shake off the dust and drear of our everyday lives. No wonder travel sections are such an important part of newspaper and magazine culture. We can float down the Nile with our favourite writer or climb to Machu Picchu in our imaginations, stirred by the luscious photos that beckon seductively as we hang from the rail of the bus on the way home from work.

While much of the copy in the travel sections is flimsy advertorial driven by the PR of the vast and powerful tourism industry, gems do abound among the thinly disguised enticements and price lists – stories that offer a different sort of travel writing altogether. These come in all shapes and sizes, often not written by people who would categorise themselves necessarily as travel writers. Helen Garner, Tim Winton, Paul McGeogh and Inga Clendinnen write occasional pieces that sometimes cross into the travel genre and would brighten any weekend. And then there are the classics like the rousing adventures of Isabella Bird, the rollicking, sensory delights of Jack Kerouac, the considered reflections of Jan Morris and the hilarious observations of Bill Bryson – stories always worth another look that trace journeys, both personal and in the larger world, challenging us to new insights about ourselves and the people we encounter in their pages.

Writing for the senses

What helps to make these stories so successful is that the writer comments on new destinations with the enjoyment of the adventurer and the freshness and perspicacity of the foreigner. She re-creates in the stories the sights, sounds and smells of the people and places she discovers. For example, Mark Mordue's enjoyment of his first trip overseas tumbles out of the pages of *Dastgah: Diary of a headtrip*,[1] the chronicle of his 1998 around-the-globe journey with his girlfriend, Lisa Nicol. This mix of travelogue, poetry and memoir takes the reader along for the ride – from a walking tour of a Paris cemetery to an S&M club in New York to an encounter in fundamentalist Iran with the colourful Azerbaijanis, re-created so vividly that we see them and hear them as if we are there:

> As for the women, my god! They're big, busty and brazen, broad-arsed as barns and loud voiced enough to fill one or even two, with dark-ringed eyes and a no-shit readiness to do business day or night so *shoo!* The women wear grey cotton raincoats and black scarves in sloppy deference to Islamic dress codes, but there's a Western trashiness to them that won't be suppressed: a polka dot handbag, a splash of peroxide blonde hair and red, red lips, a whole way of walking that suggests these women shop to kill and it's best you stay out of their goddamned, hotsie totsie way.[2]

Being aware of why you write

Mordue's prose reflects a sense of fun and openness about wandering around the world's byways that's under threat in this post 9/11 world. But, as the nightly news gets worse and ease of travel diminishes (and disappears altogether in some areas of the world), as the number of refugees forced to travel to save their own lives grows daily, is it frivolous to continue offering the fantasies of escape the travel sections are so fond of?

Writer Robyn Davidson, whose 1980 book *Tracks* took us on her solo journey by camel across nearly 3000 kilometres of the Australian Outback,[3] expressed a less than sympathetic view of travellers' tales in her 2000 essay in *Granta* where she censured all Western travel writing – for being ethnocentric, for reflecting only the interests of those with the excess leisure time and money to do it, and for increasingly embodying a longing for the exotic in an ever more 'homogenised, commercialised and trivialised world'.[4] While her words are harsh and her criticisms excessive, her clarion call for travel writers to be aware of why they are writing, and what they hope to achieve, strikes a chord. The real job of the travel writer never changes. If anything, Pico Iyer suggests, 9/11 has given a renewed sense of purpose to some 'to go and find out what these places are that we think of as our enemies'.

Telling the untold stories

Pico Iyer is a writer who tells the untold stories – stories that usually provide more than simply an escape from the mundanity of everyday life. Iyer's stories are always interesting, sometimes forcing us to engage with the underside of an unfair world or to listen to people whose stories are rarely heard. More often than not, they also act as parables, carrying universal and mythological themes.

In his essay 'The Khareef', Iyer tells a timely story. It begins with a misty description of the traveller's first impression of southern Arabia:

> In the thick fog you can hear almost nothing but the ocean sighing in the distance, and when you travel up into the mountains it's hard to see anything but women veiled in black from head to toe, only their mascara'ed eyes looking out. And locals seated on patches of green beside the road, delightedly picnicking in the rain.

The story unfolds to describe the narrator's harrowing time in Yemen, the frightening trip over the mountains in a hired car, the roadblocks, the tension. But it also reveals to the reader information about modern-day Arabia – 'goats foraged outside the broken shops and old women, at occasional red lights, came and hammered on the windows of passing cars, skinny arms extended'. Iyer unveils the country to the Western eye, layer by layer, building to a surprise conclusion that jolts us into reappraising Yemen and its inhabitants. As all good travel stories should, this is a story that makes us look twice. We can't turn our heads and pretend that this isn't a real place, that these aren't real people.

Using dialogue

Capturing conversations[5] is one of the most effective means a writer has to bring the people in a story to life – it lets the reader hear them speaking, in their own words, their own voices. Helen Garner makes no secret of her love of dialogue (see interview in Chapter 6): 'The way people speak makes me dizzy with joy – all those curls and leaps and sudden silences.'

Iyer uses dialogue sparingly but to great effect in 'The Khareef', not only to vary the narrative style and add interest, but also to move the story forward while laying the groundwork for the real point of the tale – his own reflections:

> In the Yemenia office a woman in a black veil looked out at me, preparing for hostilities, and then turned away to a friend.

'It's important that I get to Jeddah tomorrow. I'll take any flight that's available.'

'One moment,' she said, and then turned to the little girl who had appeared by her desk and joked about their friends, a birthday party coming up, perhaps.

Then, turning to the computer, she slowly tapped on a few keys and then, looking at her watch, said, 'There's a flight to the capital, but it leaves ten minutes from now.'

'I have to be out of Aden,' I said. 'There must be something leaving.' She stirred, and yawned, and went over to talk to another friend. There seemed no point in hurrying; no one was going anywhere in Aden.

Even just a snippet of conversation brings the emphasis back to the people in the story, giving the writing an immediacy – and a literary feel – that simply quoting can't achieve.

Making a point

Good travel writing crosses many genres – part travelogue, part feature, part memoir. The best of it is used by the writer to impart new insights, not just about the places visited, but about the writer's own journey through life, particularly about what she takes for granted in her own way of thinking, her own homeland both real and metaphorical. As G. K. Chesterton once said: 'The whole object of travel is not to set foot on foreign land; it is at last to set foot on one's own country as a foreign land.'

And that's what good travel writing can do. It can express the humanity of both those who write it and those whose stories it tells, with honesty, courage and integrity. Whether it's written by Bruce Chatwin, Paul Theroux, V. S. Naipaul, W. G. Sebald – or one of the emerging younger writers – the best travel writing is entertaining or moving, but always enlightening. It guides us towards compassion. Hopefully, it brings us wisdom.

Pico Iyer

Pico Iyer's books include *Video Night in Kathmandu* (which can be found on many lists of the best travel-books of the twentieth century), *The Lady and the Monk*, *The Global Soul* and *Abandon*. His piece in this volume comes from his collection of travel stories, *Sun After Dark*. Iyer studied at Eton, Oxford and Harvard. He has been reviewing and writing journalism for twenty-five years for the *New York Review of Books, The Times Literary Supplement, Tricycle: The Buddhist Review*, *Time* magazine, *Harper's, National Geographic*, the *Financial Times*, and many more. Born in England to parents from India and raised in California, he now lives in Japan – when not travelling to Easter Island, North Korea, Iceland, Paraguay and most places in between. In 1995 Iyer was named by the Utne Reader, along with the likes of Noam Chomsky and Vaclav Havel, as one of 100 visionaries worldwide who could change your life.

THE KHAREEF

Pico Iyer

***Sun After Dark*, 2004**

When the southwestern monsoon, or *khareef*, passes through the southern tip of Arabia, a heavy chill mist falls over the province of Dhofar, in southern Oman, and the temperatures fall twenty or thirty degrees below those of the rest of the Arabian peninsula. In the thick fog you can hear almost nothing but the ocean sighing in the distance, and when you travel up into the mountains it's hard to see anything but women veiled in black from head to toe, only their mascara'ed eyes looking out, and locals seated on patches of green beside the road, delightedly picnicking in the rain.

The *khareef* is an eerie, somewhat magical time in southern Oman, and its heavy fogs and rain allow the frankincense trees to grow along the foothills that run beside the sea. Drizzle is imminent nearly always, and the mist envelops everything, so that when you look down the long empty roads you see camels, and sand, and nothingness. Along one side of the road sits a Hilton hotel, but the palm trees beside it are worn, and the gusty ocean is almost entirely without color. The world has sloughed off proportion and dimension.

The smell of frankincense on the back streets, the Indian shopkeepers outside their little stalls as if they were still in Cochin – 'Foodstuff and Luxuries,' 'Watch Repair,' 'Coconut Sale,' 'Auto Cushion' – suggest somewhere entirely forgotten by the world. Everything shuts down in the middle of the day, though not for prayer; the sovereign spirits here are trade and sleep. Once the richest area in the world, Dhofar now nestles behind the mountains, unvisited, much like the last sultan, who took to his palace here for twelve years, and banned bicycles, radios, even sunglasses for locals.

I sat in my room in the deserted hotel sometimes, and watched a few American soldiers, on their Friday off, wrestle on the lawn below. The sound of Arabic curses came from the next terrace; in the lobby there were always barrel-chested Englishmen, here to train the local army, with tattoos across their forearms, pounding one fist into another, again and again and again.

The Indians sat at their desks looking wistful, sometimes wry. What had brought them here, I asked. Not adventure or dreams or anything; a shrug, an uncle now gone. They'd come to Muscat, the fairy-tale sand-city in the north, and somehow ended up here. What was there to do? A defeated smile.

In the bar, a tiny Filipina served drinks to tired blond Germans with leathery tans, who shook their bangles and tossed their heads impatiently as they waited for the grand tours they'd been promised, and groups of men from Atlanta in shorts – who knew on what mission? – cracked jokes as they sat in the thick armchairs huddled together in clusters in the lobby. 'The plural of "fish" is "fishes"?' 'A dollar for anyone in the room who can tell us what the plural of "fish" is.'

The Omanis in their long white robes sat in the vast space talking softly, their women dressed in black, so intense that they seemed apparitions of suggestiveness. A curling hand, decorated with some kind of design; a kohl-lined eye. So little could be seen of them, walking straight and regal in their black, handbags swinging from their shoulders, white clogs emerging occasionally under their robes, that their eyes carried everything. A spark, a light of mischief.

Outside my window there was dust and fog; out on the road, spotless tarmac stretching in every direction without cease. Camels by the sand, and in the distance the new port, to receive container ships. The mountains were close, but nothing but clouds now; figures appeared around curves like creatures from myth, and then disappeared again into the mist.

I arrived here after a thirty-three-hour flight from Santa Barbara to Los Angeles to London, then Abu Dhabi, to Muscat, and then Salalah; I got out at the long dusty road and walked into a room with a terrace, a view of the sea without colour. In the morning, when I went out, there was rain all over the chairs; a lone figure was somewhere behind the palm trees, walking towards the lights.

One day I hired a car and driver – a homesick man from Kerala, on his way to marry a woman he'd never met (he kept up with home at night through his FM radio) – and we drove into the hills. As we went up the mountains from the plain, the mist, already thick, began to envelop us, so we were part of it, and it of us, and the rain began to fall. Cars inched their way around turns, and at the tomb of Job, at the top, I stepped out into the lightly falling rain and followed a group of shadows, all in black, disappearing between the trees.

We drove down again, and south, and found ourselves in a paradise of sorts, a clear river running along the base of the hills, where happy shirtless boys were splashing and jumping around as if they'd found their way back to the beginning of the world. Families were gathered on carpets under the trees, one man serenading his party – a wedding party – with a set of bagpipes.

Near the Holiday Inn, a crumbling ruin not far away, archaeologists had found the remains of the place acclaimed by Marco Polo as a 'fine and great and noble city.' The Queen of Sheba had sent her dhows from here, my guide said, to Egypt and Jerusalem and Rome, bearing frankincense at a time when it was worth more than gold. Her castle was now remembered by a pile of stones.

In the lobby a Canadian engineer sat alone, looking out into the mist where the GIs organized games of touch football without a ball.

Four days later, following the so-called Incense Coast, I came to Aden, the largest port of southern Yemen, which once had seemed a centre of the world, the place where every ship from Britain to India stopped for refueling. The last time I had been here, at the age of two, in 1959 – my mother was taking me back from the Oxford where I was born to the Bombay that was her hometown – Aden had buzzed with the slightly illicit excitement that attends a port, groups of touts out to meet the tourist ships and promise everything that is possible when West first touches East. Aden, Victoria's first imperial acquisition, was the largest harbor in the world then, outside Manhattan.

Now, in the summer of 2001, the town was a biblical wasteland. Goats foraged outside the broken shops and old women, at occasional red lights, came and hammered on the windows of passing cars, skinny arms extended. I saw no shops or restaurants or anything in Aden; the children played in the street because there was nowhere else for them to play. It seemed as if the whole city was sitting on debris, waiting to see what the next wind would blow into town.

I took myself to the Crescent Hotel, near Steamer Point, where a replica of Big Ben tolled the passing hours. But when I walked into the old British haunt – a black-and-white portrait of Queen Elizabeth, when young, peering out through the unlit lobby – I quickly realized this was no place to stay. 'We have a new Crescent Hotel down the street,' the young boy at the desk offered, and I followed him to a marginally less dusty place where an aged retainer offered me a crisp military salute.

The new hotel on the beach seemed more promising, though just to walk into the lobby I had to walk through a security machine of the kind you see at airports. Going out onto the sand – pristine, and opening onto a silent, lovely bay – I noticed that I was the only person there. Then I looked more closely and saw armed soldiers on both sides of me, standing against the wall, protecting me, I could only imagine, from Aden.

When I walked out of the hotel, a sad-eyed man, apparently Indian, slouched up to me. He said hello in a fluent, almost swallowed English, and I learned that his father had been an Englishman, though born here. The man before me had applied for a passport, and the chance to live in England, but Her Majesty's Government had refused him because his father, though entirely English, was born in Aden. 'Do you want to see the cemetery?' he said.

We drove a few hundred yards to where a clump of headstones sat in the wasting heat. Their inscriptions were in German, Greek, Russian, or Chinese; Aden had once been known as the 'entrance-hall of China and the warehouse of the West.' Most of the inscriptions, though, were in English, recalling forgotten Gwendolenes and Despinas, flying officers and telegraphists. OH FOR A TOUCH OF THAT VANISHED HAND. AVE ATQUE VALE.

'We used to see them every time we went to church,' my new friend said. 'Getting buried. One or two a week.' Now St. Mary's was shuttered, and Christians such as he could worship only in secret if at all. The English had left, quite literally overnight, in 1967, the Russians had come in, and then they too had given up on Aden, leaving it to a civil war. Though technically reunited with the northern parts of the country in 1991, it had been through a two-month siege in 1994. The Frontier Hotel, burned out, had become the Mövenpick. The Mövenpick, destroyed in the next period of fighting, was now the Aden Hotel.

In the small part of town where the English had been, the signs still said, WE HOPE YOU ENJOYED YOUR STAY. PLEASE COME AGAIN at the Prince of Wales pier. A bookshop in the customs shed sold black-and-white postcards of the once bustling port, and paperbacks, forty years old, in which someone had laboriously inscribed, *Miss Sirihin Abdullah Murji, P.O. Box 1959, Mombasa.* I thought of a grandfather, difficult and vainglorious in his youth, who now has been softened by incapacity, and can almost be regarded with affection.

We drove around to see the small museum and the Rambow Tourist Restaurant and Cafeteria, where Rimbaud once had lived. And when I walked into the hotel, that evening, the man who had offered to reconfirm my ticket, to Jeddah next day, came up with a smile. 'Your flight is canceled,' he said (and having seen Aden, I was surprised they even made the pretense of flights). 'But there's another one in four days' time.'

Four days, I thought, could be forty in this wilderness, so I went outside, found an old African man with a battered car, and we drove into the deserted downtown area known as Crater. In the Yemenia office a woman in a black veil looked out at me, preparing for hostilities, and then turned away to a friend.

'It's important that I get to Jeddah tomorrow. I'll take any flight that's available.'

'One moment,' she said, and then turned to the little girl who had appeared by her desk and joked about their friends, a birthday party coming up, perhaps. Then, turning to the computer, she slowly tapped on a few keys and then, looking at her watch, said, 'There's a flight to the capital, but it leaves ten minutes from now.'

'I have to be out of Aden,' I said. 'There must be something leaving.' She stirred, and yawned, and went over to talk to another friend. There seemed no point in hurrying; no one was going anywhere in Aden.

Then, coming back and tapping away at her computer again, she said, 'There is a flight leaving in the morning. But from Sana'a, across the mountains. A six-hour drive away.' It left at 6:00 a.m., which meant that check-in was seven hours from now.

'I'll take it.'

'I can't help you with this. You must go to the other Yemenia office.'

I went out into the dark – the main street was like the cemetery – and roused the driver from his sleep; we rattled off to another Yemenia office, a few hundred yards away, where another woman in a black veil looked up at me.

This new adversary clicked away on her keyboard – computers are slow in Aden, and linked to a world no one really believes in – and then, after many blocked paths and wrong turns, she announced that a plane was leaving in the morning, from Sana'a, the capital, long enemy territory to Aden, six hours away across the mountains. Check-in was six hours from now, she said; I couldn't make it.

Time slips away in a place like Aden; space itself dissolves, as if the whole city is drifting away on the narcotic *qat* that everyone chews. The clock at the top of the Crescent Hotel clearly hadn't moved for years.

I bought a ticket from her – no price was too high – and went out to summon my driver again, to drive back to the hotel. I called the hotel in advance, from the Yemenia office, to fix up a taxi to drive to the capital, and we made our way back, at a donkey's pace, through the broken center of the city, past roadblocks and detours, the large ditches Chinese laborers were digging on behalf of the Aden Sewage Company. The city is stretched out along the coast like a piece of gum that someone has been chewing for a very long time.

At the hotel, racing to collect my things and check out, I was told that the taxi had been called for, but showed no signs of arriving; it was better to go to the taxi stand at the bus station. A young employee in a suit pushed me into a minivan, and we drove, tires squealing, across town, skidding in the dust, to a bus station that was a dingy emptiness. In front of what was optimistically called the 'taxi stand' there was darkness and silence.

At last a man appeared, smiling, in an old Peugeot, and I recognized a man who had taken me all around town two days before in search of a cemetery we never found. 'Wait over there,' he said, pointing to an even darker corner of the empty lot, and we went and sat in the silence, the night. The young man in his suit drummed his fingers on the dashboard; he looked at his watch, looked back nervously at me. Finally, the man who had cheated me before appeared, at the wheel of a very old car.

He had no interest in driving himself, he explained, through the man in the suit – the main source of income in the mountains was the kidnapping of foreigners. But he had found someone else who knew so little, or needed so much, that he had volunteered for the job: a very old man in a dirty turban loomed out of the dark. As he took his place behind the wheel, eyes closed, and visibly shaking, friends came up and patted him on the back, wished him luck, said prayers for his safe return.

He, too, before moving, closed his eyes and muttered a quick prayer, and then we were off, in the dark, the old man hardly able to see over the wheel, peering out into the night. Occasional trucks came barreling towards us on the narrow road, their headlights blinding.

The night that followed never happened, I tell myself now, it belongs to some place in the imagination. Very soon we were on a mountain road, pitch black, and though I could see nothing around us, I could tell there was a sheer drop on one side. Above us, as we climbed, there were occasional towers, medieval fortresses, set across the hillside. We turned a mountain corner, and suddenly there was noise: men with guns, turbaned boys, a clamor of faces in the dark motioning for us to stop. A flashlight in my eyes, my passport taken away, a whispered confabulation. The driver, trembling, was asked to get out and open up the back.

Then, as suddenly as they had materialized, the guns were gone again, and we were bumping along in the dark, mountains on one side of us, a precipice on the other. I tried to sleep, but every time I fell away – seven, ten times in the night – I woke to find us stopped, guns in front of us, and faces at the window. The driver shoving banknotes into a hand, or laboring out to what looked like a rebel guardpost. Boys, clamorous, full of their own strength, asking who I was, peering in to get a look.

There were painted windows made of glass in the six- or seven-storey houses beside us and when the lights were on, the panes shone like stained-glass across the darkened mountainside. Sometimes, as I slept, I woke to rain, the creaking wipers of the car moving frantically back and forth while the car skidded across the road and the man swerved furiously, so we were spinning towards the mountain. At times he turned on a radio – mad wailing in the dark – to keep himself from falling asleep, his stash of *qat* beside him.

When there was a light above us on the road, I looked at my watch – 11:41,1:53. The capital never seemed to come closer. The driver stopped, to relieve himself in a ditch. Again, to get some warmer clothing out of the back. He stopped again, to catch his breath, and I pointed angrily at my watch; he came back from his stop with a can of 7-Up, two bars of chocolate, for me.

Occasionally, we passed a sudden light in the dark mountains – a circle of figures around a shack for some reason open at 2 a.m. Then, it was only darkness again, the plain far below, the sound of thunder from the mountains. Rain, and boys waving at us to stop; guns at the window, and the air appreciably cooler in the high places, the tower-houses all around shuttered fastnesses.

As the first call to prayer rose up – 3:45, I guessed – we came to what seemed to be buildings, larger roads (the capital?), and boys who now stood at intersections in the brownish light. Guarding their turf as if in East L.A., oil drums blocking the way, and coming to our window to demand tithes, local taxes, or blood money. The driver turned left onto an empty road, then right onto an empty road, and I realized that he had no idea where he was going.

At last, long after 4:00 a.m., we saw a tower, even higher than the tower-houses all around, and I recognized the building where I had been admitted into the country a few days before, the *khareef* just behind me. A group of Chinese traders was passing through a security check; a man who slept on the sofa in his office got up to offer me Saudi rials. I got in a plane and flew to Dubai – Internet connections in the airport hotel, a seven-star hotel only a short drive away – and saw the monitors at every departure gate announcing New York, London, Tokyo.

Less than six weeks later, as it happened, two planes flew into the World Trade Center in New York, and Aden, Oman, were suddenly pulled out of the subconscious, back into the forefront of our minds. The bored soldiers I had seen in the hotel lobby began steaming towards Afghanistan, to fight, and southern Yemen, near Aden, where

Osama bin Laden was born, was taken to be the center of all evil. Aden, everyone now recalled, was the site of the most recent terrorist attack on America (the bombing of the USS *Cole* eleven months before, in the harbor outside my hotel), and a place that most of us had consigned to myth, somewhere behind the mists of the *khareef*, was suddenly dragged back into the present tense.

I sat in California and listened to the imprecations – Aden now deemed the opposite of Milton's 'Araby the Blest' – and thought back to the driver who had got out in the middle of the night to buy me chocolate, the woman turning to the little girl in the airline office, my sad-eyed guide pointing to the graves of his mother, his sister, the Indian nuns, the British officers. Many of them, I suspected, had friends and loved ones of their own in New York (even in the World Trade Center), whom they must be worried about even now. In the streets – it wasn't hard to imagine – the children would be playing tag in the dusk, their high voices rising up along the empty boulevards, while we sat in the our mansions, watching versions of their lives onscreen, and wishing destruction on them all.

Interview with Pico Iyer

Question *How did you come to write 'The Khareef'?*

Iyer As it happens – and this is often the case with the curious logic of the writing life – I had been all set on going to Yemen at the beginning of 2001. That trip fell through, and then, just three months later an editor [from *Time* magazine] called me up and said, 'You probably haven't heard of this little place, and you probably don't have the time, but would you have any interest in going to Yemen, very soon, to retrace the journeys of a eunuch navy?'

So I flew to Southern Oman and to Yemen for a few days, and wrote a short piece for the magazine for an issue on Zheng He, the fifteenth century Chinese Moslem admiral, who led his eunuch navies on seven voyages across the seas . . . And only later, when Yemen was suddenly yanked into the headlines in the wake of the 9/11 terrorist attacks six weeks after my return, did I decide to write another piece, for myself, and arising out of memory and conviction, to come at the area in a deeper way than magazine journalism would allow. What had seemed at the time a simple travel-story acquired resonances, and real-life consequences, that I could never have guessed.

How crucial is the structure of 'The Khareef' to its effectiveness?

I worked very hard on the structure, because making one's experience clear and vivid and shaped is how a writer makes a piece of writing distinctive and his own, how he turns a jumble of sensation into an attempt at lucid order, and understanding. In this piece I wanted to take the reader through the various stages of knowing a place just as I, visiting it, had been taken through them. One starts in the mist, in every sense, in a setting so haunting and foreign that it seems to belong to fairy-tale, or myth. Slowly figures appear out of the mist, and give it a human reality, a sense of something real and often poignant and bleeding. One travels deeper into the hearts and lives one meets, as around the curves of a mountain road, and finally one finds oneself beyond the boundaries of one's understanding, in something so real that it's ambiguous and throws up a sense of all one cannot know and hasn't understood.

A journey for me has its end-point somewhere in the imagination, or soul, or conscience. The last point on an itinerary is often the starting point on that second, more important journey in which we wrestle with all we have seen and felt and experienced, and try to make some sense of it. Any experience, indeed, is only as useful, a writer can believe, as the sense or shape he makes of it at his desk, taking the shards and fragments of what he has seen, and turning them into a stained-glass whole. And in this piece I wanted to take the reader, as I had been taken, from beautiful mystification, to sympathy and sadness – an engagement of the heart – to visceral terror and confusion, into what may be most important of all, a rounded and human understanding of Yemen as it exists somewhere deeper than the political sphere and in all that is left out from our headlines. I suppose the piece is about a journey into humanity, and turns on the sense that a simple traveller can see and encounter things far realer than we can get from any second-hand or mediated account.

How important is its conclusion?

An essay often works like a slow-moving fuse and here the ending is its only real point and justification. In some ways I travel in order to be turned on my head, proven wrong and confounded in every way – to be shown that the human and concrete reality of a place is an instant refutation of all my ideas about it – and in this essay I want to pass on my experience of confoundedness and even shock to the reader. So I deliberately try to lull the reader, as I was lulled, into a sense of dream-like otherworldliness when first meeting the region of 'The Khareef', and then to take her deeper into its human life and poignancy – the homesickness and loss that are its main features – and then, having drawn the reader into a sense of both enchantment and sympathy, to pull her into the present moment to show her the consequences of that sympathy and ask her what she will do with it.

I always think of the moment in Yvonne Cloetta's memoir of her life with Graham Greene (Cloetta was Greene's mistress for the final decades of his life) in which she says that, only once in their time together did Greene emerge from his study in mid-morning, during his working hours. He was looking ashen and drawn, she writes, as if he had witnessed a death of some sort.

'What's wrong, Graham?' she instantly asked. 'Are you ill? Do you need something?'

'I've just begun working on a book,' he replied, 'and now I know that I'm going to have to spend the next three years with someone I really despise.'

What makes this story interesting is that the character he had just realised he would be spending time with is Charley Fortnum, the drunken, dissolute, almost pathetically lonely Englishman abroad in *The Honorary Consul*. What is moving about the story is that anyone who reads the novel grows to feel so much for poor Charley that the drunken exile abroad becomes our place of sympathy and even beauty in the book.

Writing, that moment tells us, is about the movement from dislike through sympathy and understanding to love; you take someone you know nothing about, or may not even want to spend time with, and by bringing him your patience and attention, slowly you come to understand him, to forgive him, even to love him.

In this essay I want to win the reader's sympathy for the endlessly kind and generous people of Yemen and Oman and then, by making human contact, to question her own abstractions about the notional Yemen that we sometimes dismiss or even dislike from afar. Just as happened with me. The traveller seeks to bring places out of the mist and the world of myth and the writer tries to bewitch his reader, perhaps with a subject's otherworldly allure, only to deposit her back, in the end, very firmly, in reality.

The observations in 'The Khareef' are carefully and evocatively rendered. How important are the details to the success of this piece?

Everything is in the details when one writes – not just god, but the devils and the whole battle between them. Anyone can evoke a far-off place through memory and imagination, especially in these days when screens bring us the farthest corners of the world in living colour to our studies; what matters in the conversation between a writer and a place is nothing but the particulars. Indeed, travel and writing can both be seen as ways to move out of abstraction and the ideas behind which we hide, into the reality of what confounds.

Whenever I travel, I take voluminous notes, then and there, in full paragraphs, as if completing the first draft of an essay for myself, and not even allowing a night to intervene and dim the memory and intensity of the smells, sounds and feeling of an interaction. And then, when I get back to my desk, I decide how closely to use my notes, and how much to rely on what memory sifts and what lies between the particulars. But it's critical to get down the first impression, in all its vividness and detail, since it's always the strongest and the most disproportionately potent impression.

Part of the process involved in moving from journalism to a deeper and more lasting kind of writing is putting the notes aside at times, and calling upon memory to flavour and colour, to find the emotional logic that magazine writing might not have time or need for. But without the details, even if they only invisibly hover over a piece, one might as well stay at home!

The people in this story are very important to the way it unfolds – how important are characters to bringing a piece of creative non-fiction like this to life?

We build places through people, and the challenge is to find a person who will stand for something more than just himself, and who will become a kind of representative man, in Emerson's phrase. In Arabia, on this particular trip, I probably met dozens of individuals. But in writing about the place, I wanted to draw out, and upon, those who seemed to speak for something larger than themselves and to give a human face and complexity to what are otherwise just labels or ideas. No one in this piece is a typical citizen of Aden; and yet each, I hope, speaks for something I found in Aden that I could only have found there.

You bring novelistic techniques to your essay writing. Do those two things overlap?

I think they overlap a huge amount. And some of the great non-fictional writers I can think of right now – V. S. Naipaul, Joan Didion, W. G. Sebald – sometimes make it difficult to tell whether they are writing fiction or non-fiction. That may even be their strength – that they enter their non-fictional subjects with such depth and sympathy that these come to resemble works of the imagination. Creative non-fiction is perhaps the niece of what is often called 'the new journalism', and what is exciting about the form is the way it enlists many of the tools of fiction, in terms of storytelling, vivid characterisation, unexpected structuring and even otherworldly atmosphere to make a real subject that much realer. Few of our responses to even those people and places we know best, after all, are clear-cut or as factual and linear as traditional non-fiction makes out. If we think about the people closest to us, or the streets we know best, we realise that they compel us because they invade our imagination and memory, flee the simple clarity of something seen for the first time and acquire shadows, hidden dimensions, questions.

So when V. S. Naipaul brought out a book called *A Way in the World* a few years ago, it was released as fiction on one side of the Atlantic and non-fiction (though it consisted of exactly the same text) on the other. At roughly the same time, Paul Theroux, Naipaul's complicated and gifted friend and Boswell, started publishing stories about a character called Paul Theroux that the *New Yorker,* in its perplexity, labelled 'fact and fiction'. Bruce Chatwin's work dances around the border of what is true and what is embellished. I remember once being asked in Los Angeles who was the most memorable travel writer of the time, and I mentioned W. G. Sebald. That very same weekend, at that very same festival, Sebald was awarded the *Los Angeles Times* prize for fiction (for the same book I was extolling as non-fiction)! The lesson of the new century is that all our old divisions – between high and low, east and west, old and new – are becoming redundant, as we start living in a world of *both/and* more than of *either/or*. So, I'm happy if we reflect that new fluidity in our talk about genres, too.

I think non-fiction is the great beneficiary of this Berlin wall of genre coming down in recent times. Fiction has nearly always depended upon research and factual accuracy and other of the tools of non-fiction. Most novels I enjoy, I enjoy largely because they are leading me into an authoritative vision of the world that stands on a bedrock of fact (imagination being the light that plays over that solid stone). But creative non-fiction has grown much more artful and imaginative and daring in how it tries to do justice to the truth and make the real world seem as magical as the places in our imaginations.

Can you talk about the balance between literary techniques with the writing of fact in terms of 'The Khareef'?

A writer has to be accountable to the truth, and catching the truth of any situation is his first mandate. But the truth is not the same as the facts, as any writer of carefully fact-checked magazine articles can attest, and I think a writer has to be true to the mystery as well as the clarity of life. To some extent we live in shadow with everything around us, especially those people and places we know best, and the writer has to acknowledge some degree of agnosticism or humility along with the authority he pretends to. In every relationship that counts, with loved ones or countries or literary subjects, we're trying to catch both what one knows and understands about them and what will always remain thrillingly beyond our ken.

Writing for *Time* magazine, I came to see that you could make every word of an article true – *Time* has a large team of brilliant fact-checkers who double-check every tiny detail – and still not come close to the truth at all. While a novelist makes up a story entirely in his head to bring us closer to a truth that otherwise we never see. In the case of a piece like 'The Khareef', my only loyalty is to trying to catch this struggling, too little known nation in all its complexity and poignancy. But part of this means accepting that truth and the factual are not one and the same thing, and seeing that a true piece of writing is often one that goes beyond the facts, into the realm of the heart or the spirit.

So in putting the piece together, I compressed a harrowing night-long drive into a couple of pages, I trimmed my notes down to the bone, I excluded many encounters and moments that had moved me, in order to try to come to an emotional and atmospheric truth that sometimes gets lost in the straight transcription of 'day one: 8:00 a.m. . . . day two: 9:00 a.m.'. An unedited account of every moment is sometimes further from the truth of an encounter than something entirely made-up.

Yet it was vital to me to include no fiction in this piece. These people are real, as is their suffering, as is the way it confounds a typical traveller from abroad. I think I can say that in all the non-fiction I have written, over twenty years or more, I have worked very hard to ensure that there is no fiction in it (and my fact-checkers have worked wonderfully to try to keep me honest). Yet I would be foolish to deny that my account of, for example, the drive in this story would be very different from the driver's, or from that of the boys we met along the way.

You have written yourself into 'The Khareef' in a way that is not at all intrusive. Can you comment on your approach?

You are always trying to write to a stranger whom you have first got to grab and then you have got to hold. If you think of it in those terms, you instantly realise that babbling on about yourself is going to make the stranger turn around and go away. So you have to find that part of yourself that is going to be intriguing to the stranger – then to carry yourself with the right weight that the stranger doesn't think, 'Oh, I'm just hearing a story about Pico Iyer', but will say, 'I'm hearing a story about myself, or my friend'.

Almost any writer will tell you that writing is only as good and as strong as the depths from which it arises (indeed, writing is a wonderful test and register of those depths). You have to be tapping your wounds and your fears and your anxieties. You have to be writing from as deep inside yourself as you can. Yet you have to make it interesting to somebody who has no investment in you. The reader, picking any book up, is interested in the world and in his life, but he has very little interest usually in the author. A writer, to some extent, is only as good as his ability to render himself invisible, or at least to present his vision to the reader with a persuasive air of objectivity.

Do you see an overlap between journalism and other forms of writing?

Certainly – and many of the writers I most respect, from Graham Greene to V. S. Naipaul, keep themselves honest with their journalism, use journalism as a way to force themselves out of their homes (and their assumptions), as a way to attend to facts and the fibre of the real world, and perhaps as a way to pose to themselves the riddles that fiction tries to solve.

If you look at a Joan Didion or a Robert Stone, you realise that their entire enterprise is about trying to give a true and nuanced accounting of the world, both inner and outer, and at some point again it hardly matters whether you call their work 'fiction' or 'non-fiction'. The journalist reports faithfully on the external world, the writer reports with equal exactitude on the inner, and many of the artists we cherish are the ones who can do justice to both, and even link within and without. Indeed, some of the exciting new writers of our times – from Gabriel Garcia Marquez to Salman Rushdie – tell the story of a whole sub-continent by telling the story of themselves, and vice versa.

I went straight from graduate studies in literature to journalism, for *Time*, and one of the things I found so liberating about the move was that journalism forced me to attend to the world and to the reader. In graduate school, I often felt I was writing for an audience of two, or even of one, and so spent too much of my energy trying to amuse or impress myself. As soon as I began writing for *Time*, I was addressing 30 million readers, each of whom had no particular interest in the prose-style or talents of Pico Iyer, but just wanted to know what had happened in Beirut that week. It was a great training in clarity, in concision and even in a kind of selflessness, working towards the truth rather than merely getting lost in the excitements of self-assertion.

You have mentioned in media interviews that since September 11 you've had a renewed sense of purpose with travel writing. Could you explain that?

I feel it incumbent on me, and anyone who can gather the time and resources, to go and find out what these places are that we think of as our enemies.

Instantly, of course, we find that they are our friends; we find that we have as much in common with them as apart. I suppose my prejudice is that cultures and individuals are usually wiser than their governments.

Governments and institutions think in terms of divisions – 'us against them' – and ideologies, but human beings are more nuanced and much more ready to see that 'we' are 'they' and to travel so deep into a human connection that all sense of division dissolves. In that regard travelling, like writing, is about dreaming your way into the other.

Discussion questions

Does travel writing do more harm than good by drawing tourists to 'undiscovered' places?

Robyn Davidson says there is a need for a 'literature of movement', a genre of writing that reflects the stories of *all* those who travel, whether for leisure or out of desperate necessity. Do you agree?

Further reading

Travel writing comes in all shapes and sizes, from the traditional travel yarn to memoirs written by people spending a year in an exotic locale such as Paris or Provence. Here are some good places to start, but readers are encouraged to search out writers they love (from W. G. Sebald to Peter Moore to Frances Mayes) and lap up their engaging 'travel' stories.

Trevor Borman (compiler), *Traveller's Tales: Stories from the ABC's foreign correspondents*, ABC Books, 2004.

Patricia Craig (ed.), *The Oxford Book of Travel Stories*, Oxford University Press, 1996.

Robyn Davidson, *The Picador Book of Journeys*, Pan Macmillan, 2002.

Don George (ed.), *Salon.com's Wanderlust: Real life tales of adventure & romance*, Macmillan, 2001.

Peter Hulme and Tim Youngs (eds), *The Cambridge Companion to Travel Writing*, Cambridge University Press, 2002.

Mary Morris (ed.) with Larry O'Connor, *The Illustrated Virago Book of Women Travellers*, Virago Press, 2002.

Notes

1. News and Follow-ups

1. Robert Fisk, 'Is This Some Kind of Crusade?' *Independent On Sunday*, May 18, 1997.
2. Robert Fisk, *The Great War for Civilisation: The conquest of the Middle East*, Fourth Estate, 2005, p. 292.
3. See for example, 'Torture at Abu Ghraib: How far up does the responsibility go?', New Yorker, May 10, 2004 and 'The Gray Zone: How a secret Pentagon program came to Abu Ghraib', New Yorker, May 24, 2004.
4. David Cassidy, 'The David Kelly Affair', *New Yorker*, December, 2003.
5. David Marr, interview for *The Writer's Reader*.
6. Michael Southwell, interview for *The Writer's Reader*.
7. David Marr and Marian Wilkinson, *Dark Victory*, Allen & Unwin, 2003.

2. New Journalism and Its Legacy

1. Tom Wolfe and E. W. Johnson (eds), *The New Journalism*, Harper & Row, 1973.
2. Tom Wolfe, 'The Kandy-Kolored Tangerine-Flake Streamline Baby', cited in Wolfe and Johnson, 1973.
3. Joan Didion, *Slouching Towards Bethlehem*, Penguin, 1974 (first published 1968: Farrar, Straus and Giroux).
4. Joan Didion, *Fixed Ideas, America since 9.11*, published in booklet form, *New York Review of Books*, 2003.
5. Susan Faludi, *New York Observer*, September 17, 2001, p. 14.
6. In November 2005, Didion's new book, *The Year of Magical Thinking,* won the US National Book Award for Non-Fiction.
7. Sir Arthur Quiller-Couch, *On the Art of Writing*, Cambridge University Press, 1923, p. 203.
8. William Zinsser, *On Writing Well*, 3rd edn, Harper & Row, 1988, p. 15.
9. Cited in William Safire and Leonard Safir, *Good Advice on Writing*, Simon & Schuster, 1992, p. 71.
10. Joan Didion, 'On Keeping a Notebook', in *Slouching Towards Bethlehem*, p. 113.
11. Didion, 'On Keeping a Notebook', pp. 113–14.
12. Barry Siegel, interview for *The Writer's Reader*.

13. John Birmingham, interview for *The Writer's Reader*.
14. Siegel and Birmingham interviews.
15. Siegel interview.
16. Thanasis Lalas, 'A Wolfe in Sheep's Clothing', *HQ* magazine, March 2, 2001, p. 87.

3. Profiles

1. Tony Squires, 'Good Sport', Metropolitan, *Sydney Morning Herald*, May 4–5, 2002, p. 1.
2. Stephen King, *On Writing*, Hodder & Stoughton, 2000, p. 137.
3. Susan Chenery, 'No Ordinary Dame', *Weekend Australian*, March 13–14, 2004, p. B16.
4. David Leser, *The Whites of Their Eyes*, Allen & Unwin, 1999, p. xii.
5. Janet Malcolm, *The Journalist and the Murderer*, Bloomsbury, 1991, p. 3.
6. Malcolm interviewed Masson extensively for *In the Freud Archives*, orig. published Knopf, 1984.
7. Greg Bearup, interview for *The Writer's Reader*.

4. Investigations

1. Jessica Mitford, *The American Way of Death*, Simon & Schuster, 1963.
2. Carl Bernstein, Afterword, *The Making of a Muckraker*, Quartet Books, 1979.
3. Malcolm Knox, Journalism seminar, University of Technology, Sydney (UTS), 2005.
4. Chris Masters, *The Media Report*, Radio National, December 29, 2005.
5. Chris Masters, *Not for Publication*, ABC Books, 2002, p. ix.
6. Southwell interview.
7. I. F. Stone (1907–1989) edited the influential independent US publication *I.F. Stone's Weekly*.
8. Chris Masters, interview for *The Writer's Reader*.

5. Essays

1. 'For Love or Money: The Future of the Australian Essay', transcript, Willa McDonald (chair), Sydney Writers' Festival, 2004, *Scan, Journal of Media, Arts & Culture*, Macquarie University, <http://scan.net.au/scan/magazine/display.php?journal˙id=29>.
2. 'Of Experience', *The Essays (Les Essais)*, Bk III, ch. 13, Abel Langelier, Paris. 1595. Michel de Montaigne, *Essays*, 1580–1592, Charles Cotton (trans.), available online at *Project Gutenberg*, <http://www.gutenberg.org/etext/3600>.
3. Ralph Waldo Emerson, 'Nature', in R. W. Emerson and H. D. Thoreau, *Nature/Walking* (intro. John Elder), Beacon Press, 1991, ch. 4. ('Nature' first appeared in *Atlantic* magazine, 1836.)
4. Scott Russell Sanders, 'The Singular First Person', in Alexander J. Butrym (ed.), *Essays on the Essay: Redefining the genre,* University of Georgia Press, 1989.
5. 'Come September', *War Talk,* South End Press, Cambridge, Massachusetts, 2003.
6. John Birmingham, *He Died with a Felafel in his Hand*, Duffy & Snellgrove, 1994; *The Tasmanian Babes Fiasco*, Duffy & Snellgrove, 1997.
7. John Birmingham, *Leviathan*, Random House, 1999; 'Appeasing Jakarta', *Quarterly Essay*, Black Inc., June 2001.
8. See Birmingham's opinion piece,'Voices of Dissent Won't Destroy Us – They Can Only Make Us Stronger', *Sydney Morning Herald,* November 18, 2002.
9. Phillip Lopate, *The Art of the Personal Essay*, Anchor/Doubleday, 1994, p. xxvi.

10. William K. Zinsser, *On Writing Well: The classic guide to writing non fiction*, 25th anniversary edn, Quill/Harper, 2001, p. 214.

6. Memoir

1. Pico Iyer, Foreword to Don George (ed.), *Salon.com's Wanderlust: Real life tales of adventure and romance*, Macmillan, 2001, p. xviii.
2. Helen Garner, *The First Stone: Some questions about sex and power,* Pan Macmillan, 1995.
3. See Jenna Mead (ed.), *bodyjamming,* Random House, 1997. Garner also aroused ire because of the sympathetic letter she originally sent to the Master of Ormond College asking for an interview. It was on the basis of that letter that Mead and the two young complainants refused to cooperate with her research.
4. Helen Garner, interview for *The Writer's Reader*.
5. David Stoll, *Rigoberta Menchú and the Story of All Poor Guatemalans,* Westview Press, Boulder, 1999.
6. *I, Rigoberta Menchú: An Indian woman in Guatemala,* ed. and intro. Elisabeth Burgos-Debray, Verso, 1984.
7. There were also other grounds on which the prize was awarded.
8. For an excellent discussion of the potentially emancipatory role of the essay for women, see: Shannon Lakanen, 'Residues', Creative Writing: Non-fiction, PhD dissertation, Ohio University, 2002.
9. See the comments of Pamela Klass Mittlefehldt in '"A Weaponry of Choice": Black American Women Writers and the Essay', in Ruth-Ellen Boetcher Joeres and Elizabeth Mittman (eds), *Politics of the Essay: Feminist perspectives*, Indiana University Press, 1993, pp. 196–208.
10. Audre Lorde, 'Scratching the Surface: Some Notes on Barriers to Woman and Loving', *Sister Outsider,* Crossing Press, 1984, p. 45, quoted in Lakanen, 2002, p. 13.

7. Writing about Place

1. Ashley Hay, interview for *The Writer's Reader*.
2. Mark Tredinnick, *A Place on Earth: An anthology of nature writing from Australia and North America*, University of Nebraska Press, Lincoln & London/University of New South Wales Press, 2003.
3. See Tredinnick, 2003, p. 32.
4. Pico Iyer, *The Global Soul: Jet-lag, shopping malls and the search for home,* Bloomsbury, 2000.
5. See David Gessner's lament, 'Sick of Nature: Today's Nature Writing Is Too Often Pious, Safe, Boring. Haven't These People Re-Read Thoreau Lately?', *Boston Globe*, August 1, 2004, <http://www.boston.com/news/globe/ideas/articles/2004/08/01/sick_of_nature?pg=full>.
6. Susan Murphy, 'Zen and the City', *Heat* 9, Winter, 2005, p. 63.
7. There are several versions of Thoreau's *Walden* available online. One of the most useful is *The Thoreau Reader: The works of Henry David Thoreau, 1817–1862* (A Project in Cooperation with the Thoreau Society, © 1999–2006 Richard Lenat, all rights reserved), at <http://thoreau.eserver.org/default.html>.
8. Again, see Gessner's comments, *Boston Globe*, August 1, 2004.
9. Publisher's Summary, A. Dillard reads 'Total Eclipse', from *Teaching a Stone to Talk*, American Audio Prose Library Inc., 1989.
10. UNSW Press, 2003.

11. *The Secret: The strange marriage of Annabella Milbanke and Lord Byron*, Duffy & Snellgrove, 2000.
12. *Gum: The story of eucalypts and their champions*, Duffy & Snellgrove, 2002.

8. Travel Writing

1. Mark Mordue, *Dastgah: Diary of a headtrip*, Allen & Unwin, 2001.
2. 'The Azerbaijanis', in Mordue, *Dastgah*, p. 233.
3. Robyn Davidson, *Tracks*, Pantheon, 1980.
4. Robyn Davidson, 'Against Travel Writing', *Granta 72: Overreachers*, 2000.
5. 'Captured converstions' is a favoured term of the writing teacher Theodore A. Rees Cheney who wrote the bestselling guide *Writing Creative Nonfiction: How to use fiction techniques to make your nonfiction more interesting, dramatic, and vivid*, Ten Speed Press, 1987.

Sources

Greg Bearup, 'The Beak Wore Beads', *Sydney Morning Herald*, May 4, 2002. Copyright 2002 John Fairfax Publications Pty Ltd. Republished with permission.

John Birmingham, 'S11'. Copyright John Birmingham 2000. Republished with permission. (First appeared in P. Craven, *The Best Australian Essays 2000*, Black Inc./Schwarz Publishing, Melbourne, 2000.)

Joan Didion, 'Some Dreamers of the Golden Dream' from *Slouching Towards Bethlehem*. Copyright 1966, 1968, renewed 1996 by Joan Didion. Reprinted by permission of Farrar, Straus and Giroux, LLC and Janklow & Nesbit Associates.

Annie Dillard, 'Total Eclipse'. Copyright Annie Dillard 1983. Reprinted by permission of Russell & Volkening as agents for the author.

Kathy Evans, 'Tuesday's Child', *Sunday Age,* September 28, 2003. Copyright 2003 *Sunday Age*. Republished by permission of the copyright holder and the author whose book *Tuesday's Child* is due to be published 2007.

Robert Fisk, 'Is This Some Kind of Crusade?', *Independent On Sunday*, May 18, 1997. Copyright 1997 Independent Newspapers (UK) Ltd. All rights reserved. Reprinted with permission of the copyright holder and the author.

Helen Garner, 'The Violet Jacket'. Copyright Helen Garner 1993. Republished by permission of the author. (Included in Garner's *True Stories: Collected non-fiction*, Text Publishing, 1997.)

Ashley Hay, 'Ultramarine'. Copyright Ashley Hay 2003. Republished by permission of the author.

Pico Iyer, 'The Khareef', *Sun After Dark*. Copyright 2004 Pico Iyer. Reprinted by permission of Alfred A. Knopf, a division of Random House, Inc. and Bloomsbury Publishing Plc.

Malcolm Knox, 'Her Life as a Fake: Bestseller's Lies Exposed', *Sydney Morning Herald,* July 24, 2004. Copyright 2004 John Fairfax Publications Pty Ltd. Republished with permission of the copyright holder and the author.

David Marr and Marian Wilkinson, 'They Shall Not Land', *Sydney Morning Herald*, October 20, 2001. Copyright 2001 John Fairfax Publications Pty Ltd. Republished with permission of the copyright holder and the authors.

Jessica Mitford, 'Let Us Now Appraise Famous Writers'. Copyright Jessica Mitford, all rights reserved. Republished by permission of the Estate of Jessica Mitford.

Mark Mordue, 'Pissing in the Wind'. Copyright Mark Mordue 2004. Republished by permission of the author. (First appeared in *Purple* magazine, Paris, 1999, and then in *Overland*, 2000. Incorporated in his *Dastgah: Diary of a headtrip*, Allen & Unwin, 2001, which was released in the US by Hawthorne Books in 2004.)

Arundhati Roy, 'War Talk: Summer Games with Nuclear Bombs', *War Talk*, South End Press, 2003. Copyright Arundhati Roy 2003. Republished with permission of the copyright holder. (First appeared in *Frontline* magazine (India), vol. 19, issue 12, June 8–21, 2002.)

David Sedaris, 'Today's Special'. Copyright David Sedaris 2001. Republished by permission of Don Congdon Associates, Inc.

Barry Siegel, 'A Father's Pain, a Judge's Duty and a Justice Beyond Their Reach', *Los Angeles Times*, December 30, 2001. Copyright 2001 *Los Angeles Times*. Republished with permission of the copyright holder and the author.

Michael Southwell, 'Toxic Fallout near Alcoa', *West Australian*, September 22, 2001. 'Cancer Secret', *West Australian,* November 29, 2001. 'Alcoa Told of Health Issues', *West Australian,* May 24, 2002. Copyright West Australian Newspapers Pty Ltd. Article reproduced courtesy of the *West Australian* and the author.

Tony Squires, 'Good Sport', *Sydney Morning Herald*, May 4, 2002. Copyright 2002 John Fairfax Publications Pty Ltd. Republished with permission of the copyright holder and the author.

Index

Bearup, Greg, 78, 80, 81
  interview with, 88–91
Bernstein, Carl, 98, 101
Bird, Isabella, 198
Birmingham, John, 42, 127, 130
  interview with, 137–9
Bryson, Bill, 198
Bryson, John, 5

Capote, Truman, 5, 38
Cassidy, John, 3
Cerf, Bennett, 98, 99
Chatwin, Bruce, 149, 201
Chenery, Susan, 79
Chesterton, G. K., 201
Clendinnen, Inga, 198
Cooke, Kaz, 128
Craven, Peter, 125
creative non-fiction

Davidson, Robyn, 199
detail
  accumulation of, 4
  complex, relation to narrative, 4
  humanity in reporting and, 3
  seeking out, 2–3
  small and striking, 78
  telling of, 40–1
details
  advance of narrative and, 40
Dickinson, Emily, 174
Didion, Joan, 38, 39, 40, 43
Dillard, Annie, 175, 176, 187
direct quotes, 42

Emerson, Ralph Waldo, 126, 174
essays
  finding the right voice in, 127–8
  lineage of, 125–6
  modern, 126
  personal, 129
  structure of, 175
  use of facts in, 126–7
Evans, Kathy, 151, 153

fact
  observable, 176
facts
  assaying of, 100
  conversion into story, 2
Faludi, Susan, 39
Faulkner, William, 175
feature writing, 2, 173
features
  books as extension of, 4–5
first draft, 40
first person, 78
Fisk, Robert, 1–2, 3, 10
  interview with, 20–4
Frey, James, 149, 150

Gambotto, Antonella, 80
Garner, Helen, 5, 126, 149, 150, 151, 160, 198
  interview with, 162–6
Gessner, David, 175
Glover, Richard, 128

Harmer, Wendy, 128
Hass, Amira, 4
Hay, Ashley, 173, 176, 177
  interview with, 182–6
Hemingway, Ernest, 40
Hersh, Seymour, 3
humour, 101, 128

investigating
  versus muckraking, 99
Iyer, Pico, 149, 174, 199, 200, 202
  interview with, 209

journalism
  as great writing, 2
  celebrity, 77
  contextualising and, 2
  going beyond the givens and, 3–4
  governments post 9/11 and, 4
  investigative, 99–101
  literary, 41
  narrative, 42
journalists
  early literary, 42
  ethical duty to question authority, 4
  investigative, 99
  new, popular image of, 38
Junger, Sebastian, 5

Keillor, Garrison, 128
Kerouac, Jack, 198
Khouri, Norma, 99–100, 116, 149
King, Stephen, 79
Knox, Malcolm, 99, 116, 150
  interview with, 120–3

Leser, David, 80
Lopate, Phillip, 128
Lorde, Audre, 151
Lower, Lennie, 128

Mailer, Norman, 38
McGeogh, Paul, 198
Malcolm, Janet, 80
Marr, David, 3, 4, 5, 25
  interview with, 35–6
Masters, Chris, 100
Mead, Jenna, 150
memoir
  as distinct from novel, 150
  contract with reader in, 150
  examination of writer's life through, 148
  honesty in, 149, 150–1
  place and, 173
  taking the reader with the writer in, 151–2
  use of facts in, 149
memory, 148
Mitford, Jessica, 39, 98, 99, 101, 102
Montaigne, Michel de, 125
Mordue, Mark, 152, 167, 199
Morris, Jan, 198
Murphy, Susan, 174

Naipaul, V. S., 149, 201
narrative
  advancement of, 40
  complex, 4
  journalism, 42
  profile and, 78
nature writing
  evokation of nature in, 176
  not as safe escape, 175
  standout, 174
  structure working for content in, 176
news
  as history on the run, 2
  transformation to features, 1–2

overwriting
  dealing with, 40–1
  perils of, 39

place
  belonging to, 176
  landscape and, 174
  nature writing and, 174
  readers and, 173–4
  writing about, 173
PR spin
  assuming status of a given, 3
profiles
  details, quotes and anecdotes and, 78–9
  ethics and intrusiveness and, 79–80
  in-depth, 77
  seduction and betrayal and, 80
  story versus subject in, 77

quotes, 78–9, 80, 200
  direct, 42

reporting
  as the bedrock, 42
  as personal expression, 39
  bottom-up, 100
  investigative journalism and, 99–101
Roy, Arundhati, 127, 140
Russell, Scott, 126
Ryle, Gerard, 99

Sebald, W. G., 201
Sedaris, David, 128, 144
Siegel, Barry, 41, 42, 56
  interview with, 70–5
Simons, Margaret, 5
sources, 99, 100, 101
  anonymous, 100
Southwell, Michael, 4, 5, 6

Squires, Tony, 77, 79, 92
Stoll, David, 150
Stone, I. F. (Izzy), 101

Talese, Gay, 38
Theroux, Paul, 201
Thompson, Hunter S., 38
Thoreau, Henry David, 174, 175
Thurber, James, 128
transcendentalist movement, 174
travel writing
  awareness of reason for writing, 199–200
  dialogue not quotes in, 200–1
  learning about self through, 198
  making a point in, 201
  senses and, 199
  telling untold stories through, 200

Wilkinson, Marian, 3, 5, 25
Winton, Tim, 198
Wolfe, Tom, 38, 42
Woodward, Bob, 98
writing
  nature. *See* nature writing
  paring back of, 39
  reflective, 125
  reflective, personal stories and, 125
  travel. *See* travel writing
  vulnerability in, 128

Zinsser, William, 39, 128